LANGUAGE AND LITERACY SERIES
Dorothy S. Strickland and Celia Genishi
SERIES EDITORS

The Complete Theory-to-Practice Handbook of Adult Literacy:
Curriculum Design and Teaching Approaches
*Rena Soifer, Martha E. Irwin, Barbara M. Crumrine,
Emo Honzaki, Blair K. Simmons, and Deborah L. Young*

Literacy for a Diverse Society:
Perspectives, Practices, and Policies
Elfrieda H. Hiebert, Editor

The Child's Developing Sense of Theme:
Responses to Literature
Susan S. Lehr

The Triumph of Literature / The Fate of Literacy
English in the Secondary School Curriculum
John Willinsky

The Child as Critic: Teaching Literature in
Elementary and Middle Schools, THIRD EDITION
Glenna Davis Sloan

Process Reading and Writing:
A Literature-Based Approach
*Joan T. Feeley, Dorothy S. Strickland,
and Shelley B. Wepner, Editors*

Inside/Outside: Teacher Research and Knowledge
Marilyn Cochran-Smith and Susan L. Lytle

Literacy Events in a Community of Young Writers
Yetta M. Goodman and Sandra Wilde, Editors

The Politics of Workplace Literacy: A Case Study
Sheryl Greenwood Gowen

Whole Language Plus: Essays on Literacy
in the United States and New Zealand
Courtney B. Cazden

Social Worlds of Children Learning
to Write in an Urban Primary School
Anne Haas Dyson

Partners in Learning:
Teachers and Children in Reading Recovery
Carol A. Lyons, Gay Su Pinnell, and Diane E. DeFord

The Languages of Learning:
How Children Talk, Write, Dance, Draw,
and Sing Their Understanding of the World
Karen Gallas

PARTNERS IN LEARNING

TEACHERS AND CHILDREN IN READING RECOVERY

Carol A. Lyons
Gay Su Pinnell
Diane E. DeFord

FOREWORD BY MARIE M. CLAY

Teachers College, Columbia University
New York and London

Published by Teachers College Press, 1234 Amsterdam Avenue
New York, NY 10027

Library of Congress Cataloging-in-Publication Data

Lyons, Carol, A.
    Partners in learning : teachers and children in Reading Recovery /
Carol A. Lyons, Gay Su Pinnell, Diane E. DeFord.
      p.   cm. — (Language and literacy series)
    Includes bibliographical references (p.) and index.
    ISBN 0-8077-3298-2 (alk. paper). — ISBN 0-8077-3297-4 (pbk. :
alk. paper)
    1. Reading—Remedial teaching. 2. Reading—Remedial teaching—
Case Studies. 3. Teaching. 4. Learning.   I. Pinnell, Gay Su.
II. DeFord, Diane E. III. Title. IV. Title: Reading Recovery.
V. Series: Language and literacy series (New York, N.Y.)
LB1050.5.L96   1993
372.4'3—dc20   93-29883

ISBN 0-8077-3298-2
ISBN 0-8077-3297-4 (pbk.)

Printed on acid-free paper
Manufactured in the United States of America

99 98   7 6 5

For the Reading Recovery children, teachers, teacher leaders, and trainers of teacher leaders from whom we learn everyday; Marie Clay, who contributed so significantly to helping all children become literate; our colleagues at Ohio State University, especially Charlotte Huck and Martha King, who have provided guidance and direction over many years, and Moira McKenzie, whose research first introduced us to Marie Clay's work; and our families, who continue to support our efforts to improve the quality of life and education for children throughout the world.

Contents

Photographs appear between pages 128 and 129.

Acknowledgments

We are indebted to Professor Marie M. Clay, who has guided and challenged our thinking over many years. We are grateful to the dedicated Reading Recovery teachers, teacher leaders, and trainers of teacher leaders who shared their thinking and allowed us to understand better how children and adults think and learn. While the teachers and children in this book must remain anonymous, we believe they demonstrate the power of forming partnerships in the process of becoming literate.

We are thankful to the John D. and Catherine T. MacArthur Foundation for funding the Early Literacy Research Study that is the source of data for this book. Special appreciation goes to members of the National Advisory Board who took an active role in the project. Board members guided every phase of the research project. They assisted in the planning of the study, took an in-depth look at the rich array of data, and assisted in interpreting and evaluating the results. We express appreciation for their willingness to respond to ongoing questions as the study proceeded and to provide feedback to the many technical reports. Members of the Board included: Isabel Beck, University of Pittsburgh; Gerald Bracey, Washington, D.C.; Shirley Brice Heath, Stanford University; Robert Slavin, Johns Hopkins University; Dorothy Strickland, Rutgers University; and Richard Venezky, University of Delaware, who served as Chair. We also wish to express appreciation to Rebecca Barr, National–Louis University, and Jana Mason, University of Illinois, who acted as consultants for the research; Jeanne Chall, Harvard Graduate School of Education, who advised us during the project; and Anthony Bryk, University of Chicago, who assisted in the design and data analysis.

Most of all we wish to thank the Ohio school districts, the teachers, teacher leaders, and the children who participated in the study and whose work made it possible. We would also like to thank the following teacher leaders who added their knowledge and contributed to the data analysis in significant ways: Darcy Bradley, Rose Mary Estice, Jeanne Evans, Mary Fried,

Robin Holland, Diane Powell and Becky Shook. We would like to give a special thank you to Chava Mucino, a senior at Ohio State University, for designing and producing the figures and tables.

Finally, we want to thank Sarah Biondello, Cathy McClure, and Karl Nyberg at Teachers College Press for their helpful comments and editorial suggestions on the manuscript.

Foreword

A glance at the Dedication and Acknowledgments in this book will give the reader a sense of the collaborative expertise which is behind implementing Reading Recovery in the United States. The authors played a leading role in making the program widely accessible to U.S. children who need something extra, over and above their classroom program. They worked particularly hard to hold the program to its high standards of effective delivery, while at the same time fostering its expansion across the United States. They were assisted by the policies of the National Diffusion Network to spread a vision of the program's potential before it became diluted by changes of convenience.

I am asked whether the program in the United States is different from its counterpart in New Zealand; the answer is both "Yes" and "No". The program remains the same wherever it takes root because it was designed to give supplementary help to children from any beginning reading and writing program so that they become able to perform at average levels in their own classrooms whatever the instructional emphasis. It empowers children to learn in any good quality program. On the other hand, the program cannot be an effective intervention in an education system unless it adjusts to the characteristics of that system and its populations. The implementation must be flexible enough to work in different educational cultures and institutional structures. It is not an easy task to retain the essence of this early intervention while at the same time adapting to the exigencies of the socio-political, economic, and professional contexts.

The instructional theory that drives the program is dynamic, responding to changes in the accumulated wisdom of the psychology of learning and education. Programs and new advocacies come and go, usually with relatively short life-spans. Reading Recovery has had a longer life than most. It has existed long enough to convince many people that "what is possible" for slow learners is different from what we used to think was possible. It is my hope that it will have a long enough life to establish for all time that slow learners are slow learners only because of the ways in which we have tried to teach them. In society and in education we categorize them, and they grow to fit our categories. All we had to do was rearrange the teacher's talents, change the delivery conditions, and provide opportunities to succeed; then, slow learners caught up with their average classmates. All of it was nonsense in terms of received wisdom, and none of it was easy. The program has to remain open to new but sound information and responsive enough to make appropriate changes. All that we think we know should be tentatively held in mind and suggested changes need to be put to rigorous test.

There is a constant need to study new theories and research findings first to understand what is emerging and then to thoughtfully determine what they mean for Reading Recovery. And there is a concern to share the insights gained in this particular targeted program with general education.

This book emerges from this last concern. The MacArthur Foundation Study must be seen to be one of the best designed evaluations of Reading Recovery, in my view. It was guided by an expert panel of independent advisers. It tested the "true" form of the program against several alternate forms each of which varied the program in a specific and testable way. All five treatments were tested against each other and with a matched control group who received no extra treatment. The authors would, I am sure, be the first to acknowledge the immense value to the program of the Foundation grant they received and the guidance of its panel of experts who were probably exasperating in its insistent demands for rigor and analysis.

That study has its own report. This book makes accessible many of the insights derived during that study and subsequent to it. The authors have thoughtfully used their Reading Recovery experience and research to explore what teaching is. For me this raises a host of questions. If I conceptualize good teaching as helping children to construct their experience and their cognitive processing, then the equation of child contribution plus teacher contribution will vary between the lowest achievers and the classroom learners. I cannot suppose that what the teacher does to achieve the equation with the children who give so little, is anything like what the teachers need to do to achieve the equation with children who are actively meeting the teacher half way, or even shooting past her. I expect teaching to be different if it is sensitive to individual differences. This book introduces readers to this debate.

Marie M. Clay

Introduction

We now know enough to guarantee that virtually every child will learn to be a good reader and writer during the first two years of school. To us, as educators, that means that there are no excuses for having a large number of children who cannot read or can read very little. Our claims are based on demonstrations of reading and writing competency by more than 40,000 students, initially seen as having difficulty, who have succeeded in the Reading Recovery program. These students were enrolled in large and small rural, suburban, and urban school districts in 38 U.S. states, the District of Columbia, and 4 Canadian provinces. Many of these children are not native English speakers and they represent different cultures and ethnic backgrounds. In this book we detail how teachers create contexts that enable the vast majority of children to learn how to become independent readers and writers. We also describe how teachers learn to develop skills in accomplishing this goal.

Children's success in school depends on quality education from the start. Amid public concerns about education in general, many researchers have turned their attention to the early experiences children have in school. Here, becoming literate is a priority. It is every child's right to receive the needed level of support to be successful in their early literacy experiences and continue that success throughout their years of schooling. Meeting the needs of a diverse population of students is a challenge for educators, one that must be met if we are to maintain the quality of life of our citizens. For many children, we need to do it better. And teachers are the key to making that happen.

Recently, attention has been directed to the effectiveness of teacher education and the ongoing professional development provided for experienced teachers. The idea is to help them teach more powerfully and to be knowledgeable enough to meet the challenges inherent in modern society. The Carnegie Foundation (1986) and Holmes Group (1986) reports have raised questions about the quality of the teacher education programs and called for new structures for training career professional teachers. The reports have not made clear, however, what these new structures should look like and how they can be achieved. Nor have the reports provided evidence of effective programs or the critical theoretical understandings from which the new structures for training the professional educator can be derived.

The research presented in this book is grounded in theory and practice. We have been informed by our own teaching of Reading Recovery teachers, teacher leaders, and trainers of teacher leaders, as well as by our site visits to support the implementation of projects in a variety of settings, including urban, suburban, and rural communities throughout the United States and Canada. A most valuable source of insight has been provided by our ongoing teaching of Reading Recovery children. We hope that the observations and data included in this volume will be useful in enabling educators to understand better the learning processes involved in becoming an effective teacher of literacy.

This book is based on analysis of data from a large, statewide study of Reading Recovery and other literacy interventions. An overarching theme for the volume is attention to the nature of powerful teaching within literacy activities and the complex cognitive skills involved in learning how to teach powerfully. The first chapter provides an overview of the Reading Recovery program, including a discussion of the research and theoretical bases of the program, its goals, and the ways learning about teaching is fostered within the program. While the subject of our book is not Reading Recovery per se, this instructional setting is relevant because it provides the framework for our observations of children and teachers within reading and writing settings. This instructional setting is the vehicle for viewing teachers as dynamic decision-makers. In the second chapter, we review our study of early literacy interventions to provide a research base for the more detailed stories of teachers and children that follow. We also respond to the most frequently asked questions about the program. The third chapter presents through examples the principles of learning and teaching underlying the staff development model. We discuss the constructive view of learning and the role of language in the process.

Chapters 4 and 5 provide a focused look at teacher and student interactions that lead to accelerated reading progress. We discuss the development of reading strategies and how teachers behave in ways that effectively support that development.

Writing is the focus of Chapters 6 and 7. In these chapters, we examine what children learn about writing and the approaches teachers use to guide learners' actions within the Reading Recovery program. We discuss the connections between reading and writing and describe how teachers can help high-risk children make these connections.

In Chapters 8 and 9, we present a description, through case examples, of how teachers develop their theoretical and practical knowledge and skills over time. The emphasis here is on the development of the decisionmaking processes in relation to observing and teaching effective literacy strategies. We attempt to unravel the relationships between students' strategy learning and teachers' roles in supporting, leading, demonstrating, and probing during the process of that learning and students' role in the process.

In Chapter 10, we present implications of what we have learned about how children and teachers learn. We discuss the difficulty and the necessity for changing the educational system to meet the needs of all children. Finally, in Chapter 11, we present recommendations for restructuring literacy education in our schools and teacher education and for future research that will provide needed information to use further in the process.

This book is written for educational planners, policymakers, university faculty, and administrators who want to make a difference in the learning of high-risk children. It matters that children are provided quality programs as they begin schooling and that extra help be available to those who have difficulty in learning to read and write. It also matters what happens in those early school experiences. Programs that enable students to participate in extended reading and writing are the best context for learning and learning how to use essential skills. Appropriate materials are essential, but even more important is the way teachers and children use materials during literacy events in the classroom. The most important component is the quality of teaching. Teachers who are flexible, observant, and have a sound theoretical knowledge base that helps them know what to attend to are most effective in their instructional interactions.

We have seen how teachers develop their knowledge base and become more powerful over time as they examine their practice and engage in substantive conversation with colleagues and others who both challenge and support their learning. This research has provided insights into the teaching and learning processes; in this volume, our task was to make our own learning visible in a way that will contribute to the learning of teachers and perhaps to the design of new experiences that will help teachers learn.

Chapter 1

Reading Recovery: Weaving Learning and Teaching Together

Is it possible that a young child can feel the weight of failure in the first year of school? It was so for 6-year-old David, who said, "It's too late. Everyone is reading in my class but me. I tried to learn the letters and sounds, but I could never remember anything." And it was so for Thomas, who pretended to read, telling wonderful stories, but avoided trying to match up his "reading" to the print on the page and ultimately also saw himself as a failure. And it was so for Michelle, who struggled over each word, making sounds to go with letters in such a laborious fashion that she seemed to produce nonsensical prose.

Our interest in Reading Recovery was fired by our awareness of the large numbers of young children who daily find themselves failing in school situations. That almost always means failure in learning to read. While reading and writing do not guarantee success, literacy is a first and necessary factor that has profound effects on children's achievement, potential, and self-esteem for the rest of their school careers and lives.

We, the writers of this book, are teacher educators who listen to the frustrations of teachers on a regular basis. But we are also first-grade teachers who remember some of the frustrations, even guilt, that we faced in our own teaching. If we had succeeded in teaching David, Thomas, and Michelle how to be independent readers, what a difference it might have made to their futures! Reading Recovery, which grew out of the research of New Zealander Marie Clay, seemed to be a system that held hope for changing the lives of some children and for ourselves as teachers.

So, we set out to investigate and to implement Reading Recovery for improving education in the United States. Now, nearly a decade later, we realize that Reading Recovery is an important program not only for the children who can participate in it but also for educators who can learn from it. The subject of this book is not Reading Recovery itself. Rather, it is what we have learned about the teaching and learning processes while observing children's lessons. These processes are revealed by examining the social context of Reading Recovery lessons.

In this chapter we describe the framework, structure, and interactional systems that make up the Reading Recovery project. These include how teachers work with children but also how administrative functions and staff development surround the teaching in a supportive way. We give special emphasis to how teachers learn through their work with children and how language is used for learning. We also discuss the theoretical foundation of Reading Recovery and place it within the research on early reading. Here, we explore how we define strategies and the kinds of behavioral evidence that signal readers' use of strategies. We also present and discuss Clay's idea of the development of a self-extending system in reading, the goal of Reading Recovery instruction.

WHAT IS READING RECOVERY?

When we first became involved in Reading Recovery, we explained it as a one-on-one intervention program for children who were having difficulty in reading after one year of school. We described intensive, daily half-hour lessons taught by a specially trained teacher. Now, we realize that definition is too simplistic. The one-on-one procedures can be read about in Clay's (1985) book *The Early Detection of Reading Difficulties,* and any teacher can purchase and use a version of the diagnostic and intervention procedures. But that would not be Reading Recovery. Instead, Reading Recovery is a system-wide intervention that involves a network of education, communication, and colleagiality designed to create a culture of learning that promotes literacy for high-risk children.

New Zealand Research and Development

Reading Recovery has its roots in Marie Clay's own studies of young children's reading and writing behavior. In her doctoral work, she developed her theories and was informed by her own reading of other scholars; this process is evident in her current writing as well. Clay looked at the behavior of children just learning to read. She discovered that errors and, most importantly, self-corrections provided important evidence about how children were processing print. Clay's ideas are not easy to categorize, but she has given us a comprehensive theory of how children learn to read, one that encompasses complex kinds of learning (experiential, language, and visual) that are orchestrated in that process.

Reading Recovery was developed within a unique educational context. New Zealand had an educational system similar to that of England. Borrowing from American progressive education, New Zealand educators created some unique structures of their own. They did not imitate the U.S. trends for large financial investments in commercial reading systems, the design of semiautomated instruction, and the proliferation of testing that began in the 1950s.

New Zealand educators took a different direction for several reasons. (1) They did not have the billions of dollars needed to purchase large systems with consumable materials such as workbooks; and, in any case, educational leaders in New Zealand would not have spent funds in that way. (2) New Zealand was a relatively small educational system and therefore not a very lucrative market. (3) They were in an out-of-the-way part of the world; developments in New Zealand were based on local concerns and solutions. As Clay has said, they had a chance to think through some fads before buying into them. We know, too, that they did not *jump* into Reading Recovery either. They studied the process for several years, each time being surprised at the consistent results. The national program for Reading Recovery was implemented deliberately and with care. Only now are they getting close to national coverage.

Schools in New Zealand, however, had problems. Many children lived in rich oral cultures, but books were expensive and generally unavailable; schools needed to make reading meaningful and appealing to those children. For many children, English was not their first language. New Zealanders took the opposite of a materials approach to literacy education; the term *teacher-proof* was not heard. Instead, they looked to teacher development to provide the best literacy education for their multicultural society.

Educators in New Zealand were interested in helping teachers look closely at children and at their work in classrooms. Clay's early research and her book *Reading: The Patterning of Complex Behaviour* (1972) focused on how young children learn to read. The first edition of *The Early Detection of Reading Difficulties* (1985), published in 1972, was a small pamphlet designed simply to help teachers look more carefully at young children. The techniques that Clay devised became part of an extensive in-service project called ERIC (Early Reading Inservice Course). With a set of slides and audiotapes accompanied by a teacher's handbook, groups of teachers all over New Zealand met to participate in a 13-session course.

They read and discussed theoretical material. They gathered information about the students they taught. They learned techniques for assessing children's concepts about print, assessing language, and keeping running records. These techniques were individually administered. They provided a structure within which teachers could carefully observe children and record results, thus allowing them to be systematic in their assessment. They could not fool themselves into thinking all children were making the best progress. They had to notice every child. The assessment systems were directed toward uncovering what children know and can do; that is, to reveal their competence and their strengths as a base for instruction.

Even then, Clay was more interested in the development of teacher thinking. The wide use of observation techniques helped teachers become what in New Zealand is called "noticing teachers." They noticed what children could do; they were concerned about children who were having difficulties. They could see some children becoming more confused and lagging further behind as they waited for them to catch up. They wanted to intervene before the difficulties were compounded, and they knew the intervention had to be individually tailored for each child.

At the insistence of teachers, Clay undertook the studies that later influenced the creation of Reading Recovery. During the research project, as in all her other work, Clay worked closely with teachers. Teachers were part of a research team that watched good teachers working with individual children behind a one-way glass. Over a period of time, they gathered precise information about children's behavior and teachers' responses that seemed to help children.

Researchers selected the most powerful responses and produced a set of guidelines that teachers could use to help them make decisions while working with individual children. Many options were considered and tried. The repertoire of procedures were designed for children having the most difficulty, not for those making normal progress. Considering *each* child, teachers had to select carefully and sensitively from this repertoire. This instruction was designed to be used with the dynamic, holistic literacy program that existed in New Zealand classrooms. Clay (1972) says that what was left out of the procedures is as important as what was included in them. A limited amount of time was available for individual work, both for economic reasons and because there seemed to be an optimum amount of time that would be effective. They found that, in general, effectiveness for both teachers and children declined after 30 minutes of this intensive work. This developmental work has continued to this day, even though the basic, simple framework has remained fairly consistent.

The Program for Children

The program includes daily, one-on-one lessons for each child. These lessons continue until the child has developed the kinds of strategies that good readers use. The lessons last 30 minutes per day and are intensive. During every minute, children are actively reading or writing; the teacher works along-side and is specially trained to bring to children's attention what they are doing that is effective.

The goal of Reading Recovery is acceleration. Each child is expected to make faster than average progress so that he or she can catch up with other children in the class and thus profit from the instruction going on in the class-room. Acceleration also means having a self-improving system for reading. Children learn to use information from their experience, from what they know about language, and from the letters they see on the page, including letter–sound correspondence. They must learn to use this information to solve their reading problems and to do it on the run while reading real books.

Reading Recovery is supplementary to regular classroom programs. It is, as they say in New Zealand, "something extra." Children continue to par-ticipate in their regular classroom instruction but are taken aside for the individual lessons. Reading Recovery is a team approach. It is the combina-tion of Reading Recovery with classroom instruction that produces the accel-eration. Parents, too, are part of the team. The Reading Recovery teacher works with caregivers to help them understand the program. Every day the child takes home a book to read and a story he or she has written.

The Lesson

The lesson is organized so that students, no matter how inexperienced they are with print, will be able to act like readers and writers. They learn to read fluently, using the phrasing that good readers use, to write messages, and to look at print. They do this and meet the challenge of new text with the support of the teacher. The teacher observes the reader's strategies while read-ing and writing. Strategies are the general cognitive processes, initiated by the child, to get messages from a text (Clay, 1985). The child's strategies are analyzed throughout the lesson, that is, while reading familiar books, record-ing a running record, writing, and introducing and first reading a new book. The parts of the lesson are the same on most days; however, the particular books read, the messages written, and interactions the teacher has with the child are individually crafted to meet the needs of the particular student. Thus each lesson and the path of progress for each child are different.

Reading Familiar Books.   Each reader has a box of favorite books. Each day the child or teacher chooses from any number of them to read. The books should be easy for the child, so that he or she is able to read flu-ently. The teacher and child share the book much like a parent and child might do at bedtime, although the child will be doing the reading in this instance. The teacher comments on the story's meaning or on strategies used well, or reads with the child to support fluent reading. Depending on the length of the stories (longer ones as the child accelerates), as many as three or four books may be read quickly in this manner.

Recording a Running Record of Yesterday's New Book.   This portion of the lesson allows the child to read independently, with the teacher recording the child's reading behavior for later analysis. During and after the reading, however, the teacher makes immediate decisions about the strategies observed, selecting the most opportune times during the child's reading to help him or her learn something new. It is important for the teacher to remain neutral while taking the running record, observing the child's strategies while reading. An example of the shorthand used to capture what is read can be found later in this chapter (see Figure 1.2). This record of text reading will then be analyzed for three kinds of information: (1) text appropriateness for this particular child; (2) strategies (monitoring and searching); and (3) cues (meaning, syntactic, visual) used by the reader when making an error, having difficulty, or self-correcting. This analysis takes place after the lesson is completed, with the book and other lesson-plan materials used to inform the teacher as to the reader's use of strategies.

Writing.   The child generates a message for the writing portion of the lesson. This may come from personal experiences or from a book read at some point in the lesson. In either instance, the child and teacher work together in a highly scaffolded manner to represent the message. The child writes on unlined paper that has been made into a book (Figure 1.1). The upper portion of the book is used to practice letters, fluent writing, and sound/visual analysis, as well as to make links that may help create bridges between known and unknown words. The bottom portion of the book is where the final message is written. This page will be used for future reading experiences, so everything is written and spelled conventionally. After the child has constructed the sentence, he or she rereads the sentence while the teacher writes it on a sentence strip. The teacher cuts the sentence at word, letter, or phrase boundaries. The child then reassembles the cut-up message, and the written text becomes a reading task. The teacher records the student's sentence and underlines words and letters the child wrote unassisted, indicating the order in which the student heard and recorded each letter. The teacher indicates how the sentence was cut up, making notations about the child's ability to reconstruct the sentence.

Introduction and First Reading of a New Book.   The new book is carefully selected by the teacher to offer a challenge to the reader's developing strategies, yet be easy enough for the child to read at or above 90% accu-

FIGURE 1.1.　The Writing Book and Teacher Records

Child's book

Teacher's record

racy in the next day's running record. Although this text will support aspects of the child's language and experiences, it also offers new learning. The teacher introduces the book—drawing the child's attention to the important ideas, discussing the pictures of the whole book, and providing opportunities for the child to hear the book's language. Then the child begins reading. As the reader encounters problems, the teacher selects ways to make associations with the child's experiences, language, knowledge, and strategies to support the child in solving his or her own problem. In this way, the teacher teaches *for* strategies and guides the child in applying necessary operations. If it seems appropriate, the teacher and child may read the book one more time, the teacher pacing his or her reading to encourage fluent reading but slowing down at places where the child may need to work at a slower pace.

Teacher Decisionmaking

The Reading Recovery teacher provides a scaffold for child learning. This metaphor, first used by Wood, Bruner, and Ross (1976) and also discussed by Cazden (1988), suggests that through interaction, the teacher provides just enough support to help the child accomplish tasks that will lead to learning. While maintaining the holistic nature of tasks, such as writing a message, the teacher reduces the complexity for the child, allowing the child to achieve his or her own purposes and contribute everything possible; the teacher fills in the rest.

Teachers learn to observe quickly and analyze "on the run" while teaching, relying on a central theory—a kind of self-generating system that forms the basis for decisions. Like Clay's researchers, Reading Recovery teachers have extraordinary ability to see and interpret a student's internal strategies while reading. The example in Figure 1.2 details one teacher's recording and analysis of a child's oral reading of the book *All Fall Down* (Wildsmith, 1983).

The checkmarks indicate words the child has read correctly. Incorrect responses are recorded with the text under it. If the child succeeds in correcting a previous error, the self-correction (SC) is recorded. Rereading the sentence is recorded as a repetition (R) with an arrow indicating where the child returned to reread the text. The teacher's analysis reveals that in the first five of six errors, the child applied his oral language knowledge (structure) to make sense (meaning) and ignored visual information (visual cues from letters and words), except in two cases when the child self-corrected. And when the child substituted *fell* for *fall*, he used meaning, structural, and visual information.

Assessment and Selection of Children

Children are selected for the program using a combination of six individually administered diagnostic measures. Where required, standardized tests are used. We will briefly describe the six measures.

Letter Identification. We give a letter identification test to determine if the child can identify 54 characters of the alphabet—the upper- and lower-case letters and the printed *a* and *g*. Acceptable responses include identification of a letter by stating the alphabetic name, a sound that is acceptable for the letter, or a word for which the letter is the initial letter. Incorrect responses are recorded also. The score indicates the child's preferred way of identifying letters, any confusions he or she may have, and unknown letters.

Word Test. We ask the child to read a list of 20 isolated words drawn from a list of words frequently used in first-grade basal reading materials. The

FIGURE 1.2. Running Record Analysis

Page	Title All Fall Down	Totals E / SC		Cues used E	Cues used SC
		E 6	**SC** 2	**E**	**SC**
1	✓ ✓ ✓ ✓				
2	✓ ✓ ✓ butterfly / bee ✓ ✓ wing / butterfly	1 / 1		(m)(s)v / (m)(s)v	
3	✓ ✓ ✓ ✓ ✓ ✓ ✓ ✓ ✓ robin / bird |sc|R	1	1	(m)(s)v	ms(v)
4	✓ ✓ ✓ ✓ ✓ ✓ ✓ ✓ ✓ ✓ ✓ bunny / rabbit .|sc	1	1	(m)(s)v	ms(v)
5	✓ ✓ ✓ ✓ ✓ ✓ ✓ ✓ ✓ ✓ ✓ ✓ ✓ ✓ ✓				
6	✓ ✓ ✓ ✓ ✓ ✓ ✓ ✓ ✓ ✓ ✓ ✓ ✓ ✓ ✓ ✓ ✓ ✓				
7	They / All fell / fall ✓	1 / 1		(m)(s)v / (m)(s)(v)	

Note.
m = meaning
s = structure (language)
v = visual (letters/sounds)
E = error
SC = self correction
R = repetition

score indicates the number of high-frequency words the child has learned. Nowhere in Reading Recovery instruction do we drill children on isolated words, but we want to see the extent to which they have accumulated a reading vocabulary of the most frequently used words in first-grade basal readers.

Concepts About Print.   We assess children's concepts about print by reading one a small book developed by Clay (1979b), *Sand or Stones*. Using this small book, the teacher says, "I'll read this book. You help me." And then he or she asks the child to do things such as "Show me where I start reading. Which way do I go? Where do I go after that? Point to the words while I read." This assessment gives us information about what the child knows about print, without requiring a sophisticated language about abstract written concepts. The analysis reveals confusions the child has about conventions of our written language code, for example, problems with understanding the meaning of terms such as *letter* and *word*.

Writing Vocabulary.   Children are asked to write as many words as they can write within a 10-minute time limit, beginning with their own name and including basic vocabulary and words personal to the child's experiences. Each word written accurately is marked as correct. First-grade students at the beginning of the year can generally write 10 or more words in 10 min-

FIGURE 1.3.   Writing Vocabulary Test

Score = 1

FIGURE 1.4. Dictation Test

Score = 2

utes. Rachel, for example, wrote the word *I* and attempted to write her name *Rahl*. She had a score of 1 (Figure 1.3).

Dictation.   The dictation assessment is not a spelling test. A sentence is read to the child, and we ask him or her to try to write it. We are interested in the extent to which the child can hear sounds in words and represent them with appropriate letters. It is a test of phonemic awareness. The child is given 1 point for every sound he or she can hear and record correctly, even if the word itself may not be correct. The score indicates how many of the 37 sounds (phonemes) the child hears. Rachel's dictation score of 2 indicates that she can hear the *b* in *bus* and the *s* in *stop* (Figure 1.4).

Running Record.   The last assessment is a running record of text reading (see Figure 1.2). We find out the level of text difficulty that the child can read at 90% accuracy or better. We take down reading behavior—using a kind of shorthand—in exact detail. We analyze this behavior to find evidence of those "in-the-head" strategies that we are trying to develop. The running record is the most powerful tool of the Reading Recovery teacher. Every day, for every child, the Reading Recovery teacher takes and analyzes a running record. This provides an ongoing assessment of the strategies being developed.

STAFF DEVELOPMENT IN READING RECOVERY

While planning for wider dissemination, Clay's research team did something unique. Consistent with their theoretical view of learning as a process of constructing meaning, the researchers hypothesized that teachers must participate in constructing their own understandings, just as the researchers had constructed their theories. The original team valued the "behind-the-glass" talk on which they based their decisions, and they recommended that the preparation of teachers include this process. Alvermann (1990) has characterized Reading Recovery teacher education as an inquiry-oriented model; that is, as teachers watch each other work with individual children, they talk together, hypothesize, predict, monitor, and draw conclusions that take into account the teaching, the child's learning, and the context. They build case-by-case knowledge that forms their decisionmaking base.

Reading Recovery training can be accomplished at three levels: teacher, teacher leader, and trainers of teacher leaders. Each level includes behind-the-glass observation of teaching and a yearlong educational program. We will discuss each level here.

Teacher Training

Teachers meet in weekly sessions, usually held after school, for an entire academic year. They receive graduate-level university course credit for their participation and work, an appropriate arrangement because Reading Recovery is rigorous and demands that teachers take on and use theoretical knowledge.

The in-service program begins with diagnostic assessment training in which teachers learn to use the assessment techniques; they begin right away to administer them and to observe children closely as they do so. As teachers are guided by the assessment to improve their observational skills and to recognize knowledge and strengths that they did not realize children had, their thoughts about children begin to change immediately.

Once children are selected for the program, teachers begin working with them on a daily basis. They work with children each day in half-hour lessons for two hours; and they take turns bringing their children to the weekly in-service sessions. During these sessions, class members conduct demonstration lessons behind a one-way glass while the rest of the class observe. As they observe, they discuss the lesson. Freed from teaching, the observing group can sharpen their observational powers and gain skill in prediction, hypothesizing, and the minute-to-minute decisionmaking that makes for high-quality teaching. They learn to observe the student's processing closely, to recognize evidence of strategy development, and to teach for strategies.

Teacher-Leader Training

Teacher classes are sometimes taught on college campuses, but they usually take place in a school district or regional center. The person who teaches the staff development class is called a "teacher leader" in Canada and the United States and a "tutor" in New Zealand, Australia, and England. Teacher-leader training is a yearlong academic and practical course at a college or university. Teacher leaders learn to teach children and work with four of them each day for the entire year; they engage in behind-the-glass demonstration teaching, observation, and discussion. They complete all the training listed above for teachers, except that they are expected to think simultaneously about their own teaching of children and the nature of training for teachers.

In addition to the clinical sessions, they take seminars on learning, language, and reading and writing theory, as well as a practicum on issues of implementation. The courseload for teacher leaders is more than twice that needed for teachers and almost always requires residency at the university site. After the initial year of in-service training, teacher leaders receive considerable technical assistance from the university during their first year of working with teachers. Teacher leaders continue to teach children throughout their tenure in the role. Their work with children helps them to continue their own theory building and to operationalize it; it keeps them fresh in their staff development roles. They represent what may be a new role in education, the *practicing* professional teacher educator.

Trainers of Teacher Leaders

Teaching the teacher-leader class requires a complex range of skills that include the teaching of children; the ability to present theoretical material; and the knowledge of Clay's theory and current research in language development, reading, writing, comprehension, spelling, and educational change. The relatively few people selected to be trainers of teacher leaders learn to work with children, be instructors of teachers and teacher leaders, and study the range of leadership roles needed to provide central support for the dynamic mechanisms of the project in their state or region. They, too, continue to teach children; it is particularly important, although difficult, for university personnel to keep in contact with the fundamental level of education in Reading Recovery.

At all levels, people in Reading Recovery are involved in figuring out what is happening with individual children. The New Zealand researchers did not behave as if they already had the answer to reading problems; they continually had to think hard, to approach each child as a new puzzle, and to use their knowledge to the utmost. They did not have a prescriptive set of procedures that freed them from decisionmaking, and neither do today's Reading

Recovery teachers. As Goodlad (1990) has pointed out in *The Moral Dimensions of Teaching*, "No method or impersonal theory relieves the teacher of the burden of judgment" (p. 4). Teachers are encouraged to recognize this challenge, to put aside their assumptions, and to take a fresh look at children. Through this process, they add to their professional repertoire and their skill in decisionmaking.

IMPLEMENTING READING RECOVERY IN THE UNITED STATES

The Ohio Program

With such a powerful in-service model, it was natural that others would attempt to transplant the program to other countries. In 1984, the Ohio State University, in collaboration with the Ohio Department of Education and the Columbus public schools, brought Marie Clay and Barbara Watson, the National Director of Reading Recovery in New Zealand, to Columbus to launch the first U.S. implementation of Reading Recovery. Clay and Watson taught a group of teachers from the Columbus schools as well as a small group of teacher leaders. This pilot project was watched carefully by school district and university officials. Due to the success of the 1984–85 pilot program, the following year an agreement was made to expand the program from 6 to 12 schools and to begin a three-year longitudinal study. The lowest-performing students were randomly assigned to Reading Recovery and an alternative reading program. That first year, 74% of the 136 children served by Reading Recovery were successfully discontinued, each reading at average levels in their classrooms with independent reading strategies. While the Columbus schools were expanding the program, the Ohio General Assembly approved financial assistance to support a statewide Reading Recovery program in 1985–86. There were sites set up during the next two years with teams of teacher leaders. Each team of two teachers served a regional area with the goal of reaching at least 15% of the lowest-achieving first-grade students in the region. Since 1986, 70% to 95% of the high-risk students in each of the 22 sites have reached average reading levels and continued to learn with regular classroom instruction.

The National Program

In 1987 Reading Recovery was recognized as a program of excellence by the U.S. Department of Education's National Diffusion Network. During the 1990–91 school year, a total of 12,902 children were served by Reading Recovery teachers. Of those children, 9,486 were considered to be program children. Program children are those who received 60 or more lessons or were discontinued from the program before having 60 lessons. Eighty-seven percent or 8,295 children were discontinued from the program reading at average levels in their classrooms with independent reading strategies. In 1991–92, 3,248 teachers from 801 school districts in 38 states taught more than 13,000 high-risk students to read. At the end of 1993 the program will be operating in 44 U.S. states and 5 Canadian provinces as well as New Zealand, Australia, and England. It is estimated that in 1992–93, the number of children served will be more than 25,000 in the United States alone.

THE RESEARCH BASE FOR READING RECOVERY

New Zealand Research

New Zealand studies of Reading Recovery (Clay, 1990) indicate that regardless of sex, economic status, or sociolinguistic group, the lowest-achieving children make accelerated progress in the program and continue to make satisfactory progress after release from the program. The evidence is that gains are long-lasting. Currently, New Zealand educators are finding that after receiving Reading Recovery services, less than 1% of an age cohort need to be referred on for special service (see Clay & Tuck, 1991).

There are several reasons that the New Zealand educational system succeeds in enabling 99% of the students to learn how to read:

1. There is a flexible grade-level structure in the early years.
2. Retention is not a common practice.
3. Standardized tests are not used for wholesale assessment.
4. There is no formally established force of special remedial reading teachers allocated to serve every grade level.
5. Workbooks, worksheets, and basal reading systems are not used.

The Ohio State University Research

The U.S. Reading Recovery procedures grew out of and were consistent with typical classroom practices that included a vast amount of reading and a variety of writing experiences. In many places in the United States, however, Reading Recovery procedures represented a departure from classroom practice. There were questions as to whether the program would work at all in the United States and even more questions regarding children's ability to sustain progress after withdrawal of Reading Recovery support.

Research support for Reading Recovery comes from two sources: comparative studies and replications. Two comparative studies have been conducted to date. The first, conducted from 1986 to 1989, was a small longitudinal comparative study involving two randomly assigned groups of children in Columbus, Ohio. Longitudinal data show that, as a group, discontinued Reading Recovery children continued to perform at a level appropriate for their grade placement for three years following the Reading Recovery year (DeFord, Pinnell, Lyons, & Place, 1990).

The second study was conducted in 1988–90 and is the source of data for this book. This study involved 10 districts in Ohio and compared several treatments, including Reading Recovery, Reading Recovery with limited training, Reading Recovery teachers working with groups of students, and a skills-based tutoring program. That study showed not only that children taught by traditional Reading Recovery had greater improvement than those in the control groups but also that professional preparation and the quality of teacher decisionmaking made a difference in student success.

Replications are an even more powerful evidence for Reading Recovery. Hundreds of replications in New Zealand, Central Victoria, and Columbus, Ohio, have confirmed that cross-national replication is possible (Clay, 1987). The 1992 research results reported by the national Reading Recovery data center at the Ohio State University reveal that at least two-thirds of the U.S. children who have had a full program (60 lessons or more) can be returned to average levels of performance within their respective first-grade classrooms. While there are variations related to level of coverage, quality of implementation, and factors such as student mobility, Reading Recovery works. It does not solve *every* educational problem, nor can it be the *only* positive literacy experience children have. It does one thing very well—it teaches children to read and spell. It works.

Research on Reading Recovery continues, but it has gone beyond the program evaluation of the past. We know Reading Recovery works, but now we are trying to discover more about the factors related to success. This research will provide information to help us better understand and be more effective in our work in Reading Recovery. It may also help us in designing and refining literacy education in other settings. Preliminary analyses reveal that success in Reading Recovery is related to the decisions teachers make and their ability to make powerful moves tailored to individual children.

As we will see from the research presented in the following chapters, when procedures are applied in a ritualistic or mechanical way, success is not as likely as when flexible decisionmaking is employed. These results underscore the premise that the teacher makes the difference and illuminate some of the unique features and important concepts related to Reading Recovery teaching.

READING RECOVERY AS A SYSTEMWIDE INTERVENTION

In order to introduce and sustain a high-quality implementation of Reading Recovery in a school system, implementers must take a systemic view of change. Clay says that "an innovation cannot move into an educational system merely on the merits of what it can do for children" (1987, p. 40). That may seem a shocking statement, but innovations fail because the innovators do not take into account the preexisting organization as it interacts in complex ways with the new model. The system must learn, just as the child and teacher must learn; balance must be achieved. She emphasizes the need for a redirecting system that continually solves problems.

Reading Recovery involves a network of people, including teachers, administrators, and parents, and a process of intervention that work together to deliver the kind of instruction that will help students. It is a self-renewing system in that there are processes already in place that help everyone involved to keep on learning.

Initial Staff Development

The dynamic in-service program supports teachers' development of a system of theoretical and practical knowledge out of which their actions flow. They have a repertoire of actions, but it is a broad repertoire that does not remove the decisionmaking power of independent readers and writers. The staff development model is fully described in Chapter 3.

Continuing Professional Development

Even after the initial training, teachers continue to meet regularly, though not as frequently, for in-service sessions in which they update their knowledge and continue to grow in their understandings. There is recognition that they are building a complex knowledge base; often it is in the second year that teachers begin to say that they are truly achieving skilled teaching. Additionally, as they network with other teachers and work with children, refinements are made and the repertoire of teacher actions is better understood and widened. It is necessary to continue communication and contact with previously trained teachers so that they can constantly feel the excitement of new learning and keep their teaching and learning systems flexible.

Administrative Support and Involvement

A key administrator is the principal of the school where Reading Recovery is to be implemented; the project should not be undertaken unless the principal supports it and is willing to become fully informed. Typically, principals take an active role (along with the Reading Recovery teacher and classroom teacher) in communicating with parents. They attend some in-service sessions, often providing transportation for the children to be observed. They follow children's progress closely, making it their business to observe children while actually reading and writing.

Another key administrator is the site coordinator. One person, a school district administrator or a university faculty member or administrator, takes responsibility for the leadership role in making arrangements for the project. Those responsibilities might include supervising the facility, making arrangements for communication and selection of teachers, chairing meetings, and managing the project budget. Reading Recovery requires administrative support at every level of the district, region, or institution, or it will not be successful.

Key Role of Teacher Leaders

The key to the redirecting system is the Reading Recovery teacher leader. These teacher leaders instruct 12 new Reading Recovery teachers each year, work with four Reading Recovery children each day, provide continuing contact sessions for all previously trained teachers, and guide testing and selection of children. In addition to these responsibilities, they often conduct in-service sessions in their district or region. Teacher leaders return each year to their training sites for their own continuing contact sessions, and they participate in Reading Recovery conferences in their state or in Ohio. They are also visited by their trainers, on a regularly scheduled or request basis, especially in their first year of working with teachers, but this contact may also continue in subsequent years as necessary. Because a site report is written every year as a means of evaluating the progress of children and teachers in each site, the teacher leader conducts ongoing research as part of the national network.

READING RECOVERY CHANGE AND THE FUTURE

Educational innovations can be ephemeral. It is hard to predict the future of any educational innovation—but the safest prediction is that it will not last. Strong forces work against change. Most innovations never are tried because we have so much invested in the status quo. Sometimes they are tried, but without system support, so that existing forces continually undermine their effectiveness. Sometimes innovations are not given a long enough chance to work, or the implementers have so little power that they cannot act to solve the problems that would make the innovation successful. Even when innovations have a good long run, they can fall victim to territorial disputes, budget crises, political changes, or new personnel who enter a system with their own agendas.

Reading Recovery has already surprised some people; it has lasted longer than expected. Many problems have been solved, many barriers overcome; but there are many more. A young girl recently won an award for a review she wrote about a novel she had read. She competed against students her age from her entire region. Every student in the finals was asked to name who had helped him or her with the review. Our 9-year-old had not received help but in that blank she wrote the name of her Reading Recovery teacher from two years earlier. That same student was retained in third grade because she did not know her math facts. Surely our systems can do better for a capable reader and writer. This example tells us that we need to take a hard look at our systems. It also tells us that perhaps reading is not enough. Reading Recovery does what it is designed to do: Children learn to read and write. This ability is necessary, but it is not necessarily sufficient to ensure success throughout a child's educational career.

Those who are considering Reading Recovery can expect that involvement will provoke changes in the system. Every aspect of literacy teaching, commonly accepted practices, evaluation practices, and system of political decisionmaking will undergo scrutiny. Teachers will start to look at children and at literacy in new ways; there will be a seemingly insatiable demand for more books for children to read, and not just from Reading Recovery teachers. There may be a feeling of disequilibrium among teachers, a demand for more information and for help in promoting more reading and writing in classrooms. Reading Recovery turns things upside down. That can be a problem. But we can also expect empowered and excited teachers who are aware of the importance of what they do and students who become readers and writers.

Chapter 2

Answering Questions About the Treatment of High-Risk Children

When we began to read about and study Reading Recovery, there were some questions in our minds. Today we find these same questions arising when we meet with educators from U.S. and Canadian schools. Of course, we initially wondered whether Reading Recovery would work. There was a body of research in New Zealand that supported Reading Recovery's effectiveness, but how would it make the transition to the U.S. system? We wondered whether children would make accelerated progress and be successfully released from the program. We also wondered whether the program would have long-term implications for these children. Would they maintain their gains and go on learning at a sufficient rate to keep up with their peers?

And there were some other questions. We wondered whether *any* sound approach that used one-on-one work would have the same impact on children's progress. For example, daily, individual reading of children's literature might be just as effective, as might daily, individual work on skills. Another question arose from our concern for serving larger numbers of children. Couldn't a teacher trained in Reading Recovery implement the procedures in small groups and accomplish the same results? That would answer the economic problems involved and fit better into our system of compensatory education. Finally, we found it hard to believe that so much additional training would be needed. We had extensive teaching experience and advanced degrees in reading; couldn't we learn this process in a shorter time? Or couldn't the training be redesigned to be accomplished in something like a summer workshop? The process seemed unnecessarily long, spread-out, and costly. All of these questions indicated that we were only beginning to understand the systemic nature of Reading Recovery, but they were important questions given the educational context in which we were trying to implement the project.

In this chapter, we summarize program evaluation data for Reading Recovery in the United States and present the design and results of a statewide study designed to answer the previous questions. This study allowed us to discover more about the factors related to the program's success. As will be seen from the research presented in this chapter, Reading Recovery is effective for young, high-risk children and this success is related to the decisions teachers make and their ability to make powerful moves tailored to individual children. Success is not as likely when procedures are applied in a ritualistic or mechanical way. Flexible decisionmaking is necessary. The results of this research underscore the premise that the teacher makes the difference and illuminate some of the unique features and important concepts related to teaching in Reading Recovery.

THE OHIO READING RECOVERY STUDIES (1986–91)

We began Reading Recovery in 1984 with a small pilot project that generated excitement in our educational community in Ohio. We had an opportunity to begin to address our major questions in 1985 when the Ohio General Assembly appropriated funds to support the training program for Reading Recovery and to collect data on children's progress. The research project during 1985–86 gave us an opportunity to learn how effective the program would be in Ohio.

Purpose

The purpose of the study was to compare the progress of children involved in Reading Recovery with those involved in another compensatory program that existed in the Columbus public schools. The comparison program provided instructional assistants (paraprofessionals) who were specially trained to work with individuals and small groups on the skills that were expected in reading group work. The program was new to the district and was highly regarded; thus, it seemed appropriate for this program and Reading Recovery to share the lowest-achieving cohort of students.

Procedures

Schools and Children.   The project was implemented in 12 urban schools that had diverse populations, low achievement, and high percentages of children receiving free or reduced-price lunches. In each school, children were selected because they were, in terms of achievement, in the lowest 20% in their school. These children were randomly assigned either to Reading Recovery or to the other program, and instruction began. Children in Reading Recovery received individual lessons daily. There were 12 previously trained Reading Recovery teachers; another 20 teachers were new to the program and participated in the yearlong class during 1985–86. Each of the two training classes was taught by a teacher leader trained the previous year (pilot program). Program length for Reading Recovery children varied because students entered and left the program throughout the year; during 1985–86, Reading Recovery children received an average of 67 lessons. Of the 136 children served, 100, or 73.5%, were successfully discontinued; they were released from Reading Recovery and were not given further extra help. Children in the comparison program (N = 53) were served daily all year by the instructional assistant.

For practical purposes, we established a 60-lesson criterion for program participation; that is, a child had to have at least 60 lessons to be included as a "program child." This paralleled a similar criterion (80% attendance) that was used in the district for collecting Chapter 1 results.

Assessment Measures.   We administered several tests to children at the beginning of the year, at discontinuing time, and at the end of the school year. The first six tests make up the Diagnostic Survey (Clay, 1955): (1) letter identification, (2) word test, (3) Concepts About Print, (4) writing vocabulary, (5) dictation task, (6) text reading level. We also administered two subtests of the Comprehensive Test of Basic Skills (CTBS) (1981)—Reading Vocabulary and Reading Comprehension. To provide perspective for comparing both groups of at-risk children, we selected a random sample of first-grade students (N = 102) in project schools. These students did not qualify either for Reading Recovery or for the compensatory program; thus they represented the upper 80% of the population. This group would give us an idea of the levels that our discontinued children needed to meet. It also helped us to find an "average band" (defined as .5 standard deviation above and below the 34 mean) for "regular" classrooms. It is important to point out that this is a very conservative average band, since it is taken from the upper achievement group. The random sample of children was tested on each of the seven measures. All assessments except standardized tests were individually administered by trained testers who were unaware of Reading Recovery, comparison group, or random sample status.

Results

Means and standard deviations were calculated for each of three groups: (1) Reading Recovery children, (2) comparison children, and (3) the random sample of average first graders (May scores only). Multivariate analysis (Hotelling's T2) indicated significant differences between Reading Recovery (RR) children and comparison children. RR children excelled on the word test,

Concepts About Print, writing vocabulary, dictation, text reading, and CTBS Reading Vocabulary and Comprehension. All children achieved close to perfect performance on letter identification and the word test.

We also wanted to find out how the successfully discontinued children compared with the average group we had randomly selected. The comparison would serve as a check on the discontinuing process. Were they really reading at average levels when objectively tested by an outside researcher? We compared the end-of-year scores of successfully discontinued RR children with those of the random sample. We found that over 90% of the discontinued students met or exceeded the average range on text reading, letter identification, word test, and dictation. More than 70% met or exceeded the criteria on all other measures.

On nationally normed standardized tests, the most difficult situation for these young readers, RR children had a gain score of 8.6 compared to the comparison children's average gain score of –2.4 for Total Reading on the CTBS.

We concluded that Reading Recovery had an immediate positive effect on the children served. The Reading Recovery children reached higher levels than did comparison children; more important, the discontinued children (73.5% of program children) reached or exceeded average levels for their age cohort in project schools. Observations made at discontinuing time and at the end of the year indicated that these initially struggling readers had developed independent systems for problem solving in reading. Our next question was whether these children could maintain their progress and keep on learning without additional help.

Follow-Up Studies

All children who participated in the two treatments were followed for three years in order to provide insights into the long-range effectiveness of the Reading Recovery program. In May 1987, one year after the intervention, Reading Recovery and comparison children were assessed on their text reading ability. Again, "blind" testers administered the individual assessment. To provide perspective for the scores of both groups, a random sample of second-grade children was selected from regular classrooms in project schools and administered the same assessment. A similar testing process was conducted in May 1988, at the end of third grade, and again in May 1989, at the end of fourth grade. For the fourth-grade year, it was necessary to test a randomly selected sample of fourth-grade Reading Recovery students. An average band for text reading level was calculated for second graders in 1987, for third graders in 1988. Because of limited resources, the same third graders were again tested as fourth graders in 1989; this process resulted in a spuriously high average band but still provided valuable information. Again, the average band was defined as .5 standard deviation above and below the mean.

Our results indicated that Reading Recovery children, including both discontinued and not-discontinued students, were still far ahead of the initially equal comparison group at the end of fourth grade. Discontinued Reading Recovery children compared well with the average band. Fourth-grade Reading Recovery children demonstrated that they could read with high accuracy materials at sixth-grade level or above. Additionally, we were somewhat surprised to find that these children were excellent spellers, producing spellings closer to conventional spellings on a fifth-grade spelling test than was characteristic of the random sample population. These results provide evidence that a high proportion of successfully discontinued children continued to make progress for at least three full years after their individual Reading Recovery interventions had taken place.

We concluded that Reading Recovery has long-term positive benefits for children. The Columbus project, during those first years, was conducted in close proximity to Ohio State University (OSU). Meanwhile, the program continued to expand to other areas in Ohio, to other states, and to Canada. By 1993, Reading Recovery projects had been implemented in 44 U.S. states and 4 Canadian provinces. Each site gathers evaluation data; results of these analyses will be described in the next section.

THE NATIONAL READING RECOVERY PROJECT (1987–92)

In 1987, Reading Recovery was selected by the U.S. Department of Education's National Diffusion Network (NDN) as an exemplary program. The purpose of NDN is to make successful educational programs available to school districts throughout the nation. Selection was based on previous research documenting success; but being part of NDN provided another opportunity to gather data on the impact of Reading Recovery. Participants in Reading Recovery made the decision to collect a significant amount of information on every replication of Reading Recovery. We knew that adjustments would be needed for local conditions and populations. We also knew that now Reading Recovery would be diffused far from the original university base and would include a large variety of teachers and students. Some basic questions were:

> Would Reading Recovery continue to have positive results when promulgated by different teacher educators at distances far from the original site?
>
> Would Reading Recovery continue to have positive results for students from a variety of economic groups, geographic areas, and ethnolinguistic backgrounds?

In 1987, four educators from outside Ohio received training at osu during the 1987–88 academic year. They returned to their home states the following year to begin serving children and training teachers. During 1988–89, 679 children were served in 77 schools outside Ohio. The number of children served from 1989 to 1992 is shown in Table 2.1.

In 1992–93, Reading Recovery teachers served almost 13,000 students in over 800 school districts in 38 states in the United States and 4 provinces in Canada. The Reading Recovery network has grown to include over 5,450 trained teachers in more than 3,800 schools throughout North America. Teacher training is now provided by 263 teacher leaders, who were themselves trained at one of 18 regional Reading Recovery training centers or in New Zealand. For all these replications, the success rate has remained high, with the average percent discontinued ranging from 83% to 87%. As strength is built in regional areas and coverage increases, the success rate climbs.

For many projects, replication means a "watering down" of a program or educational innovation. A strength of Reading Recovery is that with each replication the system becomes stronger. The intensive yearlong training program followed by continuing professional development allows teachers to continue to increase their knowledge base and skills as they work with children. Teacher leaders attend a required summer institute where they encounter new research and hone their understandings through interaction. Teach-

TABLE 2.1. Number of Reading Recovery Children Served in United States, 1989–1992

Year	School Districts	Children Served	Program Children*
1989-90	332	7778	5840
1990-91	508	12902	9486
1991-92	801	22193	16313

* Children who receive 60 or more lessons or were discontinued from the program before having 60 lessons.

ers are provided conferences so that communication can take place across sites and across states and countries. In addition, site visits provide new input for continued learning. Replication results appear to support this process, since results for a single site are often better in successive years and national results seem to be improving. Moreover, there are gains beyond specific program outcomes. Reading Recovery appears to influence curriculum and policy-making within school districts.

READING RECOVERY AND SYSTEMIC CHANGE

Reading Recovery is much more than merely a particular theory or analysis of what is needed to help children who have difficulty learning. To work effectively, Reading Recovery must achieve change along four dimensions:

1. Behavioral change on the part of teachers
2. Child behavior change achieved by teaching
3. Organizational changes in schools achieved by teachers and administrators
4. Social and political changes in funding by controlling authorities

The structure of Reading Recovery recognizes the complexity of change; accordingly, many districts experience a substantial "spin-off" benefit from implementation of the program.

Systemwide Change: A Case Example

A district superintendent recently said: "The Reading Recovery program has not only reduced the number of children who are retained in first grade and placed in special education and/or remedial reading programs, it has also had a profound and lasting systemwide impact on the elementary language arts program, primary assessment practice, and primary classroom instruction in our school district." This school district serves approximately 2,400 elementary children every year. The majority of these students become proficient readers in the primary grades; however, approximately one out of every eight youngsters experiences some difficulty in learning to read in first grade. Prior to implementation of the Reading Recovery program in 1986–87, teachers had adopted a "wait-and-see" attitude; that is, they provided failing readers additional support and rich literacy experiences and then waited for them to catch up. The longer the teachers waited, however, the further the children fell behind.

When district administrators and teachers read about an early intervention program from New Zealand that helped the lowest-achieving first-grade readers reach average reading levels in 15 to 20 weeks, they decided to enroll one experienced teacher in the yearlong academic teacher-leader course at Ohio State University. This teacher leader returned to the district the following year to train the first-grade Chapter 1 teachers in Reading Recovery techniques.

District administrators and teachers realized after the first year of implementation that sending a teacher to be trained in the Reading Recovery program was a wise decision. The lowest-achieving first-grade readers did catch up to the average readers in their class. Program evaluation data over a five-year period showed that 76% of the lowest-achieving readers, those who generally "fall between the cracks," caught up with their peers and continued to learn how to read with regular classroom instruction. These results were expected. What was not expected was the dramatic decrease in the number of students retained in first grade. Prior to the introduction of the program in 1986, an average of 10 students per year were retained in first grade. In the five years since Reading Recovery began, only 17 students have been retained. These figures represent a reduction of 33 retentions over the five-year period. Not only have these first-grade students been spared years of psychological trauma associated with failing first grade, but the district has also saved approximately $170,000 through reduction of first-grade retention.

The number of first-grade students classified as learning-disabled (LD) and targeted for LD classrooms also decreased from 36% in 1986–87 to 8% in 1990–91. During that five-year period, a total of 207 students were classified by interdisciplinary teams of professionals as learning-disabled prior to their entry into Reading Recovery. After participating in the program, 167 of these students were discontinued and able to read with the average first graders in their classrooms. The remaining students (those who may indeed be learning-disabled) were referred for specialized testing and placed in LD resource rooms. The LD teachers requested in-service sessions that would enable them to continue to use similar teaching techniques with students who had made slow, steady progress in the Reading Recovery program but had not been discontinued. During these in-service sessions, the teachers learned how to administer and interpret the Diagnostic Survey (Clay, 1985) and thus become careful observers of what the children were able to learn, not what they were unable to learn. They also learned what the children should be taught from an analysis of their performance while reading whole texts rather than training in isolated visual and auditory discrimination activities.

Introducing the Reading Recovery program to the school system also reduced the number of children who were placed in Chapter 1 remedial reading programs in first through fifth grades. Chapter 1 teachers learned how to use the survey (Clay, 1985) and become familiar with some of the theory, practices, and techniques used in the Reading Recovery program. They restructured Chapter 1 classes to include more opportunities for students to engage in reading and writing whole texts. The instructional approaches used by the Chapter 1 teachers enabled approximately 50% of the students to be phased out of the first-grade Chapter 1 class at the end of the year. The remaining 50% of the first-grade students received Reading Recovery as space became available. Between May 1988 and May 1991, only 5% of the total population of second- through fifth-grade students qualified for and were served in Chapter 1 classes.

In addition to in-service sessions for LD and Chapter 1 teachers, quarterly in-service classes were also held for kindergarten and first-grade teachers. These regular education teachers learned how to be careful observers of children learning to read by administering the Diagnostic Survey (Clay, 1985). The teachers soon discovered a range of behaviors that indicated various levels of progress among the kindergarten and first-grade students. They began to realize the importance of determining the child's literacy behaviors at the onset of instruction and the value of shifting those reading behaviors from less adequate to more adequate responding early on. The teachers eventually created a Before School Reading and Writing Survey, designed to capture kindergarten and first-grade students' literacy strengths. This survey included writing vocabulary, sentence dictation, and text reading measures adapted from the Diagnostic Survey (Clay, 1985). The results of the survey revealed differences in students' abilities and provided insights into the specific kinds of literacy experiences that would be most beneficial for each student. The survey also helped teachers to identify students who would most likely need Reading Recovery screening.

The regular education teachers observed Reading Recovery lessons and had ongoing conversations with Reading Recovery teachers about the theory of the reading process and what the children should be taught to do in order to become independent processors of print. These experiences enabled regular education and support teachers to begin to understand, construct, and use specific language to describe, analyze, and assess literacy behaviors of students in their classrooms. As the teachers continued to use and understand the informal assessment measures, their focus shifted from identifying and recording students limitations and weaknesses to understanding and documenting their strengths and abilities.

The Before School Reading and Writing Survey became such a valuable observation tool for determining early reading progress that the kindergarten, first-, and second-grade teachers designed another observation instrument, the Developmental Primary Assessment, that captured emerging literacy behaviors for children in kindergarten and first and second grades. The teachers constructed a continuum of descriptors to portray the developmental levels of emergent readers and writers in order to monitor each student's literacy development and to provide goals and performance standards. Procedures for a leveled text reading assessment and a holistic writing assessment were developed for kindergarten through second grade and kept in the student Literacy Development File. The files included reading (documented in running records of text reading) and writing samples at various points in time. The samples of students' work helped teachers to capture progress over time, provide appropriate instruction, share progress with students and parents, and identify students in need of additional literacy support.

The introduction of Reading Recovery into this school district six years ago fundamentally changed teachers, administrators, students, and parents' attitudes about low-progress students at all grade levels. The program also united district personnel in their attempts to provide a comprehensive and cooperative primary language arts and assessment program that impacts Chapter 1 and learning disability programs as well.

Reading Recovery has also created systemic changes in New Zealand since the early 1980s, when it became a national program. Government figures from 1988 revealed that with approximately 20% coverage of the 6-year-old age cohort, over 90% of the children were successfully released as independent readers. A more astounding figure is that only 0.8% of the entire age cohort needed further referral and special help. These data give us some idea of what is possible and speak well of the educational system, with Reading Recovery as a vital part. "The results challenge much accumulated wisdom about literacy problems; clearly they are alterable variables for many children" (Clay, 1990, p. 69). It is our hope that, in a few years, similar figures will be reported in the United States.

A STATEWIDE STUDY IN OHIO

At the beginning of this chapter, we stated frequently asked questions that had not been addressed by the previous research. Our statewide study, supported by a grant from the John D. and Catherine T. MacArthur Foundation, was designed to address these questions. For example, since Reading Recovery is an individual program, educators and researchers have suggested that good teachers working one-on-one, whatever the approach, could achieve the same results. A second question related to the individual instruction is whether the instructional techniques could be used with groups to achieve the same results, thus substantially lowering the costs of the intervention. Another issue is related to training. Training teachers in Reading Recovery requires a full academic year and special features (such as live demonstration lessons) that are difficult for school districts to provide. Couldn't a shortened version of the training be provided that would achieve the same results?

Purpose

The purposes of this study were (1) to compare the impact of three one-on-one early intervention treatments and one small-group intervention program on the reading progress of low-achieving first-grade students; and (2) to compare the progress of Reading Recovery students taught by fully trained teachers with the progress of students tutored by teachers who received an alternative form of training. Specifically, we wanted to know:

How does Reading Recovery compare with a one-on-one basic skills instructional tutorial?

How does Reading Recovery compare with a similar program taught by partially trained teachers?

How does Reading Recovery compare with group instruction performed by trained Reading Recovery teachers?

Procedures

School Districts.   In a large midwestern state, school districts that had the highest proportions of students from families receiving Aid to Dependent Children (ADC) were asked to participate in the study. A total of 10 independent school districts representing rural, urban, and suburban settings volunteered for the study. Each school district had a Reading Recovery program already operating and at least four elementary schools that qualified for Chapter 1 services (or a free and reduced-price lunch program). Thus a total of 40 schools, four each in 10 different districts, were originally included in the study. Demographic information on these districts is presented in Table 2.2.

Students.   Student subjects for the study were first-grade students who were the lowest scorers on a standardized selection test (Metropolitan Achievement Test) and were additionally recommended by their teachers as being most in need of additional help. The sample consisted of 238 male and 165 female students. Of the total sample of students available for the study, 72 were in school districts prevented by policy from revealing information about race; the rest of the sample was divided as follows: White ($N = 244$); African American ($N = 86$); Asian ($N = 1$). In many areas, district policies prohibited the communication of information about free or reduced-price lunches; this factor resulted in missing information for 131 students. Of the remaining 272

TABLE 2.2. Demographic Information on District Sites in Early Literacy Study

Site	No. of Elem. Buildings	Type	Gender		Race		District Population
			Male	Female	White	Black	
1	15	Rural	17	16	31	1	24,328
2	5	Suburban	21	13	33	1	33,636
3	4	Rural	26	10	26	2	11,888
4	18	Urban	18	16	23	1	94,730
5	33	Urban	33	13	17	21	203,371
6	13	Urban	23	22	-	-	57,538
7	12	Urban	25	23	30	17	53,927
8	11	Urban	20	28	44	0	37,040
9	6	Suburban	26	12	17	15	7,802
10	12	Urban	29	12	23	18	56,629

subjects, 166 (61%) were receiving free lunches and 11 (4%) were receiving reduced price lunches.

Instructional Programs. Four instructional programs were compared to address the study questions: (1) Reading Recovery; (2) Reading Success (RS), an individual tutorial program modeled on Reading Recovery and taught by certified teachers who received a condensed two-week version of the Reading Recovery training; (3) Direct Instruction Skills Plan (DISP), an individual tutorial program that used systematic development of essential primary reading skills, taught by certified teachers who participated in an intensive three-day in-service course; and (4) Reading and Writing Group (RWG), a small group tutorial program that focused on reading and writing activities, taught by teachers who had been trained as Reading Recovery teachers.

Each program was compared with its own control group within the school. We accomplished this by selecting the lowest-achieving students and then randomly assigning them either to a special instructional program or to the existing compensatory education program in the school. This process allowed us to compare a set of comparisons; that is, we were examining the degree to which each special instructional program compared to the traditional program in the school. Because students were randomly assigned, they were initially equal in achievement level. The process allowed us to control for variation in students that exists across schools and school districts.

Assessment Measures. Several measures were used to assess the impact of these instructional programs. We will describe only those that were significant in distinguishing the groups. A dictation task was used to measure children's ability to represent sounds (see Clay, 1985; DeFord, Pinnell, Lyons, & Place, 1990). Children were read a sentence and asked to write the words. In scoring, children were given credit for every sound represented appropriately, thus indicating the students' ability to analyze the word for sound and letter correspondence. Several sentences were available at the first-grade level. Since students were followed into the second grade, a more elaborate sentence was constructed for use at that level.

Measures of text reading level were obtained by constructing a gradient of difficulty for text drawn originally from a basal reading system. Since the system did not include levels easy enough for many children at the beginning of the study, the first five levels were specified easy books. The scale was constructed by selecting and then testing difficulty levels with groups of children over time (see Peterson, 1991; Pinnell, DeFord, & Lyons, 1988). There were 26 levels in all, the highest level indicating approximately sixth-grade level according to the authors of the system used (see Scott, Foresman, 1979). Texts used for testing were not used for instruction; children were asked to read them without previous review of the text, moving progressively up the levels of difficulty. Children were tested by independent, trained evaluators. Individually, children were asked to read selections while the tester recorded reading behavior using Clay's running record technique (Clay, 1985) and calculated an accuracy level. Children continued reading higher levels of text until they scored below 90% accuracy on two levels of text. The test yielded a score for level of difficulty (the highest level read above 90% accuracy). Finally, children were administered the Gates–MacGinitie Reading Test (1978), a group-administered, comprehensive standardized test of skills related to reading.

Timeline. In October, students were administered the text reading and dictation assessments. Instruction in all treatments continued for 70 days before students were again tested. In February, students were administered the text reading level and dictation assessments and the Gates–MacGinitie (time 1). In October, again in December, and finally in February, lessons were videotaped and on separate occasions were observed by an OSU researcher. For two days prior to and subsequent to the videotaping, lessons were audio-taped. This procedure assured researchers a check on the representativeness of the videotaped sample. To determine whether gains were maintained, students were again tested in the fall of second grade on the second-grade version of the dictation task and the text reading level assessment. For purposes of the research, instructional programs were measured after 70 days. Reading Recovery is not a yearlong program, so services were discontinued for children around that time; Reading Success services also did not continue.

The group programs and regular compensatory programs (which served as control groups in each school) continued throughout the year. Some students were placed in Reading Recovery after the end of the experiment, and the progress of these students was also examined after the fall testing.

Results

Quantitative.   Reading Recovery was the only group for which the mean treatment effect was significant on all four measures at the conclusion of the experiment and was also the only treatment indicating lasting effects. Specifically, the analysis showed that Reading Recovery children performed significantly better than an equivalent control group and those receiving the three other special treatments. Reading Recovery was the only group that was better on all tests, showing long-term effects in reading. At the end of 70 days of instruction, when the treatment groups were disbanded and regular school services continued, Reading Recovery children were reading five levels ahead of children who had received regular remedial reading lessons. Even though the control group continued to receive lessons for the rest of the year, Reading Recovery children were still three reading levels above the remedial group average when all children were tested the following autumn. Children in two of the three special treatments, RS and DISP, were four and five levels below the Reading Recovery group average after the 7-day treatment period and only one and a half or fewer levels above their respective control groups. Children in the third treatment, RWG, which was taught by trained Reading Recovery teachers, were three levels below the Reading Recovery group. In the autumn, children receiving these special treatments were achieving about the same as those in the remedial reading group.

To put this into perspective, traditionally a child goes through four pre-primer books and a primer-level book before beginning to read a first-grade reader. The top reading group may read half of, or finish, the first reader, but the average reading group would more likely just be beginning this final book at the end of the first-grade reading program. The lowest reading group, on average, might still be in one of the preprimers. Reading Recovery children were reading the equivalent of the primer in February and were independently and comfortably reading the first-grade reader at the beginning of second grade. All other treatments and the remedial reading group were reading no higher than the third preprimer in February and were still reading, on an average, at the primer-level reader at the beginning of second grade. In the reading group scenario, Reading Recovery children would be considered to be achieving within average range, while the other children were still reading in the low range. An interesting corollary to this research project was found in the children who received Reading Recovery services *after* the experiment was over (in February, March, or April). These children were three levels ahead of children who received regular remedial reading when they were tested in the autumn. So they, too, were reading within the average as beginning second graders.

Qualitative.   In addition to gaining quantitative information about student achievement, this research project made it possible to look deeper into the processes involved in teaching and learning. Teachers in the study volunteered to be videotaped at intervals teaching the same student, and these videotapes have been a rich source of qualitative data for continuing investigations of how teachers interact with children to support the development of reading and writing strategies. Lessons have been analyzed for content and time allocations, and teachers' reflections on their own teaching have been probed to explore relationships between the teacher's knowledge base, teacher actions, and the development of students' understandings.

A total of 79 videotaped lessons were analyzed for time and content. The results, presented in Table 2.3, provide interesting comparisons for the three individual programs and two group programs.

Reading Recovery and Reading Success had the highest proportions of time spent directly on reading and writing. Time spent in the "other" category was largely talk about books, working on letter recognition, and writing for fluency. For DISP, the majority of time was spent not on reading or writing but on "other" activities, mostly exercises in listening, word recognition, and phonics worksheets, although reading to the child was included. The two group treatments, the RWG (with a trained RR teacher) and the control group, provided another interesting contrast, with the former spending more time on reading and writing. For more complete data analyses and a discussion of the quantitative and qualitative results, see Pinnell, Lyons, DeFord, Bryk, and Seltzer (in press).

Implications: The Larger Meaning

Reading Recovery owes its success to the combination of four techniques that strengthen one another. A student and teacher meet privately for a daily half-hour of intense and closely structured work. Children spend most of their lesson reading real books—not snippets from reading texts or worksheets— and writing sentences that they compose themselves. Teachers custom-tailor each student's lessons to build on the child's individual strengths, no matter how meager, showing the child how to broaden those skills and use them to master others. Finally, Reading Recovery teachers learn the program's techniques not in a quick workshop but through a yearlong course of study. The

TABLE 2.3. Instructional Time and Context for Treatment Groups

	RR	RS	DISP	R/WG	CG
Number of Lessons	18	18	18	13	12
Setting	Individual	Individual	Individual	Small Group (4-6)	Small Group (4-6)
Allotted Time	30 min.	30 min.	30 min.	30-45 min.	45 min.
Average Actual Time	00:31:21 (00:24:20- 00:41:48)	00:27:23 (00:16:33- 00:37:52)	00:26:49 (00:20:13- 00:33:20)	00:31:43 (00:26:18- 00:41:26)	00:26:39 (00:19:22- 00:32:18)
Average % of Time Reading Text	60.2%	62.3%	29.9%	26.8%	21.0%
Average % of Time Writing Text	25.3%	28.8%	.3%	23.4%	3.1%
Average % of Time-other	14.5%	8.9%	69.8%	49.8%	75.9%
Books Read by Children	94	84	4	31	16
Average no. Books/per Lesson	5.22	4.60	.22	2.38	1.33

RR = Reading Recovery
RS = Reading Success
DISP = Direct Instruction Skills Plan
RWG = Reading/Writing Group
CG = Control Group

course includes extensive practice teaching, which is critiqued by experienced Reading Recovery teachers. Back in the schools, teacher leaders help working Reading Recovery teachers to catch and correct weaknesses in their work and to find new ways to be even more effective.

The results of this study make it clear that the success of Reading Recovery is due to more than the individual factor and the instructional emphasis factor. The time allocations for Reading Recovery and Reading Success were quite similar, and they used the same framework for instruction; but as a group, the Reading Recovery teachers had higher student outcomes. It is clear that another factor made the difference: the intensity and effectiveness of the teaching within the Reading Recovery framework. The use of time, materials, and the one-on-one factor are necessary; however, teachers' ability to make spontaneous and effective decisions, supply sustaining feedback, and provide prompts that simplify the demands of the task is even more important. More research is needed to uncover the nature of the learning–teaching relationship, but the Reading Recovery training model and continuing contact among teachers may be critical factors in assuring student success. Reading Recovery emphasizes the role of the teacher as an informed, autonomous decisionmaker who is responsible for and controls both curriculum and instruction for each student. In order to provide opportunities for students to develop as independent readers and writers, the teacher must follow the student's thinking, recognize "teachable moments," and attend to the most memorable and powerful examples that will help learning to occur. The ability to understand and conceptualize learning and instruction at the cognitive and sociolinguistic levels takes reflection, practice, and time. Reflective opportunities, over time, with knowledgeable peers are inherent in the Reading Recovery training program and the system of support that surrounds teachers who participate.

This study confirms the previous findings—that, as an integrated system, Reading Recovery works. Individual instruction, instructional emphasis, and training—all are factors in the success of Reading Recovery; but information is needed beyond these surface factors. Solving the problems related to reading failure in the United States may ultimately depend on our willingness to examine programmatic outcomes in ways that take into account the multiple, interacting factors that may mean success for our high-risk students.

Results of this study provided insight into why Reading Recovery works. These data also reveal that Reading Recovery is not a quick-fix alternative. Rather, it is a complex program. It is obvious from our studies that even with the full training program, the carefully structured and supervised follow-up assistance, the network of support, and the collection of outcome data, there are variations in the success of Reading Recovery. This variation *cannot* be laid at the doorstep of the children and families involved; in many sites with low-income populations, Reading Recovery works quite well. We theorize that when the implementation is in place in a quality way, the degree of success is related to coverage, to circumstances in the educational system, and to the skill of the teachers.

In this study, we gathered valuable information about individual instruction, instructional emphases, and the nature of effective teacher education as they impact on successful tutoring programs for at-risk first graders. We also discovered that we need information beyond these surface factors. Solving the problems related to reading failure in the United States may ultimately depend on our willingness to continue to peel away the layers of complexity surrounding the teaching and learning act. The rest of this book reveals our progress toward this goal.

Chapter 3

Learning and Teaching: Language Processes

Reading Recovery is usually described as an early intervention program designed to undercut reading failure. It is also a dynamic and intensive professional development process for teachers. Since Reading Recovery is based on teacher decisionmaking rather than step-by-step routines or packages of materials, the staff development model is the key to success in the program. In Reading Recovery, teachers see their own teaching as an opportunity to learn, and they extend their learning through careful observation and interaction with others. In this chapter, we describe the staff development model and the yearlong teacher in-service course. We offer examples of powerful learning situations that inform and extend teachers' understandings. We describe teachers' learning by examining six key principles that underlie the learning process: (1) a constructive view of learning, (2) using language to learn, (3) valuing tentativeness, (4) flexibility, (5) creating supportive networks to extend learning, and (6) ongoing learning. The chapter concludes with a discussion of what we have learned in studying the Reading Recovery staff development model.

READING RECOVERY STAFF DEVELOPMENT MODEL

Research on teacher education usually focuses on "learning to teach," but the Reading Recovery model could just as easily be characterized as "teaching to learn." The heart of the program is not lesson plans or curriculum guides; instead, it is professional decisionmaking within the act of teaching. The success of Reading Recovery for any child depends on the teacher's ability to select and use examples. Clay (1985) stated:

> It is not enough with problem readers for the teacher to have rapport, to generate interesting tasks and generally to be a good teacher. The teacher must be

able to design a superbly sequenced program determined by the child's performance, and to make highly skilled decisions moment by moment during the lesson. (p. 53)

The language used to describe teaching in Reading Recovery is "following the child." In doing this, the teacher uses whatever opportunities arise from the books children read, their responses to the books, and messages composed by the student to craft teachable moments. Ongoing records provide a background of information for the teacher. In the act of teaching, however, the teacher selects and draws attention to the "most powerful, memorable examples" to help the young student construct an inner understanding of processes involved in reading and writing (Clay, 1985). At the core of a teacher's work with each child is the belief that readers construct an "inner control" by engaging in problem solving (Clay, 1991). They construct meaning within experiences with written language. In so doing, children connect their own knowledge of the world and of language with print, the visual representation of language.

The adult plays an important role in supporting the learner's active problem solving. While the teacher and child collaboratively participate in reading and writing, instruction is carried out in a dialogic interchange. The student takes the lead, performing operations as independently as possible; but it is the teacher who helps the learner work effectively. Clay and Cazden (1990) have described this relationship from a Vygotskian point of view, claiming that the teacher provides a "scaffold" that allows the learner to work within the zone of proximal development.

As teachers learn how to teach in this manner, a shared language and a unique stance to their learning is established. In this culture, teachers are encouraged to see their teaching as an opportunity to learn. This stance is promoted by particular aspects of the staff development model, including (1) careful observation of children, (2) reflecting on and talking about teaching, and (3) interacting with others during the process. However, we want to make it clear that such learning is never finished. All of us continually try to add to our knowledge and skills. Reading Recovery teachers are started on their way with an intensive in-service course, but they soon learn the value of remaining lifelong learners.

The program for children and teachers is supported by a systemic approach for reasons that are clear in this statement by Clay (1987): "An innovation cannot move into an educational system based solely on what it can do for children" (p. 38). Reading Recovery has a network of communication that links teachers and teacher leaders from different sites and promotes continued dialogue. Regular staff development opportunities are provided at all levels, with participants moving increasingly toward independent problem solving. Data on each child are systematically collected. Program evaluation includes both quantitative and qualitative data, which is collected and analyzed by teachers and teacher leaders. Each year, teacher leaders produce a site report that is used for program improvement and problem solving. This system is not only supportive; it is designed to be self-renewing. The communication system allows for updating of knowledge as new research becomes available. Providing the teacher training requires the minimum of a five-year implementation plan with built-in evaluation and continuing contact. Inherent in this plan is the concept of Reading Recovery as a systemic intervention.

THE YEARLONG IN-SERVICE COURSE: AN OVERVIEW

Reading Recovery training takes an entire year. First, teachers learn the observation procedures that are used to help the teacher start daily work with children; then, they learn the framework of the lesson and begin to develop a repertoire of procedures. The process is strongly supported theoretically, but it takes time for teachers to get beneath the surface and become flexible in their learning. At first, they may simply go through the motions. Wiley (1992) reflected on her process in a piece written for the Reading Recovery teacher newsletter, *The Running Record*.

> As a novice Reading Recovery teacher, I was beginning to understand the terminology; but I was not certain how to put the procedures into practice or how to help Lazonna develop a forward thrust as a reader and writer. Phrases such as "orchestration of cues," "teaching for strategies," and "self extending system" all made sense to me. Yet I continued to work and teach from older scripts that had been successful in the past. Instead, I needed to help Lazonna by observing and understanding her abilities to such a degree that I would not do anything for her that she could learn to do for herself. (p. 3)

Reading Recovery requires a radical shift in teachers' views, adjustments in the system to accommodate unusual practices, a different approach to serving the lowest-achieving population of children, and a wider view of the teacher's role and teacher education. Meyer (1988) provided this observation from her research on implementing effective reading programs:

> Even simple behavioral changes are difficult to achieve. When we ask or demand that teachers change how they teach, particularly when new techniques are different ideologically and behaviorally from those they learned and accepted in college, we are asking for what Kuhn (1970) called a paradigm shift. Changes of

this magnitude are difficult to accomplish, but they can be expected if teachers have adequate feedback and support while they are learning new things. (p. 56)

Knowledge is built through a yearlong program that makes extensive use of a two-way mirror. Weekly, teacher groups meet in seminar sessions to watch members of the class teaching lessons behind the mirror. Typically, the group observes lessons conducted by two members of the class, one after another. Two lessons are considered essential because the idea is not to provide specific feedback to an individual teacher but to draw out important principles of learning from the two observed "cases." The one-way glass allows the observers to see the lesson at close range and to hear the teacher–child interactions. They observe closely, developing the ability to notice minute shifts in children's behavior and to quickly make inferences about the internal processing that the behaviors might signal. For example, the teachers might notice that the child stops using his or her finger to check that what is said matches the printed word. This behavior suggests that the child is gaining control of serial order; that is, the child is beginning to develop the internal processing for searching visually word by word in sequence using his or her eyes.

The observation is not silent. While they observe, teachers in the class engage in an extended conversation during which they are encouraged to think out loud, describe behavior, and try out their hypotheses about the ongoing process. They intimately participate in the lesson and the inherent instructional decisions without having to assume the responsibility for acting; thus they can concentrate on the development of their thinking as teachers. In a sense, the demonstrating teacher is providing a case, a common experience, around which his or her peers can focus their talk.

The demonstration lessons that occur behind the one-way mirror, then, serve to clarify understandings. In the talk behind the glass, teachers are guided to state observations, make their meanings clear, back up assertions with evidence, and reflect on their own experiences.

Admittedly, the first behind-the-glass experiences can cause uneasiness. American teachers are not accustomed to displaying their practice for their peers. Even observing can be a demanding experience; silent, passive observation is not allowed. Everyone is expected to contribute. Jo Ann Talwar (1989) wrote about her first experience during the teacher leader training course at Ohio State:

> The schedule for teaching "behind the glass" was being decided. People were volunteering quickly. Would it be better to do it soon and get it over with? I knew I hadn't yet had time to learn what we'd been practicing, reading about, and hearing. That was going to take time: Maybe it would be better to wait, give

myself time. I had thought that they would give us a few weeks with the kids to try and "orchestrate" all the various aspects of the program. What if I am teaching and everything goes wrong? How come I hadn't thought this part through? I realized that I had repressed any thoughts of how I might feel about teaching in front of others . . . this is supposed to help me learn . . . and I can't ask others to do this if I don't learn to do it myself. I raised my hand.

As an observing participant, I noted that "behind the glass" had demonstrated how the teaching could be done. There was a lot of incidental learning that one picked up in addition to what was highlighted by the questions from the teacher leaders. Following the lessons there was a discussion that was provocative, reassuring and stimulating. It was such a rich learning experience that questions I had wondered about, problems I had encountered and concerns I had only felt were addressed both implicitly and explicitly. I was convinced that this was a valuable experience for me as a member of the group who was engaged in the discussion while observing the lessons. Monday came and I took my turn "behind the glass." As the person on the spot, I didn't learn the same things I did as a participating observer, but I felt more confident for having survived. Actually, I noted that I could put the audience out of my mind once I started working with Robin; what was distracting was the mirror effect of the one-way glass and having it right in front of me. Even that, I hope will not be so distracting another time. I suppose I am likely to be nervous each time I do this, because there are so many aspects of the Reading Recovery program that I have to learn to integrate and orchestrate into my personal repertoire; but now I feel that I can do it, I know why I am doing it, I'm a part of a group, we are all doing it. I'm learning from the "behind the glass" activity . . . both sides of it. (pp. 3–4)

After many such experiences, teachers lose their defensiveness and begin to focus all their attention on taking on the child's point of view. They learn that by analyzing others' teaching, they gain insights to help their own teaching. The whole experience builds a culture in which people are not afraid to examine their existing teaching beliefs, their own teaching, and that of others for the greater gain to students. Geeke (1988) described this culture:

The interview data show that most of the participating teachers had their existing beliefs shaken during the early in-service sessions. They were quickly persuaded that their current methods of teaching reading and writing were based on false assumptions about teaching and learning. Subsequently, on the basis of their observations of children and their experiences during in-service sessions, they developed new beliefs about teaching and learning. This set of beliefs then acted as a framework into which the specific teaching practices of Reading Recovery could be placed. . . .

. . . the teaching procedures were not given to the teachers as a set of "ideas" for teaching literacy. Instead, the teachers were expected to use the procedures in a way that reflected the set of basic beliefs which were being developed at the same time. The ultimate aim of the training program seems to have been the development of a dynamic relationship between belief and practice; with belief acting as an individualizing influence on instruction.

. . . It seems that real teacher change is unlikely to be achieved by simply introducing a "new method of instruction" in some curriculum area. The new "method" will only be really effective if teachers have thoroughly accepted the underlying principles of the program as well as its teaching practices. The techniques employed by Reading Recovery to achieve this result deserve close examination, especially as it appears to have been much more successful than usual in achieving teacher change in the group immediately involved. (pp. 144–145)

After the two lessons, the teachers bring their group reflections into a new focus as they discuss what they observed with the demonstrating teachers. Pinnell (1991) has described this interactive model as facilitative of problem solving, supportive, and providing for ongoing learning.

The outcome of effective staff development must be the growth of a set of theoretical understandings, based on which the teacher will make decisions and take action. Lists of "good" teaching behaviors, performed in mechanical ways in response to supervisors' observations, are useless without this underlying knowledge. The problem to be faced by teacher educators is *how* to help teachers develop theories of learning that support the model of literacy underlying Reading Recovery and change their disposition and interactions with students to support this model of literacy.

LEARNING THROUGH BEHIND-THE-GLASS CONVERSATION

Observing and discussing lessons taught behind a two-way mirror has been a powerful way to change teachers' dispositions and interactions, to bring them in line with the model of literacy inherent in the Reading Recovery program. Teachers are provided opportunities to analyze and discuss specific actions and behaviors while at the same time conducting intensive reflections and holding conversations about the teaching and learning processes they are observing. The conversations are specific to the problems teachers see in the here and now—both their own teaching and the cases that are presented to them via the experience of the two-way mirror.

Below is a brief example of behind-the-glass talk. This conversation took place during one of the two behind-the-glass lessons in a teacher class in January, half-way through the training year. Twelve teachers were in the class, and during the lesson all contributed comments. In this brief segment (about three minutes of talking while observing), five class members entered the discussion.

On one side of the glass Ken, the Reading Recovery teacher, is working with Pam, who is reading *The Chick and the Duckling* (Ginsburg, 1972), categorized as Reading Recovery level six. Pam is working to achieve control of word-by-word matching in reading, but in this case, she is placing her finger on top of the words and sliding it along while reciting a rendition of the text, largely from memory. Her teacher says, "Pam, when you are reading *The Chick and the Duckling,* your finger can help you. Make sure it points under the words you are reading so you can see them." Then the teacher demonstrates the process. "Now you read it with your finger," he says. Pam begins again. This time, she attends closely to the print while she reads the story. On page 16, the text says: "'I am going for a swim,' said the duckling. 'Me too,' said the chick." Pam reads, "'I'm going for a swim,' said the duckling. 'So am . . .'" Then she hesitates. Pam knows the word *me*. She goes back to the beginning of the line and, pointing, reads "'Me too,' said the chick." Ken says, "I liked the way you were reading with your finger and checking on yourself. You knew that was the word *me*, didn't you?"

The interchange described above took only a few minutes. Simultaneously, on the other side of the glass, this conversation was taking place between Meredith, the teacher leader, and several teachers who are observing the lesson.

MEREDITH:　Make some comments about what you are seeing.

DEBORAH:　She needs to get control of word-by-word matching. Ken should make her point to the words.

MEREDITH:　What makes you say that?

DEBORAH:　Well, look, she's not doing it.

BOB:　Wait, she can match. She's pointing at each one but just not reading what's on the page. I think it might be that her strong language knowledge is overriding. That's the way kids would talk. It seems like she's inventing the story.

SARAH:　I wonder if she thinks reading is just remembering language.

MEREDITH:　Sarah, do you agree with Bob? Can she match what she says to what she reads?

SARAH:　I think she can because she was pointing to each word as she read along.

MEREDITH:　Then what do you think Ken needs to help Pam do?

BOB:　Show her how to match under the words.

DEBORAH:　Make sure that her finger is precisely under the words instead of on top so she can see them.

MEREDITH:　How will that help?

BOB: It'll help her attend to the words as she reads.

MEREDITH: Say more. How else can Ken help her?

ANGELA: Right now, he's encouraging her to point under the words. I like the ways he demonstrated this so she could see the task.

MEREDITH: Do you agree, Sarah?

SARAH: Yes, and he talked about what Pam was supposed to do while he demonstrated it for her.

ANGELA: He did a good job explaining the pointing to Pam.

MEREDITH: Beyond showing her how to point to each word as she reads the word, what else should Ken do to help Pam?

ANGELA: He needs to teach her how to check her predictions with something she knows about print.

MEREDITH: Let's watch to see if that is happening.

SARAH: Yes, it is. It appears that she's cross-checking. She just self-corrected because she noticed *me*? She knows that word.

DEBORAH: Ken did a good job pointing out when Pam was doing the right thing?

MEREDITH: What did you like about Ken's comments?

ANGELA: He demonstrated and he was explicit.

BOB: She's [Pam] learning by looking and then doing it.

MEREDITH: Was it productive teaching?

SEVERAL: Yes!

MEREDITH: Why?

DEBORAH: Because she finally got it right?

MEREDITH: Let's say more about that. Is being right the purpose?

SARAH: No, not really. It's getting her to cross-check and use visual information. It's the cross-checking that's important even if she didn't get it right.

ANGELA: I agree with Sarah, that's what we have to pay attention to.

DEBORAH: The child made a shift there.

MEREDITH: What are we asking the child to do when we say to "read it with your finger"?

ANGELA: Coordinate oral language with visual information on the page.

MEREDITH: Why is that important?

SARAH: It helps her move along in reading.

ANGELA: She can do her own work and checking and not just depend on remembering. There's evidence that she is getting more independent.

BOB: But you've got to be careful to keep her reading fluently.

KATHY: Voice pointing is normal at this stage, isn't it? We don't want her to go so fast that her language overrides attention to print.

ANGELA: Pam knows some words and some beginning sounds. This will help her know how to use that information in reading.

MEREDITH: Oh, Angela has brought up a new point. Let's watch to see if we can find more evidence of Pam's using this kind of knowledge in reading.

The discussion took place quickly, with group members initiating ideas and offering comments. This group had been working together with the leader for several months. Each had had at least two turns teaching behind the glass. They were past defensiveness and ready to "dive in" with their analyses of the lesson. After the lesson, they would talk with the demonstrating teacher about their observations. The leader had to simultaneously watch the lesson and respond to the group. She could not pick up on every comment but had to focus continually on the teaching so that important concepts could be touched on (for example, cross-checking and the use of word-by-word matching).

PRINCIPLES OF THE LEARNING UNDERLYING THE STAFF DEVELOPMENT MODEL

In the behind-the-glass discussion presented above, we can see operational evidence of several of the key principles upon which the Reading Recovery staff development model is based. We explore six of these principles in the section below: (1) a constructive view of learning, (2) using language to learn, (3) valuing tentativeness, (4) flexibility, (5) creating supportive networks to extend learning, and (6) ongoing learning.

A Constructive View of Learning

A constructive point of view suggests that when people learn, they build theories that explain what is happening in the world around them. Language interactions with others support this process. The whole setting for the Reading Recovery in-service course supports construction of knowledge. Participants look closely at the children and try to construct understandings to match their observations. In behind-the-glass talk, teachers make their own theories explicit and help others do the same. In the preceding dialogue, several participants offered explanations for Pam's reading behavior. They stated hypotheses backed by evidence. Several group members revised their theories in conversation with others. They worked from a simplistic explanation (matching word by word) to a more complex analysis of what the student did and what the teacher needed to do to help the student move forward. Angela moved from evaluating teaching by whether the child got it "right" to watching for evidence of how the teacher supported internal processing, regardless of "right" answers. Five members of the 12-person group contributed to the co-construction of knowledge in this brief interchange.

From exchanges such as these, teachers shift in their beliefs as they listen to their colleagues provide examples for what they are witnessing. They compare these statements with their previously held beliefs; sometimes clashes occur. But over time, and with continued work with children and conversations with peers, new beliefs and practices become established.

Using Language to Learn

The setting in which dialogue is carried on while teachers simultaneously observe lessons is based on the assumption that language is a key factor in building theories. In this way, language is used to represent our experiences to others and to refine and extend it for ourselves. Through language interactions with others in the group, we try out our ideas to formulate or reformulate understandings of a particular phenomenon. The process is rooted in what Halliday (1975) has described as "learning how to mean."

Throughout the teaching process, whether with children or adults, dialogue is central to the learning situation. Language is consciously used to support learning. A central process within the in-service course is verbal challenge (see Shannon, 1990). The leader's role is to challenge teachers to make statements and to back them up during the talking-while-observing sessions. Teachers are challenged at several levels; Shannon has identified three: (1) to articulate what is observed, (2) to explain what is observed, and (3) to justify one's explanations. This process, as Clay indicates, places high linguistic and cognitive demands on the teachers.

In the example above, Bob challenged Deborah's assertions that (1) the child had a problem with word-by-word matching and (2) teaching for matching should be the teacher's focus. In response, Deborah shifted in her view. The leader also offered challenges. For example, when Angela identified productive teaching with helping the child get the "right" answer, the leader invited discrepant views and the discussion that followed moved deeper into the process.

Using language to learn is a characteristic that permeates the teacher–child conversations in Reading Recovery lessons. In behind-the-glass sessions, teachers attend to language interactions and the powerful way they support learning. Teacher leaders consciously attend to the use of language and the negotiation of meaning that teachers use to acquire and integrate knowledge. During the course, they learn a language that they can use to talk with one another. This language is demonstrated and supported through the talking-while-observing sessions and the reflective discussion. Their talk is intimately tied to practice. Once they have experienced the training, Reading Recovery teachers can instantly begin to negotiate meaning with others from any part of the world.

Valuing Tentativeness

Reading Recovery teachers try to remain tentative in their definition of good teaching; this hesitancy reflects (1) valuing ongoing inquiry and (2) recognizing the complexity of students' learning and its relationship to the social context.

Duckworth (1987) has commented that it is hard for a teacher to let go of a plan of how things are expected to proceed and just "follow the child." But for the sake of the learner, "we must come to accept surprise, puzzlement, excitement, patience, caution, honest attempts and wrong outcomes as legitimate and important elements of learning" (p. 69). This stance furthers children's development and establishes the virtue, on our part, of *not knowing*. In essence, we must suspend our beliefs and expectations to learn from our children.

Just because a teaching action is suggested in Clay's (1985) *The Early Detection of Reading Difficulties* does not mean that it will be effective all the time for all children. Clay's suggestions are meant to be applied in the light of a teacher's analysis of the child's response and background knowledge, as well as the task at hand. The language used in class sessions deliberately includes phrases such as "seems to be," "is evidence of," "could be," and so forth. For example, even in his challenge to Deborah, Bob put forward his theory tentatively, saying, "She seems to be . . ." In saying "she could be cross-checking," Sarah was referring to behavioral evidence that to her indicated internal processes. The teacher leader fosters the use of tentative language as a constant reminder that we cannot know precisely what is going on in the learner's head. We are always acting on our best hypotheses. The tentative stance represents a difficult change in thinking for most teachers.

Flexibility

Reading Recovery teachers also try to remain flexible in their work with children. Ken, who was teaching in front of the glass, demonstrated flexibility in his lesson with Pam. While teaching, Ken might have been testing several hypotheses as to what Pam knew and what she was trying to control. Ken came to the same conclusions as did the observing teachers in their conversation behind the glass. Pam needed to use several sources of information rather than just word-by-word matching. First, Ken helped Pam refine her pointing movements so that it would be easier to attend. Then, he attended to her cross-checking behaviors to help her move forward in what she needed to do. He praised her for the processing rather than getting the right word. Both the demonstrating teacher and the observers had to move from idea to idea, simultaneously observing the child to enlighten their theories. Angela noticed Ken's flexibility when she talked about the way he adjusted to and commented on Pam's self-correcting behaviors.

The feeling behind this tentativeness is captured in the following statement by Carl Rogers (1969):

> I find that another way of learning for me is to state my own uncertainties, to try to clarify my puzzlement, and thus get close to the meaning that my experience actually seems to have. The whole train of experiencing, and the meanings that I have thus far discovered in it, seem to have launched me on a process which is both fascinating and at times a little frightening. It seems to mean letting my experiences carry me on, in a direction which appears to be forward, toward goals that I can but dimly define, as I try to understand at least the current meaning of that experience. The sensation is that of floating with a complex stream of experience, with the fascinating possibility of trying to comprehend its ever-changing complexity. (p. 154)

Creating Supportive Networks for Learning

Talking together in class sessions is a first step toward creating supportive networks for learning. These networks are extended through individual consultations between the teacher leader and teachers during the training year and afterwards, as well as by colleague visits that extend learning among experienced teachers. Schön (1991) talks about "reflection-in-action," or thinking about what you are doing while doing it. Most often, this process occurs in situations of uncertainty, uniqueness, and conflict. The tradition in educational institutions is to separate research and theory from practice, leaving no room for reflection-in-action. Such polarization creates a dilemma of rigor and relevance. Schön (1991) suggests that colleges of education should "learn from such deviant institutions as studios of art and design, conservatories of music and dance, athletics coaching and apprenticeships in crafts, all of which emphasize coaching and learning by doing" (p. xii). The dynamics of the individual teacher visits in Reading Recovery capture both the spontaneity of a concert and the coaching qualities of studio art. The teacher visit described below is reconstructed from extensive notes of a visit conducted in 1990–91. This example shows Meredith, the teacher leader, visiting an experienced Reading Recovery teacher.

A week after the behind-the-glass experience, Meredith went to Ken's school to observe him teaching Pam and one other student. By this time, Pam was reading books on level 7 and was consistently showing evidence of cross-checking predictions from her meaning base with the visual information on the page. They began the conference by looking at Ken's records. The previous two running records provided evidence of Pam's ability to cross-reference information. For example, on the previous day, Pam had easily read her new book *Mary Wore Her Red Dress and Henry Wore His Green Sneakers* (Peek, 1985). Looking at the lesson records over the last six days, Meredith and Ken noticed that Pam was consistently reading above 95% accuracy and that she had read a series of highly patterned books. Meredith asked Ken to select several books that might be good books to introduce to Pam today. Ken chose *Mrs. Wishy-Washy* (Cowley, 1980) and *The Lion's Tale* (Scott, Foresman, 1979). Then, Meredith suggested that he observe Pam carefully during the lesson to determine what she did at point of difficulty and at point of error. Meredith was trying to help Ken notice productive "reading work" on the part of the child and to work with a text that would offer sufficient challenge.

Meredith observed the lesson while Pam read several familiar books and composed and wrote a story. She had little difficulty; her running record, taken on *Mary Wore Her Red Dress . . .*, was almost perfect. Ken had opportunity to notice that Pam was able to read almost all the books relying on her memory of the patterns. While she was tracking and checking most of her responses with print, the texts offered little challenge. He selected *The Lion's Tale,* a book with more complex written text, to introduce at the end of the lesson. Later Ken said, "I asked myself whether I was seeing evidence of problem solving. I decided she needed a harder book with less patterned language." This one-on-one coaching helped Ken to become a better problem solver himself as he worked with individual readers.

As they become more experienced, Reading Recovery teachers learn to help one another extend their understandings. Wiley (1992) has described such a colleague visit.

> Toward the end of Lazonna's program, I invited three Reading Recovery colleagues to observe my lesson with Lazonna. . . . The colleague visit helped me to see that I need to teach to the individual child *for the individual moment.* Just as the child needs to process on-the-run, I need to make decisions on the run. In this manner education becomes individual and timely. It was this kind of thinking that paralleled Clay's (1979a) description of a good teacher:
>
> > "Good teachers know what to look for. They set time aside for observation of what individual children are doing. They know the direction in which a child had been moving; and they keep brief but continuing records of the changes that occur. They are sensitive observers of change in early reading behaviors. They know which new attempts are pointing in the right direction and they foster these with praise." (p. 212)

Having colleagues visit is mutually supportive. I am the novice learning to see the world differently, and as experienced Reading Recovery teachers, my colleagues bring not only an objective view but also a more expert perspective. Our understanding is strengthened by our collaboration as we remember always to think in the now. (p. 3)

Ongoing Learning

Through interactive staff development, teachers are expected to change their views of the children they teach and of themselves and what they do. The leader's goal is to help teachers become independent learners who will keep on seeking the answers they need. The seeking, called "sifting and sorting" in New Zealand, is probably the most important component of the adult learning mode. It suggests that teachers must tolerate the ambiguity inherent in teaching. It is often said by teacher leaders that a good Reading Recovery teacher never feels "finished." Perhaps it is not the final learning of procedures or even becoming a very polished teacher that really makes the difference for students; it may be the act of inquiry on the part of a "not-finished" teacher.

While the initial training lasts only for one calendar year, teachers continued to meet regularly (although not as often) in subsequent years. They are assisted by the teacher leader, who may even bring in other leaders to offer additional challenges and new views. Many teachers report that during the second year, they really feel a shift in understanding. Teachers become much more independent of the leader; colleague visits help them to extend their understandings without formal staff development. As Shulman (1987) has said, teachers and staff developers must be prepared to invest time and unusual effort in the learning process. This time and effort pay off not only in student learning but also in a continually revitalized school staff.

Diane DeFord talked about this continual learning process in an address to a group of teachers:

When I first read, or attempted to read, Clay's book *Reading: The Patterning of Complex Behavior* (1979a), I was immediately put off by the cognitive psychologist language and terms like *confusion*. Consequently, in 1980, I put this book away on my shelf. In 1985, I was asked to observe a Reading Recovery lesson at Ohio State University. I was fascinated as I observed the half-hour lesson, and by turns, brought up short by things I "didn't like." I could see the child in front of me had made startling gains in both reading and writing, was happy, excited about books, and engaged in learning new things. When his teacher talked about his early reading and writing, a different picture emerged: a child who was passive in new learning settings and who, the classroom teacher felt, would fail first grade. My curiosity overcame my initial discomfort with aspects of the program, and I became actively involved in learning about Reading Recovery. At first, the practices I agreed with were easy, and I tried to find ways around using the practices I disagreed with. But during the six years I have been teaching children in Reading Recovery, I have put my disagreements on hold to try to see the sense of particular practices with some children. Daily, I am forced to reconsider my beliefs in light of what I see children and teachers doing, but I have also continued to fill out my belief in early literacy learning. I had to take off my "theoretical high heels," so to speak, and replace them with walking shoes that are now quite comfortable.

As teachers, then, we have beliefs in action that are based on empirical knowledge, whether informed by others or by self and experience. These beliefs can be explored, compared with evidence and observation, put aside, or extended. However, the core of accumulated beliefs and experiences establishes what we see, as well as how we analyze and respond to the challenges that occur as we consider the unique and unexpected (Smith, 1988). They mold what can be regarded as right and wrong in thought and action (Rokeach, 1979). Before change can occur, however, we need to understand the roots of theory building. It is important for professional educators to understand that while logic can influence what we believe as teachers, experience accumulated during teaching is central to the evolution of theory.

RESEARCH ON READING RECOVERY STAFF DEVELOPMENT

Research on the staff development program (Pinnell et al., 1988; Pinnell et al., in press) indicates that when the program is implemented as described, including the teacher training and implementation, results for both students and teachers are positive. The staff development process sets up an interactive system in which the learner is acting, observing, talking, responding, and negotiating. The model is consistent with recommendations for programs that emphasize the teacher's own learning (Berliner, 1986; Shulman, 1987) and awareness of such learning (Duckworth, 1987). Berliner (1986) recommends a "pedagogical laboratory," which includes a range of inquiry-oriented activities.

Research on teachers' participation in Reading Recovery provides evidence that the training program has a powerful impact. Individuals generally experience a shift in theoretical orientation, moving from a skills-oriented view of reading, which focuses on materials and sequential learning of specific aspects of reading, toward a whole-language orientation, which suggests that children begin to "orchestrate" a range of skills and knowledge when they learn how to read and write (see DeFord, 1993).

A yearlong qualitative study of one group of teachers revealed continuous shifts in teachers' focus of attention throughout the training period (Pinnell & Woolsey, 1985). For one full year, the researchers transcribed informal discussions held after the teacher class. This oral language transcript provided a window on change in the way teachers thought about their learning experience. At the beginning of their training, teachers tended to focus on the mechanics. They wanted to be told how to do it, how to use materials and procedures outlined in *The Early Detection of Reading Difficulties* (Clay, 1985); and they were concerned with doing it "right." Management was their general focus, and they also wanted to talk about the stresses and strains associated with change. This surface-level discussion continued for several months, indicating one reason why it may be so difficult to make lasting change through two-week workshops or short-term university courses.

Eventually, the focus of discussion shifted to descriptions of the children they were teaching. Members of the group got to know Tim, and Ivie, and Jason, and to ask for progress reports. As often happens in teacher support groups, they told stories of children's behavior and created shared ways of talking about children.

Toward the end of the year, the discussion took on a new character. Stories were still evident in the discussions, but teachers began to enter into more philosophical and theoretical discussions. Sometimes they argued about the process of development, using their stories as evidence. All had now experienced daily teaching and analysis of eight to ten children and had viewed about 40 behind-the-glass cases. They began to link their case-by-case knowledge into broader generalizations. This process took a long time and was finished at the end of the training year. A member of that training class, interviewed four years later, said:

Looking back, it almost seems as though I knew so little that first year. I was learning a lot, but now we are going so much deeper into the processes. There are new understandings. I see much more when I observe behind the glass and participate in the discussion following the observation session. I think my teaching is getting better because I am noticing new things and understanding the reading process at a different level.

Alvermann (1990) has characterized Reading Recovery training as an inquiry-oriented model for teacher education. She claims that teachers' professional knowledge is currently being recognized as far more complex than previously thought. Instead of focusing on techniques, researchers are beginning to be interested in how teachers acquire knowledge and use theories to guide their instructional decisions. Reading Recovery training challenges teachers to make their implicit ideas explicit, to examine them, and to link them to practice. The setting for training, demonstration teaching, behind-the-glass discussions, colleague visits, discussions with previously trained teachers, and weekly discussions with teacher leaders about children's progress facilitate this analytic process and helps teachers to develop new understandings that translate directly into their daily teaching responses.

Chapter 4

Teaching for Problem Solving in Reading

The teacher's goal is to help young readers learn to move continuously through text, reading for meaning and attending as needed to lower-level details such as words or letters. These beginning readers must learn to use effectively their previously developed knowledge as they problem solve while reading. Knowledge of the child informs teachers and helps them focus attention on the memorable examples that will help the child extend his or her understanding of how reading works. A program that stresses attention at the right moment is more efficient than one that puts all children through the same sequence of activities whatever their knowledge base or focus of attention. Independent reading depends on the kind of "inner control" of operations that work together so that the reader can problem solve in search of meaning. The teacher has in mind the behavioral evidence that signals the construction of independent reading strategies, but students may take many different possible routes to learning. Clay (1991) describes the teacher as having a map of possibilities but watching the child closely and going "the child's way to the teacher's goals" (p. 286).

To understand teaching, we are required to take into account the complexity of the social context within which instruction occurs. Teachers do not make their moves in isolation; instead, they affect and are affected by the children with whom they interact, by the texts being read or written, and by underlying priorities related to expectations. In this chapter we take a closer look at teaching during the reading components of Reading Recovery lessons. We report the results of our analyses of the use of time and content and of teacher behaviors that appear to be more and less effective. And we discuss some of our observations of teacher–student interactions. Finally, we explore the process holistically through the eyes of expert Reading Recovery teacher leaders.

THE SEARCH FOR WHAT WORKS

Much research has been conducted to determine what works in reading instruction. A diversity of opinion is evident in the literature. According to Barr (1984), the answer is not simply a choice between method or materials. We have devoted much debate to stating which activities (e.g., phonics exercises or literature experiences) are effective in helping students learn to read. Just as powerfully influential, however, are the ways teachers and students act *within* those activities. Studies of classroom instruction (see Rosenshine & Stevens, 1984) have revealed the importance of teachers' questions and feedback to student responses. Lesson pace is also important (Brophy & Good, 1986; Good & Beckerman, 1978), as are the amount of content covered (Barr, 1973/1974) and the amount of attention students give to a task (Chall & Feldman, 1967).

For eight years in the United States, program evaluation data have been collected on every child served by Reading Recovery. Analysis of data across hundreds of sites in North America indicates that something is "working" in the program. Our controlled study, reported in this volume, supports and extends this program evaluation data by comparing several treatments that reveal the impact of underlying components of Reading Recovery. Three factors, in combination, appeared to be related to the successful outcomes of Reading Recovery: the lesson framework, individual instruction, and teacher education.

Of the three, teacher education emerged as the most powerful factor. Teachers who had participated in the Reading Recovery training program appeared to teach more effectively than those prepared in an alternative model. Individual instruction, characteristic of three of our treatments, was a necessary but not sufficient factor. There were three one-to-one treatments: Direct Instruction Skills Plan (DISP), Reading Success (RS), and Reading Recovery (RR). Of those three, the first two had unsatisfactory results. Reading Success, which utilized the Reading Recovery lesson framework and provided teacher training and follow-up support, was more successful than Direct Instruction Skills Plan, but fell far short of moving children to independent reading. Only Reading Recovery, with teachers who had participated in the full training, had long-term results for students. Reading Recovery children were more likely to make accelerated progress; that is, with the 70-day period, they could read texts at much higher levels than children served in the other treatments. Reading Recovery children also continued to make progress after the treatments were withdrawn, evidence of the development of problem-solving strategies. These children had developed networks of understandings that worked together for further learning.

Our study provides evidence that cautions educators against a wait-and-see approach for children having difficulty in the first grade. Although rich environments and opportunities to read and write contribute to student learning, more is needed. Not all children need the one-on-one instruction of Reading Recovery—that should be reserved for the very most at risk. But many children need highly skilled and supportive teaching. Most need teachers who notice significant behaviors and interpret them in the light of theory, then interact in ways that make reading and writing processes visible to the learner. According to Clay (1991), it is the teacher's responsibility to know the range of possible routes to independent reading, to analyze the behavior of the particular student, and to respond to that learner in a way that supports and extends effective learning. Reading Recovery teachers take that charge very seriously.

STUDYING TEACHING WITHIN THE READING RECOVERY LESSON

In the larger study, outcome data from pre- and post-test measures were used to determine higher and lower student outcomes that could be attributed to the application of the instructional model. Student ability level was not a factor, since differences were derived by comparing each group, within schools, with its own randomly assigned control group. Results of the study indicated that, as a group, Reading Recovery teachers were using the most effective model; yet within that group, variations in effectiveness could be observed by examining student outcomes and descriptive data. We identified lessons associated with higher and lower student outcomes in order to look within the model, fine-tune it, and extend our understanding of teaching and learning. This look at the most successful teachers was designed to provide important information for the teacher education component of the program. It also offers insights into the kind of powerful teacher–student interactions that can provide the scaffold for learning reading strategies.

Investigations that take a deeper look into teacher–child interactions have indicated that successful teachers tend to prompt for the use of balanced sets of information but keep the primary focus on meaning (see DeFord, Tancock, & White, 1990; Lyons, 1991a; Lyons & White, 1990). Prompting and reinforcing statements by teachers support the child's use of the full range of information needed for reading: meaning, language syntax, and visual information. Teachers who experience lower success rates in Reading Recovery tend to focus attention in unbalanced ways. For example, they sometimes emphasize the use of letter–sound relationships and neglect other information sources. The most successful teachers are more likely to teach intensively; that is, to exhibit high energy and efficiency, thus covering more content within the 30-minute lesson period. More successful teachers are also judged by

expert observers to be more likely to support children's use of effective strategies and to require independent action on the part of the children. Lyons
(1991a) has stated that Reading Recovery teachers are distinguished from partially trained teachers by subtle differences in the opportunities they provide
for the student to negotiate meaning through talk.

Teachers in Reading Recovery select opportunities that provide productive examples to help children build systems of understanding. In the Reading Recovery staff development course, teachers become highly aware of their
interactions with young students. The process of following the child requires
that teachers use ongoing observation, as well as accumulated knowledge about
a particular child, to guide their interactions and the focus of attention during lessons. Observation is a key.

> Sensitive and systematic observation of young children's reading and writing
> behaviors provides teachers with feedback which can shape their next teaching
> moves. Teaching can then be likened to a conversation in which you listen to the
> speaker carefully before you reply. (Clay, 1985, p. 6)

Thinking about teaching as conversation helps us get beyond the typical
arguments that surround literacy education in the first years of school. Educators argue as to whether teachers should directly instruct children or simply encourage and support their efforts. In some contexts, simplistic interpretations of either position have resulted in unsound educational practice.
Some proponents of direct instruction have created tedious drills that risk
making learning dull, meaningless, and repetitious. Those proponents of natural learning who support a purely facilitative stance run the risk of paralyzing
teachers so that they assume a passive role, afraid to tell the child anything.
Natural conversation assumes that there is some telling, some demonstrating,
some encouraging, some suggesting, some praising, and all other types of
human interactions. The child is making imperfect, approximate attempts to
which the more expert adult responds by praising the attempt and acting in
a way that helps the learner to expand and refine the response.

Within the naturally occurring interactions in the home, children's caregivers constantly provide feedback, encouragement, and suggestions that help
to extend the child's repertoire. The difference between these caregivers and
teachers is that teachers are explicitly aware of the way interactions can support learning. They use observation as a guide for selecting ways to support
children's responses. Initially, teachers may think consciously of these behaviors; but as they work with children, they build a foundation of knowledge
from which their moment-to-moment responses emanate. This knowledge base
forms an in-process theory of learning that guides the interaction. The following example illustrates instructional interactions early in a child's program.

Marianne is reading *Space Journey* (Cutting, 1988b), an easy book with repetitive patterns. The book is one of the easiest levels on the Reading Recovery book list, yet it poses some challenges for this young student. When tested for Reading Recovery, Marianne could recognize 18 letters and write her name and one other word, *I*. She was able to join in on texts with repetitive patterns but paid little attention to print. After 10 days of "roaming around the known," during which time the teacher introduces no new learning (see Chapter 1) and four Reading Recovery lessons, Marianne was just getting control of word-by-word matching in reading. She had also written some simple stories, which she had read many times. She had written words such as *see* and *can* and read them in other stories, although her teacher would not expect her to recognize them in isolation. She had also learned the word *the*, which she could write independently and locate in text. The running record represents her reading and the teacher's analysis (Figure 4.1).

Marianne is beginning to use her strength in language to predict what she will read in the story. After reading "I can" for the first two words, she stops, perhaps noticing the word *the*, which she knows. Then, she returns to the beginning of the line to try again, this time self-correcting. After reading "moon" for *stars,* she checks the picture and returns again to the beginning of the line to reread it. This young reader has been predicting, checking, and searching again to problem solve this line of text. She has made sure that her reading is a possible language pattern, that it matches the meaning (as illustrated by the pictures), and that it matches aspects of print that are within her power to notice. The known word *the* serves as an anchor for her, an "island of certainty," that allows her to use visual information as a check.

While taking the running record, the teacher assumes the neutral position of an observer. At one point, she tells Marianne the difficult word *planet* so that the reading can continue. But she observes that Marianne handles the book well and is working independently. The teacher is not looking for accuracy but for evidence that Marianne is using what she knows to problem solve during the reading. She notices the good reading work on the first two pages, work that enables Marianne to continue confidently to the end of the text with very little assistance. She also notices that Marianne, as evidenced by pointing behavior, is making a good voice–print match.

After the reading, the teacher makes a quick positive comment on the reading, emphasizing the way Marianne has "made it match," and then goes back to page one for more specific praise.

TEACHER: I like the way you really worked on this page. (The teacher points to the first two words.) You read "I can" and then what did you notice?

MARIANNE: "The."

FIGURE 4.1.   Running Record and Teacher's Analysis—*Space Journey*

Page	Title	Totals		Cues Used	
	Space Journey	E	SC	E	SC
1	I can|R|sc moon |R²|sc See the stars.	I	I	m̶s̶v	ms(v)
		I	I	m̶s̶v	ms(v)
2	See the (w) planets. | T				
3	See the sun.				
4	See the moon.				
5	See the earth.				
6	Home!				

Note.
Marianne's substitutions written above text

m = meaning
s = structure (language)
v = visual (letters/sounds)
E = error
SC = self correction
R = repetition
W = wait
T = told

TEACHER: Yes. You know that word, don't you? And you went back and fixed it up. Read it once again.

MARIANNE: Yeah. (She reads the page again, checking the picture as she finishes.)

TEACHER: Were you right?

MARIANNE: Yeah.

The teacher points out that the picture has stars in it, and then they talk a few more seconds about Marianne's favorite part of that book. The interchange illustrated here took only a minute or two, but it helped to focus Marianne's attention on some very productive problem-solving work she had done. It pointed out how she could use her knowledge of the world and of print to check on her own reading. There is no one right way to respond to a reading example like this one. The teacher's focus of attention depends on the priorities for that child at the particular time.

The next day, Marianne reads *Space Journey* again as one of her familiar reading selections. The book is much easier for her, and the teacher notes that Marianne has good control of the language patterns of the book. They have a brief conversation during the reading, once about the way the moon looked and once about Marianne's going back to confirm her reading by repeating a line. Coming to the word *planet,* Marianne substitutes "moon," then stops and appeals.

TEACHER: I like the way you were noticing that word. It could be the moon, but does it start like *moon*?

MARIANNE: No, that would be an *m*.

TEACHER: Could it be *planet*?

MARIANNE: Yeah.

TEACHER: How do you know the word could be *planet*?

MARIANNE: Because planet starts with a *p*.

TEACHER: Does *planet* sound right and make sense?

MARIANNE: Yeah.

TEACHER: (The teacher points to the word *planet*.) Does this word look right?

MARIANNE: Yeah.

The teacher was asking Marianne to be more active in confirming that *planet* was the word in the text by checking three sources of information: meaning, language structure, and visual information. This book would continue to be a potential selection for several more days or it might be sent home.

The next example comes from later in Marianne's program. By her fortieth lesson, she was reading much more difficult books and behaving independently. Early strategies such as matching were well under control, and she was reading fluently. By this time, easy reading for her was about the middle of first-grade level. She was reading *Letters for Mr. James* (Cowley, 1987b), a level-13 book that she had previously read twice (Figure 4.2). The story focuses on an old man whose friends, noticing that he gets no mail, write letters to him.

The teacher compliments Marianne for her fluent reading and for making it sound like "talking," and after the story is over, they talk briefly about why Mr. James would feel so happy about the letters. The teacher points out Marianne's good problem solving on the last page.

> TEACHER: You knew *they* didn't you? And you figured out *they're*. Did it make sense?"
> MARIANNE: Yes, that did make sense.
> TEACHER: Did it sound right and look right?
> MARIANNE: Yes, so it had to be *they're*.

The questions encouraged Marianne to check the line again, confirming her reading for meaning. Marianne's behavior when she came to the words *they're* and *friends* demonstrated her ability to approach words analytically without losing meaning. Moving fluently through the text, she attended briefly to details as needed in search of meaning. This problem-solving ability was also evident with new texts, and it was initiated by Marianne without the teacher's prompting. All of these behaviors signaled a developing inner control of the processes involved in reading. Marianne would soon be ready to be released from Reading Recovery. She was well on the way to developing a self-extending system.

The examples described above were only three of hundreds of conversational interchanges between Marianne and her teacher. To put this into perspective, we should realize that by the fortieth lesson, Marianne had read over 200 books, approximately 60 different titles and several rereadings of many of them. Each text encountered offered opportunities for the teacher and child to focus attention on productive examples. The teacher ignored some behavior and attended to others. In the first example, her priority was to help Marianne notice discrepancies between her reading and the print because the child needed to learn to monitor her own reading and to use visual information. In the second example, priorities were reading fluently and problem solving. In both examples, the teacher rewarded partially correct responses that had strategic value and did not spend time on examples that would not have any payoff in terms of helping the child learn how to assist herself.

The hardest shift for teachers to make is to think about teaching as assisting the student's problem solving. In Reading Recovery, we would refer

FIGURE 4.2.   Running Record and Teacher's Analysis—*Letters for Mr. James*

Page	Title Letters for Mr. James

14

    "Letters!" called the mail carrier.

    "Letters, ⌐Mr. James!"

    "They can't be for me,"

    said Mr. James.

    "I ~~don't~~ (H) never get any letters."

    "They've got your name on them,"

    said the mail carrier.

    "They are for me!"

    Mr. James said.

    When /sc
    "Where did they all come from?"

15

    They   (stopped, shaking her head)
    "They're   T: What's wrong

                S: That's not they

    They /sc   T: Try that again and look all the way through the word.
    ·They're from all your friends,

    Mr. James," said the mail carrier. *R* ←

Note.

Marianne's insertions and substitutions written above text.

H = Hestitation; SC = self correction; R = repetition
S = Student; T = Teacher

to this interchange as "teaching *for* strategies." While we cannot directly teach strategies, we can, through conversation, support the reader's use of productive strategies. The goal is to enable the student to take over the process, eventually working alone. Marianne was already engaging in much independent, strategic behavior; the teacher was working to help her extend her power over the reading process.

Teacher behavior is significant in determining the outcomes of Reading Recovery. Our large comparative study revealed the importance of teaching but told us little about the nature of teaching within Reading Recovery. Only qualitative analysis of teaching could be expected to provide the information needed to understand better teaching behavior. To gain detailed information about teaching, we videotaped teachers' lessons at several points in time. These videotapes provided a way to take an in-depth look at the instruction.

IN-DEPTH ANALYSIS OF
TEACHER–STUDENT INTERACTIONS

Videotapes of the reading portion of the Reading Recovery lesson were analyzed in several ways. First, we looked at the content of the lessons and then asked how much time was spent on reading, writing, and other activities. Our time and content analysis for all treatments in the study indicated that Reading Recovery teachers spent more time on reading and writing than did teachers in other treatments. Would there be a difference among Reading Recovery teachers? Next, we transcribed the videotapes and prepared transcripts so that we could view the tapes and follow the transcripts.

Three expert Reading Recovery teacher leaders were asked to help in analyzing the tapes. A training program for analyzing the videotapes helped the research team to coordinate their efforts. This program involved the teacher leaders and two faculty researchers in viewing sample tapes of one-on-one lessons and engaging in discussions that linked program tenets to specific actions. They first viewed one tape together, stopping at critical points to talk about the teacher–student interactions they had observed. From this process, categories emerged that helped to codify the teacher behavior. Then, the team of raters independently viewed a sample tape with transcript. They used the categories they had created as a group. Their individual coding was checked for reliability, and the category definitions were renegotiated and refined. Finally, the tape was independently coded by each rater, and the reliability was calculated. In the coding of several hundred interactions, the raters agreed 80% of the time, a sufficiently high reliability to confirm the categories they had created working together to analyze the lessons.

The categories generated referred to teacher behavior and teacher language. For example, when a teacher complimented a child for stopping and noticing a discrepancy in his or her reading, that behavior was categorized as reinforcing monitoring. The teacher might ask the child to start again and think "what would make sense," a behavior that would be categorized as prompting the child to search for meaning. Or the teacher might suggest that the child check again to "be sure what you read looks right and sounds right," indicating a prompt to search using visual information as well as language syntax. We assumed that teacher behavior was influenced by the child's immediate responses, the history of the child's progress, and the potential in the particular text being read.

Teachers' Statements

Teacher language was first categorized as prompts, reinforcements, or general comments. Prompts involved initiating topics with children. Teachers appeared to observe the child's behavior, waiting for a chance to demonstrate or tell the child what would be effective in the process of reading. These prompts were not preplanned; instead, they were highly related to the context. They simultaneously asked the child to act in the process of reading, to access prior knowledge, to search, to check, and to discover. For example, at a point of difficulty, the teacher might remind the child to check the picture and think what the text might be saying.

Reinforcing statements occurred when a teacher commented on or attended to a desirable reading behavior used by the child. The teacher appeared to be observing the child's reading behavior to discover useful actions that they wanted to encourage further. A teacher might say, "I like the way you were checking the picture and thinking what would make sense there." Teachers also made general comments that were related to managing the lesson, and they gave general directions and encouragement; for example, saying "good job" or "keep on going." Finally, teachers occasionally told the child the word while reading in order to keep the process going. While teachers tried to keep "tolds" to a minimum, they had to use discretion to increase efficiency. Results of this analysis revealed that 50.3% of teacher statements were prompts, 12.4% were reinforcements, 27.0% were "other," and 10.3% were "tolds." To analyze the content of teacher actions, we used only reinforcing and prompting statements and combined these two specific teaching actions.

Categorizing Teachers' Actions

The team of coders initially used 14 categories to code the prompts and reinforcements they observed (see Pinnell, DeFord, & Lyons, 1990, for a complete list of categories). The coded transcripts were then collated and frequencies calculated for the entire group, for different subgroups, and for different points in time. Additionally, transcripts were searched for examples of the different teacher actions that appeared to typify the instructional approaches. Essentially, we looked at teacher moves within three broad categories that represented three different ways to focus attention.

Directional Movement/Matching. When they begin to read, children must learn and use important conventions about the way print works. For example, they learn that they need to move from left to right across the line of print and sweep back to the left at the end of the line. Another important concept is that of word-by-word matching. According to Clay (1991), children must make a time and space transformation to match the oral stream of language to the visual presentation of letters and spaces on the page. They must learn how space is used to define words in print. In the beginning stages, while the child is just developing control, the finger helps the eye in tracking print while reading.

Teachers assist children in developing control of directional movement and word-by-word matching by demonstrating the process, by complimenting children on their pointing and reading, and by prompting children to "make it match." A teacher might also compliment a child, saying, "I like the way you made it match." Or a teacher might suggest using word-by-word matching to monitor reading, for example, "Did it match? Try it again and make sure it matches." Often, when oral rendition and print do not come out even, a child will hesitate, having "run out of words." A teacher might say, "What's wrong?" and compliment the child on noticing something important about print. Once control of print conventions is achieved, the process is fast and automatic, and the teacher no longer needs to attend to matching or directionality but can direct more attention to higher level strategies.

Operations Using Words and/or Letters. As they develop control and learn to focus on individual words, children begin to notice visual detail and to relate those details to the sound system of the language. In early reading experiences, the child notices some known words while reading texts, and these "islands of certainty" help the reader to monitor and check while reading. To solve problems in decontextualized print, children must eventually be able to read individual words and to analyze them visually, but words are not presented to be learned in isolated form. It is the *use* of words while reading that makes them strategically valuable.

During the course of problem solving on text, teachers draw attention to visual information and/or letter–sound relationships in the service of moving on to discover meaning in the text. They also help children use examples of successful word solving as a way to build knowledge of ways to analyze words. For example, if a child knows a letter–sound relationship, the teacher might help him or her use that information to solve words. The prompt might be to "Get your mouth ready for it." Or the child might be complimented on substitutions (such as Matthew's substitution of *friend* for free in the example later in this chapter) that indicate use of letter–sound relationships. The teacher might ask a child to check reading by saying something such as, "Does that look right?" Or there might be some word teaching using magnetic letters to break apart and re-form a word or to analyze parts of words. In the beginning, the teacher might also help the child develop a vocabulary of a few words that are known in every detail and can be used as anchors to monitor and check reading. All of these teacher moves help the student develop ways of working on words that will later become fast and efficient.

Text-Level Strategies. The goal of reading is to move continuously through text, reading for meaning. To accomplish this goal, readers bring their language systems to bear on the task. They use their knowledge of the world and of language to predict, search, and monitor. These systems help them confirm or disconfirm their reading in complex ways. Good readers use several different kinds of information simultaneously, but at the same time they work efficiently, so that reading goes along quickly enough to make sense. Thus it is important for readers not only to solve words but also to make reading sound like meaningful language.

During reading activities, teachers can help by reminding children to use the knowledge of language that they already have. They might ask questions such as, "Did that make sense?" or "Can we say it that way?" Or they might prompt for fluency, for example, saying, "Make it sound like talking!" After the child has checked a text in one way (e.g., thinking about whether the word looked right), the teacher might ask him or her to read it again just to be sure it made sense. In that case, the teacher is asking the child to check more than one source of information. Reading Recovery teachers would call such action teaching *for* cross-checking. Teachers might also prompt the child to monitor, saying, "Were you right?" Or, at point of difficulty, a teacher might ask "What's wrong?" to get an idea of what the child is attending to. The teacher might compliment the child for searching or monitoring even if the child cannot go on independently to solve the problem. The idea is to support and prompt for strategic processes rather than accuracy. Clay (1991) describes the teacher's role as follows:

> The teacher is more concerned to reinforce how the child worked to get the response than whether the child arrived at the precise correct response. In this

way the teacher is responding to the learner's construction of strategic control over reading and writing processes. (p. 343)

Discussions of Teaching

To capture the complexity of Reading Recovery lessons, we had to go beyond the categorization of teacher behaviors. Teacher behaviors must be considered in combination with student response during lessons and with the knowledge and profile of progress of the individual child. Every day, teachers take notes on student behaviors, based on their informal observations, and they systematically take running records of reading, which they analyze to build a foundation of knowledge about each child. When teachers make their moment-to-moment instructional decisions, they are supposed to consider the opportunities inherent in the interaction with the text, what the child already knows and is able to do, and the particular response of the child at the time. The teacher thinks about past behavior and his or her own predictions for the child's progress. So teaching techniques are not followed like a script; they are, instead, a menu carefully selected with the young learner in mind.

When our expert teacher leaders watched tapes as part of their training process, they found themselves bringing to the situation the observational strengths they used every day to help teachers work more powerfully with students. They were looking for and labeling those responses to children that they expected to see when leading a discussion of behind-the-glass teaching demonstrations or when visiting individual teachers. Even without full information on every child, coders found themselves making informal comments about the teaching, such as:

"She's working for the flexibility he needs."
"Teaching for fluency there is mixing the child up."
"She should be going for more independent behavior."
"I would try to question for cross-checking after the running record."
"That's a good decision for this child on this text."
"That's okay, but it's not the most powerful thing she could do."
"She needs to help him get word-by-word matching under control."

It became obvious that simply taking on the language of Reading Recovery or exhibiting the activities and techniques would not capture the process. Research on instruction must take into account the social setting in which it occurs (Green & Wallat, 1987). Accordingly, the last analysis to be reported in this chapter involved the observing teacher leaders in an analytic critique of the lessons on tape.

FINE-TUNING THE TEACHING PROCESS

All teachers in our analysis were using the same instructional framework, and, as a group, they had the most positive results in the study. To increase our knowledge of powerful teaching, however, we looked within our group of Reading Recovery teachers. This analysis allowed us to collect information about how very successful teachers make those instructional decisions within the lesson framework. We could think about this information as useful in fine-tuning the teaching process.

Assuming that productive teaching would be evidenced by faster student progress, we took a detailed look at the interactions in lessons associated with higher student outcomes; videotapes of four teachers were observed and analyzed. We contrasted those actions with lessons in which teachers and students were having more difficulty; here, too, four teachers were observed and analyzed. All of these teachers were using the model of instruction demonstrating the greatest impact on students overall. We were probing subtle differences that would help us better describe the minute moves involved in teaching.

Time and Content Analysis

The first step in fine-tuning our knowledge of this teaching process was to analyze systematically the literacy events in the lessons in our study. For this process, we used the videotapes that were collected for Reading Recovery teachers. First, we analyzed them for time and content so that comparisons could be made (Table 4.1).

For the Reading Recovery lessons available on videotape, the average length of time was 33 minutes, 21 seconds, slightly longer than the specified 30 minutes. Of that time, the average proportion devoted to reading was 60.2% and the average proportion of time spent on writing was 25.3%, with 14.5% spent on the category called "other." Time spent on other activities was further broken down into the following proportions: talk about books (63.2%); letter–sound work, or phonics (15.0%); word fluency practice (12.4%); letter identification work (3.9%); teacher reading to the child (3.5%); and general (2.0%).

The greatest proportion of "other" time involved teachers and children talking together about the books they were reading. Fluency practice on writing words occurred when words were taken from the writing portion of the lesson and written several times; these words were not taken from a preplanned list. Phonics work was usually related to the writing portion also. The activity called "hearing sounds in words" was a regular part of the lesson; also, visual

TABLE 4.1.   Time and Content for Reading Recovery

	Reading Recovery (RR)
Number of Lessons Analyzed	18
Average length of Time	00:33:21 (00:24:20 - 00:41:48)
Average % of Time Reading Text	60.2%
Average % of Time Writing Text	25.3%
Average % of Time Other	14.5%
Content of "other" category	talk about books 63.2% letter/sound work 15% word fluency practice 12.4% letter ident. work 3.9% teacher reading to child 3.5% general talk 2.0%
Books Read By Children	94
Average no. of books per lesson	5.22

analysis of words during reading was fostered by the use of magnetic letters. A total of 94 books (5.22 books per lesson) were read by children in the 18 lessons that were videotaped.

Teachers with Higher and Lower Student Outcomes. Results of the time and content analysis for Reading Recovery teachers who had students with higher and lower results (as determined by the level of text reading when the students were released from the program) were examined. The results revealed that in the lessons observed, teachers with higher student outcomes seemed to be giving slightly more instructional time to the students. They exceeded the recommended instructional time, whereas teachers with lower student outcomes had slightly shorter lessons. We do not interpret these results to mean that Reading Recovery lessons should be lengthened. On average, there were only three minutes difference between the two. While further research would be necessary to explore fully the time factor, we suspect that effectiveness had more to do with the pacing and intensity within a time frame-work that could vary from day to day but would average around 30 minutes. More productive time analyses were available when we looked at the allocation of time within lessons.

In the first observation (Figure 4.3), teachers with higher student outcomes during the first time period (Time 1) tended to spend more time on writing (44%) as compared to teachers with lower student outcomes (29%) and less time on reading (37%) than teachers with lower student outcomes (52%). During the second time period (Time 2), for the lessons analyzed, teachers with higher student outcomes spent a higher proportion of time on reading (61% compared to 49%), less time on writing (28% compared to 31%), and less time on "other" activities (11% compared to 20%). Our interpretation of these results centers on the importance of writing in early lessons. It may be that writing can be used very effectively to help children develop early strategies and concepts about print. Teachers who used writing to the full potential might have been more successful in working for early learning gains. Writing will be further explored in Chapters 6 and 7.

Focus of Teaching Behavior

Through their prompting and reinforcing statements, teachers took the initiative to draw students' attention to behaviors related to different aspects of the reading process: (1) making it match (achieving one-to-one correspondence between spoken and written words); (2) problem solving on letters and words; and (3) problem solving at the level of text. While students are engaged in reading continuous text, teachers use conversation to make suggestions or

FIGURE 4.3.   Content of Lessons for Higher and Lower Student Outcomes at Two Points In Time

Higher Outcomes

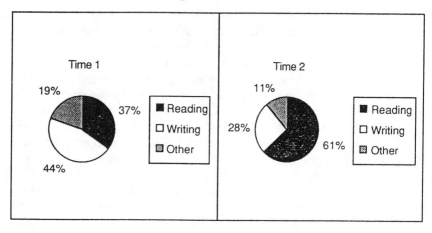

Lower Outcomes

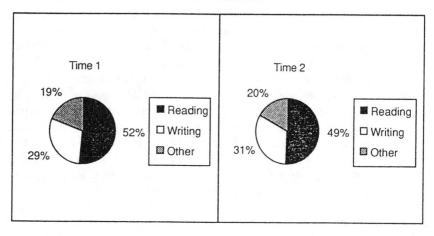

to comment on observed behaviors. Deciding where and when to intervene is the most difficult part of teaching in Reading Recovery lessons because inappropriate or excessive intervention could interfere with the student's reading. And the intervention should take the form of conversation. A teacher leader recently wrote this comment after visiting a Reading Recovery teacher: "She interacted with Ariel in a powerful way while he was reading, selecting memorable examples that would help him get better at the process, but the conversation seemed casual and natural. They were having fun reading."

Teachers with Higher and Lower Student Outcomes. When we compared teaching associated with higher and lower student outcomes, we found that the focus of teacher attention differed (Figure 4.4). For this analysis, we combined prompting and reinforcing statements. The overall patterns of response reveal that in Times 1 and 2, lessons associated with higher student outcomes showed a balanced approach, with greater teacher attention to text-level strategies and less attention to the letter and word level. In comparison, teachers in lessons associated with lower student outcomes tended to focus attention at the letter and word level, with less attention to the text level. They also tended to prompt more for word-by-word matching than did teachers with higher outcomes; however, this analysis did not reveal whether this prompting enabled this particular child develop a self-extending system of behaviors.

FIGURE 4.4. Focus of Teacher Behavior for Higher and Lower Student Outcomes at Two Points in Time

Higher Outcomes

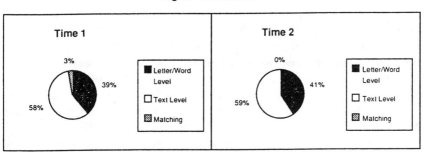

Lower Outcomes

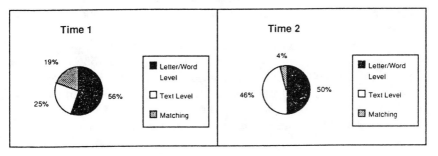

We also looked at changes over time. This analysis revealed that for Reading Recovery teachers who provided lessons with higher student outcomes, prompting for matching decreased to zero during Time 2. As students achieved full control of the early strategies, teachers would cease teaching to support this kind of learning. Efficiency would require a shift to other types of prompts. In the example presented earlier, Marianne's teacher exhibited a shift in priority and attention from Time 1 to Time 2. During the second reading, she did not need to attend to early strategies that had long since become automatic routines for the student. The teacher ignored some discrepancies between Marianne's reading and the text because her errors at that point made no difference in meaning; moreover, she knew that Marianne could attend to the details of words if needed. Her reading would be inefficient if she overcorrected insignificant errors. Following Marianne's lead, the teacher focused on the productive problem solving in which the child was engaged. She asked questions such as "What's wrong?" and prompted her to "Try it again." These prompts communicated to Marianne that the teacher believed that Marianne could problem solve on her own.

Teachers with lower student outcomes were attending to matching during Time 1 (19%), and although the behavior decreased, they were still prompting for matching during the second observation (4%). This situation indicated either that the earlier prompting was ineffective or that the teaching continued long after it was needed by the student.

Teachers with higher student outcomes tended to focus on text-level strategies the majority of the time (Time 1 = 58%; Time 2 = 59%) but also gave attention to letters and words (Time 1 = 39%; Time 2 = 41%). Within the letter and word category, teachers with higher student outcomes were more likely to prompt for word analysis, whereas those with lower outcomes were more likely to prompt for letter–sound work. Teachers did not separate attention in these two categories. Examination of the lesson transcripts revealed that they quickly and flexibly moved from one kind of attention to the other. When the attention was given to letters or words, it occurred within the context of experiencing the whole text. Items (specific words or parts of words) were given attention briefly and intensively; then, the attention returned to the meaning. This kind of teaching was illustrated by the example of Marianne's reading.

During the first observation (Time 1), teachers with lower outcomes focused primarily on letters, words, and visual information (56%) and less on text-level strategies (25%). During the second observation (Time 2), these same teachers slightly decreased attention to letters and words (50%) and increased attention to text-level strategies (46%); however, the majority of attention was still devoted to letters and words. Using *Space Journey* and *Letters for*

Mr. James, we present two simulated examples of the kinds of interactions we observed in lessons with lower student outcomes (Figures 4.5 and 4.6).

Like Marianne, George was using his strong sense of language to check on his own reading. He was dealing with the complicated language of the story and doing some problem solving. After the running record, the teacher praised his reading and then went back to page two, saying, "You made some mistakes here, George. What's the first word?" When George was unable to identify the word, the teacher asked him to sound it out; although he was able to make the first sound, he was confused, first saying "s" and then "I see." Finally, the teacher told him the word. This interaction was repeated for each error in the story. The teacher's objective appeared to be to help George correct

FIGURE 4.5. George's Running Record, Time 1

page	Title	Totals E	Totals SC	Cues Used E	Cues Used SC
1	I can see the stars / See the stars.	4	0	(m)(S) v (m)(S) v (m)(S) v (m)(S) v	
2	I ✓ ✓ ✓ / . See the planets.	1		(m)(S) v	
3	I ✓ ✓ ✓ / . See the sun.	1		(m)(S) v	
4	I ✓ ✓ ✓ / . See the moon.	1		(m)(S) v	
5	I ✓ ✓ moon / . See the earth.	2		(m)(S) v (m)(S) v	
6	✓ / Home!				

Note:

M = meaning
S = structure (language)
V = visual (letters/sounds)

FIGURE 4.6. George's Running Record, Time 2

Page	Title
13	Letters for Mr. James

That ✓ morning ✓

all ✓ the ✓ children ✓ wrote ✓ letters ✓

to ✓ Mr. James. ✓ They ✓ wrote ✓

big ✓ letters ✓ and ✓ little ✓ letters, ✓

~~f f fit~~ ✓ _thing_ ✓
fat letters and think letters,

letters ✓ with ✓ pictures _p...p_ Ⓐ

and ✓ letters ✓ with ✓ jokes, _H_

	T: What does it start with?
	S: "j"
	T: Sound it out.
	S: j..j..j..
✓ _little_	T: jokes
and letters	

✓ _k... k .. kitten._
with kisses

Note.

A = Appeal
H = hesitation
T = teacher
S = student

his reading and attend to visual information; that goal was partially achieved, but she was not helping him to use information strategically. She paid little attention to the good work he was doing in matching oral and written language. Figure 4.6 demonstrates that this teacher's patterns of response did not change as George progressed through the program.

The teacher had not taught George how to problem solve on his own and was reduced to telling George each word. As a result, his reading broke down, with George doing little problem solving on his own. The teacher went back to read the page in unison with George, which helped him to get the language of the story but did little to support independent reading behavior. The danger here is that George might think of reading as one of two things, sounding out individual words or memorizing what the story says. Neither theory would lead to the kind of orchestration that makes for a self-extending system. George was not developing the kind of strength that would allow him to read more difficult texts. In fact, the text he was given was too hard for him to do effective problem solving. Without a chance to do this reading work, children will have difficulty in developing effective strategies. The teacher pictured here was overly concerned with accuracy as an end in itself, and she neglected opportunities to support strategic problem solving.

A BALANCE OF TEACHING

Highly successful teachers appeared to have a bias toward prompting for text-level strategies; however, they did not neglect the use of visual information or attention to words. They seemed to be helping students to analyze words using larger "chunks" of information in addition to letter–sound correspondence. This balance of attention was consistent across observations.

Teachers with lower student outcomes tended to focus more on letters and words and less on text-level strategies in both observations. Their attention to letter–sound correspondence was high; yet they did not appear to work toward helping the student use word analysis "on the run" while reading continuous text.

The results of these analyses indicate that Reading Recovery is not a single method or approach. Simply using the Reading Recovery framework and engaging in the recommended behaviors will not guarantee a high level of success. Perhaps that is why supervisors' use of checklists to code teacher behavior will not guarantee higher student achievement. Teachers must observe children carefully and do so "on the run," while teaching. They have to have priorities for each child; they must tailor their responses to the individual child's revealed strengths. We coded the teacher behavior and found some interesting differences, but when experts looked at lessons in a more holistic way, applying their powers of critical evaluation, we learned much more.

Learning About Teaching in the Lesson Context

The teacher leader's role is complex; their most important responsibility is the continual examination of teaching, which they do through their own work with children and through the analytical critique of lessons taught by teachers in their classes. They become expert in analyzing, interpreting, and evaluating Reading Recovery lessons. Because of this expertise, teacher leaders were a natural extension of the data collection for our in-depth study of teaching. Their explanations and perspectives helped us to understand not only these individual lessons but how teachers think about lessons in ways that extend their knowledge base.

For an illustration of how a leader assists teachers, let us revisit an example from earlier in this chapter. This time, however, we look at the example as a behind-the-glass lesson. Remember that Marianne was reading *Space Journey*. Before the lesson, the teacher leader provided some information about Marianne to the observing teachers but did not tell her entire case history. She wanted the teachers to observe closely and state their interpretations of behavior. The teachers watched the familiar reading, noting that Marianne was exhibiting control of word-by-word matching on texts with one or two lines of print. While she occasionally approximated text using her strong language skills, she was beginning to check on herself consistently. During the lesson, the teacher took the running record shown in Figure 4.1.

As Marianne was reading, the teacher leader asked teachers to make comments about her control of early strategies. Here are some of the statements elicited:

TEACHER 1:   She's doing well on matching.
TEACHER 2:   This text is easy for her.
TEACHER 3:   I notice that she was really predicting a language pattern that would be more typical than the one in the text, but she knew that there was a discrepancy.
LEADER: Why is that important?
TEACHER 3:   Because she is starting to check on her own reading.
TEACHER 2:   She's monitoring.
TEACHER 4:   She knows *the*. That may be why she stopped.
TEACHER 5:   I'd go back and praise her for that.
LEADER: Does anyone agree with that recommendation?
TEACHER 2:   Yes.
LEADER: What would be powerful about that teaching response?

TEACHER 3: It would let her know that she is solving her own problems and she might go on doing more of it.

LEADER: Why is that important for Marianne?

TEACHER 2: She is just beginning to link up oral language and the visual information in print, so she is getting more control by doing it on easy books.

LEADER: Is this a good book for her?

TEACHER 3: Yes, it doesn't have much print, but she knows the ideas in it.

TEACHER 1: There are some problems but she can handle it.

LEADER: Do we want reading that's completely accurate?

TEACHER 1: No.

LEADER: Why not?

TEACHER 5: Because it's not the words, it's the way she uses anchors as a check in reading.

It would take many more pages to provide a fuller picture of the teachers' talk, but it should be obvious from this example that they were following Marianne's lesson closely and learning to analyze the processes of teaching. They were predicting the teacher's instructional decisions based on their own analyses of Marianne's understandings at this point in her program. The leader plays a key role in guiding teachers' social interactions through their negotiation of meaning.

The leader's observation of teaching also takes place in school settings. Several times during the training year and thereafter, the teacher leader makes individual visits to teachers to observe and offer assistance. At an individual school visit, after Marianne's lesson, the leader might have asked the teacher to talk about the reader and analyze the miscues, noticing the child's strengths. She might have pointed out the powerful teaching moves made by the teacher and suggested some future moves that might help Marianne be more independent. Together, they might have selected Marianne's new book and talked about the orientation with the intention of providing her with a greater challenge.

Analysis of Teaching for Strategies in Context

Reading Recovery teacher leaders are accustomed to using their analyses to help teachers increase their observational powers and make better instructional decisions. In our study, three expert teacher leaders applied their knowledge holistically to our videotapes of Reading Recovery teaching. The example presented here illustrates the complex nature of teacher–child interactions. Teachers' prompts were swift strings of comments that both responded to the child's behavior and directed attention to cues that would be helpful in enabling the child to resolve his own conflicts.

Let us look at an extended example of Matthew's reading of *The Poor Sore Paw* (Cowley, 1987c).

MATTHEW: "Sam move the" [Text: *Sam moved the wood on the bridge.*]
TEACHER: What did he move?
MATTHEW: "Move the"
TEACHER: Get your mouth ready.
MATTHEW: "Moved the"
TEACHER: (Pointing to the picture of the wood.) What do you call this?
MATTHEW: A wall.
TEACHER: I don't think it would be a kind of wall. It starts like wall, though. What did he move right here? What is this?
MATTHEW: "Moved the"
TEACHER: Could that word be *wood*?
MATTHEW: Yeah, *wood*.

When the teacher leaders discussed this section of the lesson, they noticed that the teacher was prompting Matthew to notice a variety of cues, including meaning, structure, and letter–sound relationships. She was flexible in her prompting, basing her questions on a very quick analysis of what the child had used and what he had neglected.

MATTHEW: "Wood . . . wood of the bridge." (Matthew continued reading.) "The, the poor sore paw came out of the friend." [Text: *The poor sore paw came out. The dog was free.*]
TEACHER: You're starting it. It begins like *friend*. Let's see, what would make sense? Stretch it with me.
MATTHEW: "Free."
TEACHER: Read it and see if it makes sense.
MATTHEW: "The dog was free."
TEACHER: Was he? Did he get his paw out? And the last part read quickly.

The teacher noticed the productive work Matthew did in using the first letters of *free*, but she challenged him to check his use of visual information against his knowledge of what would make sense. She also asked him to look through the word as he searched, and he successfully read the word. She then took him back to meaning and language syntax by asking him to read it again to confirm.

MATTHEW: "The dog and goat and cow and the farmer got how."
[Text: *The dog and goat and the farmer stopped howling.*]
TEACHER: Is that what they were doing?
MATTHEW: "How"—yeah.
TEACHER: *How.* Take a look at the word. Is there a little chunk on the end of it?
MATTHEW: "Howling."
TEACHER: *Howling.* Good, Matthew.
MATTHEW: "They went over the bridge and they all went home for their lunch, dinner." [Text: *They went over the bridge and they all went home for their dinner.*]
TEACHER: You almost said "lunch." Would that have made sense?
MATTHEW: No.
TEACHER: Look at it. All went home to eat their lunch. Would that make sense?
MATTHEW: Yeah.
TEACHER: Why did you change it to "dinner"?
MATTHEW: Because it wasn't *lunch.*
TEACHER: But what did you notice about *dinner?*
MATTHEW: It had a *d.*

The teacher in this example was prompting the child to use strategies; in just a few minutes, she had prompted the student to search for various kinds of information. She knew when to provide information and when to ask him to act, coming up with support when necessary to help him search further. She praised the hard work he did in the lesson. She had asked him to confirm his attempts using meaning, language syntax, or visual information. She had noticed the way he was using his knowledge (e.g., he substituted words that had the same letter as the word in the text) and confirmed that as a strategy, but she asked him to think further and to make his reading make sense.

This sample represents highly active teaching during the first reading of a new book. The teacher was working to help the child solve problems at a difficult point. At other points in the lesson, observers noticed that the teacher might be less active and her emphasis might be on reading for fluency and independence. For example, earlier in the lesson he had read fluently and accurately *Little Pig* (Melser, 1981), a book that was easy for him.

MATTHEW: "'Go home,' said the dog. 'No,' said little pig."
TEACHER: He doesn't want to go home, does he?
MATTHEW: "'Go home,' said the cow. 'No,' said little pig. 'Go home,' said the sheep. 'No,' said little pig. 'Go home,' said the butcher. 'Or I'll make you into sausage.'"
TEACHER: Think he'll go home?

MATTHEW: "'Yes, I will,' said little pig."

TEACHER: He sure did. And look at those talking marks we've got
again. And the little pig says, "Yes, I will." And all of those words
are what the little pig said, weren't they? You read it again. Let's
get really excited. Let your voice show excitement. Try it again.
Let's get real excited.

In reading *Little Pig,* there were few problems for the child to solve. He
was reading quickly and fluently. The teacher confirmed his reading and
encouraged him to use phrasing and fluency.

The examples above illustrate the quick responses made by the teacher;
they also show that these responses are interconnected with the child's
responses and with previous reading. In a way, the teacher and child are creating an oral language text that supports the child's reading of written language.

Characteristics of Teachers with Higher Student Outcomes

The Reading Recovery teacher leaders who coded the tapes suggested
in their ongoing dialogue that the decisions and interventions that help students consist of much more than a list of the desired behaviors to be checked
off. When teacher leaders observed the taped lessons, they did so with recognition of the complexities of the social context, and their informal discussion was rich in meanings that could not be accounted for in the coding of
behaviors into categories.

The team of experts discussed all videotapes, including those of teachers
with higher and lower student outcomes. They did not have access to student
outcome data but were encouraged to use their ability to evaluate critically
the lessons just as they would in behind-the-glass sessions. The result was a
list of descriptors for each lesson; these are presented in Tables 4.2 and 4.3
for teachers with higher and lower student outcomes.

In general, teachers with higher student outcomes were described as more
specific and more attentive to problem-solving strategies—both those initiated by children and those for which they prompted after observing a potential opportunity. These lessons were not perfect; our experts had many critical comments, for example, "She's losing some power there." But they also
noted that teachers were being selective:

"She knows when to be quiet and let him work independently."
"She's supporting the child's strategic moves."
"She's helping him use oral reading and rehearing to get a feedback sys-
    tem going."

TABLE 4.2. Characteristics of Teachers with Higher Student Outcomes

WORKING FOR INDEPENDENCE AND ACTIVE LEARNING

- Allows time for independent problem-solving; knows when to be quiet.
- Persistent in questioning and prompting students to do what they know.
- Requires students to problem-solve while reading.
- Questions in a way that makes children think and act.
- Asks the child to evaluate him/herself
- Asks children to be responsible for checking.

WORKING FOR STRATEGIC OPERATIONS

- Questions in a way that helps children check several different sources of information.
- Helps children discount or verify their predictions based on a closer visual look.
- Helps children use oral reading and rehearing to get a feedback system going.
- Uses specific praise to confirm children's strategic behavior.

CREATING A SUPPORTIVE SOCIAL CONTEXT

- Is a warm and friendly in the interaction.
- Accepts the child's efforts, even those partially right.
- Observes and responds to the child's moves.
- Personalizes the story for the individual child.
- Sounds positive and reassuring that the child has done something good.

TABLE 4.3. Characteristics of Teachers with Lower Student Outcomes

WORKING FOR INDEPENDENCE AND ACTIVE LEARNING

- Seems to tell instead of supporting the child's working it out.
- Inconsistent in requiring child to problem-solve.
- Reinforces the child's looking at teacher for confirmation.

WORKING FOR STRATEGIC OPERATIONS

- Tends to tell and repeat.
- Prompts child to "remember" instead of problem-solve.
- Overly attends to words; preteaches words; book selection revolves around words.
- Consistently works at the letter-sound level; teaches sounds in isolation.
- Neglects monitoring; doesn't support self-monitoring.
- Does not help children check on themselves.
- Appears to be overly concerned with accuracy.
- Overuses verbalization which could get in the way.
- Does not help child use meaning and language structure as a feedback system.

CREATING A SUPPORTIVE SOCIAL CONTEXT

- Questions in ways that are inappropriate for the particular child.
- Does not "tune in" to where the child is.
- Does not interact enough with students.
- Tends to move the lesson at a slow, uninteresting pace.

"The main power of this teaching is the initial focus on meaning, accep-
tance of the child's efforts."
"She's very skillful in helping him to discount or verify his prediction
based on a closer visual look."

In contrast, comments made during the viewing of lessons associated with
lower student outcomes described teachers' actions as less specific and more
targeted on items rather than strategies.

"She keeps asking students to remember rather than to problem solve
on their own."
"She is teaching items (such as words) in isolation."
"She is consistently working at the letter and sound level."
"They only got through the problem on that page."
"She isn't working to let him to apply that to another situation."
"She is telling him what to do and when it is right."
"She is monitoring for the student."

This analysis proved to be highly productive in helping us to understand
the teacher–child interactions within the reading portion of Reading Recovery lessons. In the next chapter, we continue to look at teacher and student
interactions during reading and apply some of these understandings to a general discussion of teaching reading in Reading Recovery as well as in classroom settings.

Chapter 5

Working Toward More Effective Teaching

In Reading Recovery lessons, children experience texts at varying levels of difficulty, and they work with them in different ways. Teachers also play different roles at various points within the lesson framework. Sometimes they are active in sharing the problem solving going on. Sometimes they retreat to the neutral position of observer, asking the child to work independently. They shift their behavior as the student grows in understanding. While their conversational interactions provide support, the child is left with challenging work to do. The teacher is more than a support; often he or she demonstrates or directs the child's attention. But it is clear that it is the child's job to construct the internal understandings necessary for strategic reading. The combination of the lesson framework and effective instructional interactions based on observation provide the basis for accelerated progress in Reading Recovery. Classroom teachers have concerns paralleling those of Reading Recovery teachers: (1) the activities they plan and provide for children in their classes and (2) the way they converse and guide children within those activities. And Reading Recovery teachers and classroom teachers have similar long-term goals—helping children construct their own self-extending systems for reading. In this chapter we discuss some important theoretical concepts related to learning to read as well as teaching tools such as the use of running records, book selection, and providing story orientations.

INDEPENDENCE: THE GOAL OF READING INSTRUCTION

We understand reading to be a problem-solving process by which an individual creates meaning through interacting with a text. When readers encounter stories, written directions, personal letters, notes, signs, menus, and any other texts, they re-create them in their heads while perusing the visual information. There is information in the text, represented by graphic symbols. But meaning for the reader is created as he or she brings prior knowledge and personal meanings to the experience. No two readers create exactly the same meanings even though they are reading the same piece of written language.

Readers simultaneously participate in a variety of complex in-the-head activities. Cued by the visual information in print, readers access their knowledge of language and the world. These cognitive strategies cannot be directly observed, but there is evidence that they exist. For younger readers, some overt behaviors, such as self-correction and starting over, provide evidence that internal monitoring, searching, and checking processes are at work. Older competent readers provide little information about what they actually are doing, a circumstance that makes it difficult for young children to figure out what is going on when people read.

When we interviewed a group of kindergarten children in another study, we asked them to show a teddy bear how to read (see Pinnell, Bradley, & Button, 1990). A substantial number of them simply said, "Watch me and do what I do," then took a book and looked at it silently, moving the head from right to left. The first graders who participated in the study reported here were also interviewed. These children, designated as the lowest readers in their classes, were more likely to identify good behavior, such as being quiet, listening to the teacher, or hand raising, as the characteristics of a "good reader" than to talk about anything specific (Pinnell, Bradley, & Button, 1990). As Meek (1982) has said, "one of the greatest problems for the beginner is that he cannot tell by watching them what readers are actually doing." (p. 20)

For Reading Recovery teachers, Clay (1991) provides this definition of reading: "a message-gaining, problem-solving activity that increases in power and flexibility the more it is practiced" (p. 6). First, the goal of reading is to gain meaning; meaning is gained through in-the-head problem-solving activity undertaken by the reader. We cannot know exactly what is going on in the reader's head, but we assume that a dynamic process, involving the eyes, is underway, always in search of meaning. Through engaging in this problem-solving process, the reader builds systems of understanding that make up what Clay has called a "self-extending system," one that fuels its own learning.

To understand this kind of system better, think of yourself as a reader. Perhaps in recent years you have been required to read something that seemed difficult, perhaps in an unfamiliar subject-matter area or a genre of literature you had not read often. At first, the reading might have gone slowly. You had to back up, reread, and check one part of the text with another. Gradually, though, if you read more and more in the same area, the going got easier. As a good reader, you have the ability to teach yourself to read better and better. As you encounter new kinds of texts, new content, and new vocabulary, you not only learn new words but you learn how to read that kind of material more efficiently.

Good readers have self-extending systems that allow them to extend their knowledge and abilities constantly. They are seldom aware of this largely unconscious process; they provide little evidence of it in their overt behavior. In the example in the last chapter, young Matthew was engaging in the kind of problem-solving work that will help him to build his self-extending system for reading. It is easy to see evidence of his problem solving because he is just beginning to build the system. Reading Recovery teachers learn to observe children carefully to detect behavioral evidence of this "reading work."

How Teachers Look at Children's Reading

In Chapter 4, we presented an example of Matthew's reading of *The Poor Sore Paw* (Cowley, 1987c). We revisit a segment of the reading here, with some further description of nonverbal behavior, in order to show how his Reading Recovery teacher would interpret the behavior.

MATTHEW: (Hesitating.) "The, the poor sore paw came out of the friend." [Text: *The poor sore paw came out. The dog was free.*]
TEACHER: You're starting it. It begins like *friend*. Let's see, what would make sense? (Placing her finger under the beginning of the word.) Say it slowly, stretch it with me. Stretch it with me.
MATTHEW: "Free."
TEACHER: Read it and see if it makes sense.
MATTHEW: "The dog was free."
TEACHER: Was he? Did he get his paw out?
MATTHEW: Yeah, he got his paw out.

Here is the way a Reading Recovery teacher might describe and interpret Matthew's behavior.

Matthew was reading fluently, without pointing, and was consistently checking the pictures to confirm his reading. On the word *friend,* he seemed to use the visual information, the *f* and *r*, to predict the word. That shows that he is able to analyze words visually. But it appears that he was monitoring his reading using meaning and his knowledge of how a sentence is supposed to sound. He stopped when it didn't make sense and didn't fit his knowledge of syntax. That indicates to me that he is monitoring his own reading.

In *The Early Detection of Reading Difficulties,* Clay (1985) asks teachers to think about three kinds of cueing systems that readers use to problem solve while reading text. Cues, in her definition, are sources of information that the reader accesses. Two, meaning and syntax, are essentially language systems. The third, visual information, refers to the print.

Meaning.   Readers use their background of knowledge about the world and about language to predict and monitor while reading. Through interacting with others in the social context of home and community, they have learned to express meanings in oral language. Thus children bring this system of meanings, expressed in language, to the reading of written language.

Syntax.   Readers come to the task with a system of rules for their oral language. These rules are not rules of grammar as we have encountered them in school. They are the rules by which words are strung together in sentences that make sense. Children come to school understanding and producing the syntax of their own oral language. If they have heard many stories read aloud, they may also have a sense of the syntax of written language, which is different in some ways from that of oral language. This knowledge is evident in the "talking like a book" that many prereaders, even very young ones, exhibit. They expect their renditions of texts to be consistent with what they know about language syntax.

Visual Information.   Readers are able to distinguish letters one from another and know that clusters of letters represent meaning-carrying elements such as syllables, words, and word endings. The visual symbols are related to the phonemic system that readers use in their oral language; thus, letter–sound relationships provide a valuable resource in figuring out words. Readers use the visual information in the print to check the predictions they make based on the other two cueing systems and to solve words when other cues are insufficient.

Readers use all three of these systems as sources of information while reading for meaning. The reader is moving visually left to right and top to bottom through the written text and at the same time is selectively attending to whatever system of information is needed to make sense of the text. A reader may be focusing on the meaning of the passage but, encountering difficulty, stop momentarily to attend to visual detail or to think whether the sentence fits his or her notions of the rules of syntax. Clay (1991) talks about these processes as attending to serial order and hierarchical order, describing them as the "twin puzzles" of reading acquisition.

Thus readers are always asking themselves questions; for example, Did that make sense? Did it sound right? Did it look right? Although it is not usually a conscious process, we could almost hear Matthew thinking something like: "That word looks like *friend* but it didn't sound right. And it didn't make sense. A paw couldn't come out of a *friend*. What else could it be?" Young readers need a chance to engage in this problem-solving process. They need opportunities to work on texts that are interesting and easy enough to assure that meaning can be carried through; but they also need a chance to encounter a little difficulty so that they can use their problem-solving strategies and, in the process, build independent, self-extending systems that will allow them to increase their skills while reading for meaning.

A NEW WAY OF LOOKING AT TEACHING

It appears that the system of strategies must, ultimately, be constructed by the reader. What is the role of the parent or teacher? If exposed to print and hearing written language read aloud, will children just naturally begin to figure out reading? For some children, that may be the case. With almost minimal demonstrations, they seem to grasp the essential processes and begin to read. Most children, however, need some level of adult support to build internal processes. This support level varies for individuals, depending on the accumulation of wisdom from experiences they have had previous to school and the attention they have given those experiences.

Every child comes to school having experienced "literacy events" at home and in the community. When we talk about literacy events, we usually think about hearing favorite stories read at bedtime or "writing" messages with scribbles, letters, and emerging use of print conventions. Literacy events also included everyday functional encounters with print. Children notice menu items in restaurants, play with the mail that arrives at their homes, or listen and interact as adults read advertisements or the sports page. Any encounter with print in a social context can constitute a literacy event and can support children's growing concepts of what reading and writing are all about.

Emergent literacy behaviors have been described by many researchers (see Ferriero & Teberosky, 1982; Harste, Woodward & Burke, 1984; Teale & Sulzby, 1986). All of this research indicates that the social setting is an important factor in literacy learning. In every interaction surrounding literacy events, parents, caregivers, and teachers are demonstrating or telling children something about the complex actions that make up reading.

Research on language learning has provided powerful evidence of the influence of caregivers on children's learning (Cazden, 1988; Snow, 1983). In learning language, caregivers act as supporters by involving the child as a conversational partner. Even before they can use words, children learn important social conventions, such as turn taking, and caregivers respond to their attempts in a way that helps them extend these understandings. Building on a suggestion from Bruner (Wood et al., 1976), Cazden (1988) has character- ized caregivers as providing a "scaffold" that gradually shifts as the child's knowledge base is built and expanded.

Through demonstrations of all kinds of functional reading and also through reading stories to children, parents and other caregivers usually encourage children when they make their own attempts to retell stories by looking at pictures. When they read with their parents, many young children practice searching for information in pictures, using the syntax of written lan- guage, and remembering how the story goes. Because preschool children are not expected to read, they are free to work out the process over time, with adult praise and support. When children enter school, however, expectations begin to change, and soon they are expected to read print with few discrep- ancies between their oral renditions and the precise message.

The child depends on what he or she is told and sees. Having a person to talk with while exploring the complex task of reading provides a support system, a temporary context, that assists in making the transition to literacy. Research by Board (1982) indicates that these interactions with others are especially important for children who find it initially difficult to perform the tasks related to literacy in the school setting. These children, he says, may be more vulnerable to the influence of instructional interactions.

Teachers provide important support for young readers through a reper- toire of interactional behaviors that help to weave meaning around the lit- eracy event. They demonstrate processes to the child through reading and through seemingly casual conversation that make visible some ways to go about solving a problem. A teacher might say, "Let's read it again to make sure it makes sense" or "Let's check the picture." Teachers also remind children to access their own sources of information. For example, a teacher might say, "Have you checked the picture" or "Did that sound right?" or "Did that look right?"

Matthew's teacher, for example, provided support at the point where he encountered difficulty. According to Clay (1985), what teachers notice is a powerful influence on children; that is, children attend to what teachers attend to. First, she noticed that Matthew was using his knowledge of letter–sound relationships to begin a left-to-right analysis of the word *free*. She hypoth- esized that he noticed the *fr* and guessed the word *friend*, a familiar one to him. But she also noticed that he stopped, possibly because his reading sud- denly did not make sense. She demonstrated the process of searching for meaning by saying, "Let's see. What would make sense?" Simultaneously, she asked him to look through the word visually. Matthew quickly came up with the word *free*, but the teacher did not stop there. She asked him to read it again and check to see whether his reading made sense. After he did so, she asked him to reflect briefly by saying, "Was he? Did he get his paw out?" In this brief interaction, taking only a few seconds, the teacher was supporting Matthew's problem-solving processes and helping him become flexible in searching.

Active teaching in this sense is not the same as planned direct instruction. Like direct instruction, teachers take the initiative to draw students' attention to critical elements in the reading process. But unlike direct instruction, teachers' moves must conform to students' responses and repertoire. Making the decisions related to their active teaching is the most difficult challenge for Reading Recovery teachers.

Meeting Students' Needs in Classrooms

In classroom situations, too, teachers are faced with the challenge of supporting children's problem-solving actions. Prescriptive programs, which take children through preordained steps, may not leave enough room for these young students to engage in problem solving while reading text. For example, in some programs students spend most of their time learning items, such as letters and letter–sound relationships in a particular order, and that learning may be successful regarding the particular piece of information. They may, through practice, learn a repertoire of words, but the most important thing to learn is *how to use that information while reading.* Clay (1991) points out that some children learn item knowledge in orchestrated ways. Whatever the approach, they know what to do with the information. In these times, however, when reading opportunities outside school may not be extensive, it is important to provide demonstrations and activities that help young readers understand the purposes and processes of reading.

It is not necessary for classroom instruction to require the development of a large amount of item knowledge before engaging the child in authentic reading. From the beginning, it is possible to provide opportunities for children not only to learn about the details of print but also to use that information in strategic ways while reading text. Recent curriculum developments, such as unison reading of "big books" and interactive writing, provide demonstrations and involve children. Many classrooms are provisioned with a large number of simple stories that children have no trouble reading on their own after the teacher has provided some introduction. These transition texts have characteristics of literature in that they usually provide stories with interesting illustration, but they are especially designed to help young readers sort out their beginning ideas about reading. The easiest ones have only one, two, or three lines of text, language close to the child's own oral language, and very supportive illustrations. Working with the teacher, with partners, or alone, even beginning first graders can behave like readers, using what they know to search, check, and confirm before they have a large store of item knowledge. As Clay (1991) has said, "A few items and a powerful strategy might make it very easy to learn a great deal more" (p. 331).

Using Running Records to Inform Teaching. Both Reading Recovery teachers and classroom teachers can keep track of children's progress and guide their own instructional moves by observing reading behavior. The running record is a powerful tool in this process. This assessment procedure was originally developed to help classroom teachers become better observers of children's reading. It is extensively used in New Zealand classrooms to keep records of children's reading and is expanding in use in the United States and Canada.

The running record provides an easy but precise way to record reading behavior while it is occurring. The teacher does not need to tape the reading and listen to it later. The shorthand technique of running records is quick and easy to read back; no pretyping of text is necessary. Sitting beside the child and looking at the text, the teacher makes a check for every word in the text that the child reads accurately, conforming the marks to the layout of the text on each page. The teacher also records behavior such as substitutions, omissions, insertions, and repetitions. This behavior can later be analyzed as the teacher reflects on the reading and develops hypotheses as to the kinds of cues the child was using. Once the record is completed, the teacher can make statements about the kind of evidence it shows about how the child problem solves and uses strategies to resolve his or her own conflicts.

It is possible for teachers to take a running record on any book the child picks up to read. All that is necessary is the ability to see the text at the same time the child is reading it. For materials, all the teacher needs is a pencil and paper. Teachers can use their shorthand notes to analyze instantly some aspects of reading behavior and can respond to the child right away. In individual conferences in the classroom or in Reading Recovery lessons, teachers can use running records as a guide to focusing the child's attention. The following example illustrates:

Phillip was reading *Little Pig* (Melser, 1981), a book with a simple, predictable text and supportive pictures. He had read the book several times before.

PHILLIP: "'Go home,' said the butcher, 'or I'll turn you into sausages.'"
[Text: *"Go home," said the butcher "or I'll make you into sausages."*] (Hesitating and looking at the teacher.)
TEACHER: Try to read the sentence again.
PHILLIP: "'Go home,' said the butcher, 'or I'll make you into sausages.'"
TEACHER: (Pointing to the word *make.*) What did you notice about that word?
PHILLIP: The *m*, so it has to be *make.*

TEACHER: Yes, you are right. And does *make* sound right and make
sense in the story.

PHILLIP: Yes.

TEACHER: Good checking, Phillip.

Later in the lesson, Phillip read yesterday's new book, *The Trolley Ride*
(Butler, 1988), while the teacher took a running record of his reading. During this section of the lesson, the child operates as independently as possible
while the teacher observes closely, helping only when necessary to keep the
process going. Figure 5.1 shows a section of the teacher's running record of
Phillip reading *The Trolley Ride.*

In this example, the teacher quickly noted some interesting behavior on
Phillip's part. After the reading, she turned back to page three and said, "I
really liked how you worked on this. Read it again." Phillip read the page
quickly, with phrasing. The teacher complimented his problem-solving work
and self-correction. Then, she moved to the last page, again complimenting
the child, and noticing how he was looking closely at the words and checking
to see if what he read looked right and sounded right. Finally, she asked Phillip
to build *the, they,* and *then* several times using magnetic letters. She was teaching for word analysis after Phillip had done some successful work with those
words in text. Her running records guided the process and helped her respond
to the particular student's behavior.

Reading Recovery teachers use running records daily to assess student
progress and gain evidence of the child's developing problem-solving abilities. We have previously discussed how they consult running records as they
try to identify priorities and establish the knowledge base needed to interact
effectively with the child. They also can use records to evaluate their choice
of a particular book for an individual. A general guide is to select a book that
a child can read at about 90% accuracy so that the reader can be effective
and flexible in problem solving. Achieving this goal depends on text selection
and story orientation, two concepts that will be discussed later in this chapter.

Classroom teachers do not use running records as extensively as do Reading Recovery teachers, but they have important classroom uses. Classroom
teachers use running records to evaluate texts, both their level of difficulty
for particular students and the appropriateness of their language. Running
records are an important tool in portfolio assessment. For example, systematic use of these records can provide a way for teachers to look at progress
over time. The records not only can show that children are reading more difficult texts but also can reveal increasing evidence of strategic reading.

Selecting Books to Help Young Readers.   Books are an important
part of any reading program, whether in individualized tutoring or in the class-

FIGURE 5.1. Running Record and Teacher's Analysis—*The Trolley Ride*

Page	Title	Totals		Cues Used	
	The Trolley Ride	E	SC	E	SC
8	✓ ✓ ✓ ✓ ✓ ✓ The cat got on the trolley.				
9	<u>The /sc)</u>R — _ away Then the trolley zoomed off.	I	I	ⓜⓢv | ms ⓥ ⓜⓢv	
10	<u>Then the /sc</u> ✓ ✓ ✓ ✓ A monster got on the trolley.	I	I	ⓜⓢv mⓢv | msⓥ	
11	<u>the/sc</u> Then . . .	I	I	m sⓥ | ⓜⓢⓥ	
12	✓ ✓ ✓ ✓ ✓ ✓ . . . the turtle got off the trolley.				
13	✓ ✓ ✓ ✓ ✓ ✓ The chicken got off the trolley.				
(The story continues as all the animals get off the trolley.)					
15	✓ ✓ ✓ ✓ ✓ ✓ ✓ Even the driver got off the trolley.				
16	<u>The /sc</u> ✓ ✓ ✓ ✓ Then they all zoomed off.	I	I	ⓜⓢv | msⓥ	

<u>Note.</u>

Phillip's substitutions are written above the text.

m = meaning
s   = structure (language)
v   = visual (letters/sounds)
E = error
SC = self correction
R   = repetition

room library. In Reading Recovery, two kinds of books are available: (1) those the child has previously read and (2) new books selected daily by the teacher. In familiar reading, the child reads books that he or she has successfully encountered in previous lessons. Drawing out several of these books, the teacher may ask the child to select one or two. Or the teacher may purposely select for the child. The purpose of the selection is to facilitate phrased fluent reading and to provide opportunities for conversation about the text.

The teacher selects each new book very carefully. This book will be introduced to the child on one day and read for the first time. That same book will be used for the running record assessment the next day. Text selection and the orientation both have impact on the independent reading work revealed by the running record. The teacher knows the child's interests, background of experience, control of language, and knowledge about print. He or she also knows the language patterns and concepts in the text. All of those factors are considered in text selection and in thinking about the opportunities offered by the text to support the child's current strategies as well as to offer unique challenges that will help to develop control of new strategies. The notion of challenge is important; the teacher juxtaposes that which the child already knows and novel information that the child is just beginning to know. The teacher considers what the child can "get to" using his or her current strategies and information. Then the teacher supports links between known and unknown sources of information.

This process has different implications at different points in the child's program. For example, in selecting *Space Journey* for Marianne, the example discussed in Chapter 4, the teacher was successful in finding a text that was interesting to the child. Marianne knew the concepts in the book and was visibly interested in pointing to the illustrations of stars, the moon, and planets. The teacher also had to find a text that Marianne would find accessible. This one had one of Marianne's known words in it; it was a predictable pattern; and there was only one line of text, an important characteristic because she was just beginning to use word-by-word matching and the return sweep in reading. Later in her program, the layout of text would not be so important.

In another example, the selection of A *Trolley Ride* was important for Phillip. The text had a cumulative pattern that assisted his reading but offered some tricky parts that challenged him to attend closely. The story was enjoyable; the pictures provided solid cues but did not carry the entire message. Since Phillip had full control of matching and did not need to point while reading, he could deal with several lines of text per page and layout was not so important as it had been in his early lessons.

In classroom teaching, too, the selection of texts is important. Here, text selection involves the collection of a variety of texts that will support reading in different ways. The teacher must choose texts to read aloud to the group; these will provide a rich language background and are generally more difficult than children will be expected to read by themselves. Teachers also think about the potential of read-aloud books for use as a foundation for interactive writing, a collaborative group writing experience.

Another area to consider in book selection is those texts to be used in group guided reading. These are introduced to children, and they are assisted in their first attempts to read them; later, they become books for independent reading. Children also select books for themselves. Some may be difficult, the kinds of books in which children enjoy pictures and recall and reconstruct the story without attending much to print. Others, they will work to read with more precision, problem solving their way through and learning about reading in the process. Still others may be easy and provide opportunities for fluent reading. In classrooms with many opportunities to read, the types of reading may be self-selected; but we caution teachers to monitor children's reading experiences carefully and, as appropriate, provide guided reading that challenges them and demands problem solving. Some children, although able, may be inclined to do only very easy reading or to approximate texts rather than do reading work. Loosely organizing the classroom collection along a gradient of difficulty will help teachers assess student progress and guide them in selection (see Peterson, 1991).

Using Story Orientations to Promote Independence.   In *Becoming Literate: The Construction of Inner Control,* Clay (1991) states that the child has a "right" to an orientation before reading a new text. She stresses the importance of talking with children before they read a new book, helping them to understand the overall meaning and structure of the story, perhaps letting them hear some of the difficult language patterns, and often locating some new and important words. Reading Recovery teachers and classroom teachers provide story orientations for students, although in Reading Recovery they are usually more thorough and are specially tailored to the individual child.

In both cases, story orientations sound less like instruction and more like conversation. Teachers do not ask question after question as if they are testing the child; instead, they share interesting aspects of the story, inviting the child to enter into discussion. The child's language and nonverbal responses tell the teacher something about how hard or easy books will be for the child to read.

Here is a short segment of the teacher's introduction of *The Poor Sore Paw* (Cowley, 1987c) to Matthew:

The teacher and Matthew are going through the book looking at the pictures and talking about the story. On the last page of the story, the illustration shows two children helping the dog get his poor sore paw out from between the cracks in the bridge.

TEACHER: Look, they squeezed! Look at them with all their mouths open. They did just what Horace did. They howled and they howled until finally what did Jessie and Sam do?

MATTHEW: Walk over.

TEACHER: They walked over and look. He took his hand and he moved the wood on the bridge and what, what happened to the dog? Could he get his sore paw out?

MATTHEW: Yeah.

TEACHER: It came out and they went home in time for. . . .

MATTHEW: Lunch!

TEACHER: . . . or dinner. They went home for dinner. What letter would you expect to see at the beginning of *dinner*?

MATTHEW: A *d*.

TEACHER: Find the word *dinner*. You got it! Are you right?

MATTHEW: Yeah.

TEACHER: How do you know you are right?

MATTHEW: Because *dinner* makes sense and it looks right.

TEACHER: Good checking, Matthew.

It is easy to see how this orientation paved the way for Matthew's problem solving during his reading of a text that he found difficult in places. Throughout his reading of *The Poor Sore Paw*, he kept the meaning in mind while doing quite a bit of problem solving. As discussed in Chapter 4, he substituted *wall* for *wood,* and then, with the teacher's help and prompting, worked on the passage trying to make sense. He substituted *lunch* for *dinner* on the last page, then, noticing the *d*, self-corrected. The teacher's introduction was highly supportive. It helped Matthew be flexible in attending to different levels of language from the meaning to the letters. But the introduction did not provide so much support that Matthew had nothing left to do on his own. He still had some productive, strategic work to do that would contribute to developing a self-extending system.

THE CRITICAL ROLE OF TEACHING

Throughout this volume we have emphasized the role of the learner in constructing meaning from text. We have said that we cannot know precisely what is going on in the reader's head and that, ultimately, he or she must read independently, without help. Yet we have also talked extensively about the teacher's critical role. Recognizing children's potential to learn from text and to power their own learning does not deny the need for help on occasion.

Reading Recovery children need extensive support of a particular kind. It is especially important that these children, who are vulnerable to instruction, are the recipients of a good, balanced teaching approach. The Reading Recovery teacher tailors his or her instruction to meet the students' individual learning needs.

It is also important for children in classrooms to experience good teaching. While they may not need consistent attention because they can profit from the social group, they do need memorable demonstrations and the opportunity to engage at their individual level of learning. They need teachers who notice their behavior and can interpret it in terms of knowledge of the processes. They need teachers who can observe student strengths and their attempts to make sense. They need teachers who will provide them many opportunities to use what they know and to become fluent and flexible with it.

In this chapter we have discussed the use of running records in helping teachers notice important behavioral signals of children's development of internal processes. We have highlighted three important aspects of teaching, both for Reading Recovery teachers and for classroom teachers: (1) running records and their use in informing teaching and supporting instructional conversation, (2) book selection, and (3) story orientation. In the next two chapters, we discuss the important role of writing in helping children learn to read.

Chapter 6

Learning About Written Language

According to Tharp and Gallimore (1988), the development of literacy is inseparable from the development of language. "When language splits from an exclusively verbal stream to form a written branch as well, certain profound changes occur in the relationship between speaking and thinking" (p. 104).

At home, concepts and language develop through joint activity in a highly supportive context around meaningful experiences. Some school contexts, however, decontextualize and make abstract the very language and experiences a child might have found familiar. For example, in a typical workbook activity, a child is presented a picture of a rainbow, a box, and a rabbit and asked to draw a circle around the ones that begin with *r*. If the child only predicts "bunny" as a label for the picture and has difficulty detecting and manipulating specific phonemes, as most first graders do (Goswami & Bryant, 1990), this task becomes difficult. Such constraints are not considered by developers of commercially produced instructional materials. Even highly supportive school settings demand more of the child in terms of working with print in decontextualized ways.

Literacy education in the primary grades requires a shift in the child's attention from sign–object relationships to sign–sign relationships (Wertsch, 1985). This need to manipulate language in more abstract, decontextualized settings is what sets schooling apart from literacy and language-learning events in the home. Vygotsky suggests that schooling frees the symbol systems of reading, writing, mathematics, and science for use as tools, thus allowing forms of thinking different from those of everyday life (in Tharp & Gallimore, 1988).

Tharp and Gallimore go on to describe the tension that exists between the detached systemic tools of schooled verbal symbols and everyday language and learning encounters that children have previously experienced. The dialectic of everyday language juxtaposed with schooled verbal symbols helps children become aware of the symbolic nature of written language and makes verbal and written symbols usable as a tool in practical thinking. Tharp and Gallimore (1988) argue that "the instructional task of the school is to facilitate that developmental process by teaching the schooled language of reading and writing, and facilitating the constant conjunction of these systems with those of everyday concepts" (p. 108). By making links between familiar concepts and new ones, the school can capture the power of the young child's learning process.

In this chapter we explore what children know about written language and how the Reading Recovery teacher explores the boundaries of this learning. We review pertinent literature on children's writing development before school begins, knowledge of which forms the basis for decisionmaking in instructional conversations in Reading Recovery. We also focus on what children may know when they enter school, what the school may require that they do in the name of learning about writing, and how the writing in Reading Recovery lessons relates to these contexts for learning.

LANGUAGE: THE FOUNDATION FOR WRITING

As we studied the instructional conversations between Reading Recovery teachers and their children, we were reminded again of the similarity between mother–child dyads in daily activities and the instructional conversations teachers and children had during writing. As a means of understanding teaching and learning in writing, we examine here the transition from home to school for emergent writers.

Oral language is learned within a speech community as the child and caregivers interact within common, daily routines. Neither the parent nor the child has the intention of "teaching" or "learning" language; neither children nor caregivers regard their interactions as a language-learning process (Ochs, 1983). Rather, language is the vehicle through which they communicate in order to accomplish their goals, and both teaching and learning occur within this frame of goal-directed activity. Language is learned as a means to an end (Tharp & Gallimore, 1988).

Writing, as another literacy-learning event in the home, provides a similar context in which to learn about writing. Clay (1975) reports one interaction between a mother and a child around a written product:

NATASHA TO MOTHER: What does this say?
MOTHER (sounding out the first line):   Sahspno!
NATASHA (thoughtful and satisfied):   I did it. (p. 3)

By responding to the child's intention to write as this mother did, she furthered the child's understanding that people draw (or write) not only things, but also speech (Vygotsky, 1978). In the above instance, the mother demonstrated to the child that her writing consisted of signs that designated sounds for spoken language. It is in this way that a child's first writing efforts may be given new meaning as they are responded to by others (Dyson, 1989). In home settings, writing can be part of everyday literacy experiences as children are encouraged to print their names and write headings on pictures, make shopping lists, write letters and notes, produce signs, and produce other written materials as part of their play (setting up a lemonade stand or a restaurant, etc.). These events occur almost always in a social, collaborative setting.

The characteristics of parent assistance and what children learn about reading and writing through the goal-directed activities in the home have particular import to an understanding of children's continued learning about written language in school settings and in Reading Recovery:

> How parents respond to children's emerging literacy seems to influence the course of language and literacy development (Snow, 1983). Parents (or other competent individuals) can enhance language and literacy development if they respond to children's early reading and writing attempts in ways that are semantically contingent and assist higher levels of performance. Snow (1983) has hypothesized that experiences with "decontextualized language" might also be critical for school success. Such language is more abstract, less rooted in the immediate context of a situation, and is used to recall previous experiences and relate them to present situations. It is the type of language children must develop if they are to be successful in school. Children who have neither this kind of language nor emergent literacy experiences will require . . . language- and literacy-development conversations as a routine in the classroom activity setting. (Tharp & Gallimore, 1988, p. 104)

The very basis of what occurs in instructional conversations within the writing component in Reading Recovery, the writing routine itself and the instructional moves the teacher and child make, is a more formalized use of the assisted conversations held between children and caregivers. Within these writing lessons, the teacher seeks to weave an instructional program around what the children know and extends that knowledge base in order to allow them to learn with their peers, to learn more about writing through classroom encounters with reading and writing. In the next section we explore what knowledge children bring to school writing tasks.

WRITING AS A SYMBOLIC AND SOCIAL TOOL

Understanding what writing is, how it is accomplished, and the purposes it serves are the practical learning that children accomplish before and during the first few years of school. For the children who enter Reading Recovery, the experiences they have had with writing in the home form the basis of the teacher's instructional program. The teacher will pay close attention to each child's current understandings of writing as a symbol system and as a process for communicating their messages.

The roots of their learning are in play, gesture, drawing, and the making of visual signs (Vygotsky, 1978). Early on in a child's history with written language, scribbles, drawings, and letterlike shapes represent the basic function of writing. These writing movements are supported by talk and establish a communicative event that illustrates basic concepts the child is able to initiate (Clay, 1975; DeFord, 1981; Harste et al., 1984). The child employs such communication strategies as scribbling, letterlike shapes, invented spelling, known words, and pictures to produce sentences, messages, and stories (DeFord, 1981). "As children develop as visual symbolizers, talk is an accompaniment to and then an organizer of their symbolic action. . . . Here speech may serve to guide and even to invest the visual symbol with meaning" (Dyson, 1990, p. 5). When children discover that people draw not only things but also speech (Vygotsky, 1978), speech itself forms the raw material for representing graphic symbols (Dyson, 1989).

Luria (1983) suggests that children's discoveries about written symbols are linked to their grasp of the specific function of print as an aid for recalling messages—and for others to do the same. Figure 6.1 illustrates this point. David, age 5, handed a map to Diane. He had met her in Ohio, but he saw her again when she was visiting Texas. While she had flown to Texas, David assumed she would have traveled by car, as he had with his parents the previous year.

DAVID: Here is a map . . . to get you back home.
DIANE: Why, thank you, David. Tell me about your map.
DAVID: You're here, in Texas, and you have to cross the Mississippi to get to Ohio. (Points to the line drawn in the center of the map.)
DIANE: That's a big help to me, David. Tell me, you have shown another way to go . . . here. (Points to a more direct line on the map.) Where will this take me?
DAVID: It's a short cut.
DIANE: What city will it take me through?
DAVID: Uh, Los Angeles, I think.

As David talked about getting to Ohio using a "short-cut" through Los Angeles, his conception of the meaning behind the visual representation expanded. Through conversation with Diane, David was able to use his experiences and hypotheses surrounding driving and map reading in a unique way to explain the signs on his map and their function. Vygotsky (1978) states that

FIGURE 6.1. David's Map

meaning is established interpersonally (with others) before it becomes intra-personal (inside the child): "Understanding of written language is first effected through spoken language, but gradually this path is curtailed and spoken language disappears as the intermediate link. To judge from all the available evidence, written language becomes direct symbolism that is perceived in the same way as spoken language" (p. 116). The map and subsequent conversation illustrates how David internalized the functions and forms of writing for his personal use. Vygotsky (1978) describes the process of internalization as a series of transformations:

a) An operation that initially represents an external activity is reconstructed and begins to occur internally.
b) An interpersonal process is transformed into an intrapersonal one.
c) The transformation of an interpersonal process into an intrapersonal one is the result of a long series of developmental events. (pp. 56–57)

THE WRITING SYSTEM

Between 1975 and 1990, there was an explosion of research on early writing development (Calkins, 1980, 1983; Clay, 1975; DeFord, 1980, 1981; Graves, 1983; Harste et al., 1984; King & Rentel, 1981, 1982, 1983). This research has helped educators understand the nature of children's learning about writing that is critical to school success. There are key concepts, or principles, that children learn about writing that form the basis of a self-extending system. There are also understandings that children develop about the phonological system, before and during their first year of school, that have an impact on reading progress as well as writing. Children who have adequate experiences with books and written language prior to school have developed a firm foundation in these basic principles about writing as a symbol system. For the at-risk child, however, these basic understandings must be incorporated into an instructional program. In early studies of children's writing development, Clay (1975) found the following:

Early learning is both approximate and specific . . . any one new insight may change the child's perception of the entire system drastically, or may even disorganize it. This seems to be because, at first, there is so little system and so much that is new. (p. 15)

The notion that children approximate is not new. Vygotsky (1978) and Sully (1986) showed that children do not strive for representation; they are much more symbolists than naturalists and are in no way concerned with complete and exact similarity. When writing something as meaningful as their name, however, children may reject all but one specific sign (Clay, 1975). David, for example, did not recognize his name unless each letter was capitalized. When the teacher wrote his name as *David,* he insisted that she change it. Calkins (1983), in observing children's writing over time, discussed the value of maintaining a file of student work so that the teacher could learn lessons from each child.

Figure 6.2 illustrates the different ways children explore print forms and how print functions to communicate for the emergent writer. In Figure 6.2a, a 3-year-old said "These are my aunts and my uncles" as she wrote a line of circles under her picture. In Figure 6.2b, a 6-year-old reread her text as a letter. Another first grader formed his text as a label under a drawing of his house (Figure 6.2c). Using letterlike shapes, and some of the letters from his name, he read "Me and my brother play at home." From early experiences with writing, children form concepts about how writing operates and how they can represent their messages for others to read.

Concepts and Principles

In the book *What Did I Write?* (1975), Clay discusses a child's gradual development of a perceptual awareness of those arbitrary customs used in written English. Using samples of children's work, she describes children's progress in learning the complexity of the writing system in approximate ways at first and later with considerable skill. As children work with a teacher in Reading Recovery, they will explore many of these underlying principles of written language:

1. The recurring principle refers to the child's developing concept that language and language forms recur in written language. A child who only knows a few letters, for example, learns to use these letters again and again to construct a long message.
2. Children learn directional principles when they discover that English text has directional conventions within space of left to right and top to bottom.
3. As children learn some elements, with different plans for combining or arranging them, they begin to generate new items, or to use the generating principle. This particular principle is an adaptation of the recurring principle, in that it adds the principle of variability to the child's understanding of written patterns.
4. Children also itemize what they have learned, illustrating the inventory principle, a form of systematic practice.
5. As children order their knowledge of print, they may begin to compare circle shapes with line shapes in letter learning, which suggests that they are acquiring the contrasting principle.

FIGURE 6.2. Young Children's Writing Samples

(A)

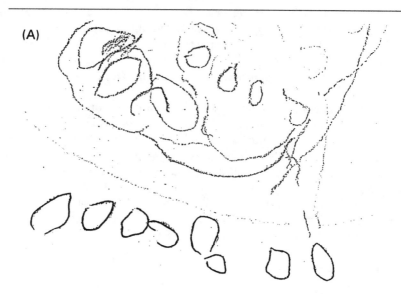

These are my aunts and my uncles.   Kathy--Age 3

(B)

Mary--Age 6

FIGURE 6.2. (*continued*)

(C)

Me and my brothers play at home.   Steve--Age 6

---

6. These comparisons set up contrasting sets and help children develop the flexibility principle, the concept that written language varies within certain limits.

In order for children to develop a self-extending system as writers, they must recognize that letters, words, and stories form the basis of written language. They must gain power from each encounter with print so as to generate new knowledge, using what they know to solve new problems as writers. As children are engaged in purposeful writing activities within a social setting, they come to understand signs in written language, to organize the written code, and to express themselves in writing within these meaningful interactions. The above generalizations and approximations that children make when they write provide a foundation for a network of understandings about writing as a process and as a symbol system. The task of writing instruction in schools is to assess the general principles a child has begun to initiate and to use this information to guide further instruction. The school will play a critical role in helping young learners know how to use writing as a means of communication.

Phonological Awareness

In addition to the above general concepts about how our written symbol system operates, young children begin to attend to how the phonological system operates. The phonological system is comprised of the sounds of speech that are also represented in the symbolic form of written language. The child's growing sense of how this system works is usually termed phonological awareness. Goswami and Bryant (1990) state: "When children learn to talk, their interest naturally is in the meaning of the words that they speak and hear. The fact that these words can be analyzed in a different way—that each word consists of a unique sequence of identifiable sounds—is of little importance" (p. 1).

However, by the time children enter school, they do have some basic facility with the phonological system. Learning to read and write also helps children learn more about the smaller constituent sounds within our language. It is important to understand what they can do easily and what tasks might be difficult at school entry.

There are three ways of breaking up a word into its smaller sound units. First, syllables offer an easy way for children to break words into parts. If asked to clap word parts, most 5-year-olds will do this successfully. Another common way to divide words into smaller units is at the phoneme level. "A phoneme is the smallest unit of sound that can change the meaning of a word. *Cat* and *mat* sound different and have different meanings because they differ in terms of one phoneme" (Goswami & Bryant, 1990, p. 2). This particular principle is a basic one within the traditional phonics approach to teaching reading. Goswami and Bryant argue that "children are not particularly sensitive to the existence of phonemes in words at the time when they begin to learn to read" (p. 26). To many children, "peanut butter and jelly" is one unit, since they have not formed a concept of words as a specific unit in speech or written language. Children who have not yet learned to read have great difficulty with tasks in which they have to detect and manipulate phonemes, unless the phoneme is at the beginning of a word and they are given some training in the task (Goswami & Bryant, 1990).

The third way words can be analyzed is through onset and rime. These are forms of intrasyllabic units, with the onset being the beginning phoneme or cluster and the rime being the end unit (c-at in *cat*; str-ing in *string*). Children are sensitive to rhyme and alliteration, and they can categorize words that have the same onset or the same rime (Goswami & Bryant, 1990). Therefore, manipulating sound components of syllables and onset and rime (building on a strong sense of rhyme and alliteration) has been shown to be easier for children who have not learned to read. These strengths can be used by teachers to help children make generalizations about words and smaller word parts that facilitate their learning to read and write. The ability to manipulate phonemes seems to develop as a result of learning to read and write and can be facilitated through writing instruction in particular. There is little evidence, for example, that young children use graphic-to-sound information in reading, but they are able to represent sound-to-graphic information, especially onset and rime in writing. They can easily categorize information learned in writing about onset and rime and, through analogy, associate and extend their knowledge about words with common onsets and common rimes; and they can begin to apply this information to reading. Goswami and Bryant (1990) describe this process in the following way:

> As children write, they form categories of words and when they begin to read they soon recognize that words in the same categories often have spelling patterns in common and that this spelling sequence represents the common sound. As soon as they realize this, they can make inferences about new words, and they do. (p. 147)

Figure 6.3 illustrates children's explorations of this phonological system. As Mark wrote "In . . . I like to ride my bike," he carefully articulated each word and used his knowledge of both print and numbers to construct his message without using spaces between word units (Figure 6.3a). Angela combined known words with sound analysis to form the message "The Christmas tree is pretty. It is green" (Figure 6.3b). Both children illustrate the notion of approximation in sound analysis and in their use of conventions.

Reading is difficult when it is presented to children as an abstract and hard-to-do-task of going from graphic information to sound information. It is more appropriate to build on writing–reading relationships, using the strength that children have in hearing and representing sounds, and through analogy, helping them apply this information gradually to reading. Skill with this level of language manipulation usually begins with language play, as children learn language, play with language, and use language to meet common ends (Lindfors, 1987). As we have discussed, within this process adult–child interactions are a catalyst for the children's deliberations about print (Dyson, 1990).

WRITING IN SCHOOL SETTINGS

There is a great deal of variation in writing instruction in our schools today. "In some classrooms, writing is not encouraged, except for some copy-

FIGURE 6.3.   Children's Explorations of the Phonological System

(A)

In...I like to ride my bike.   Mark--Age 6

(B)

The Christmas tree is pretty.   It is green.
Angela--Age 6

ing and letter formation exercises. The teacher is in charge, giving direct instruction. Most of this instruction is about basic skills. Such classrooms appear to be antithetical to encouraging the themes that take place in literacy rich homes" (Sulzby, Teale, & Kamberelis, 1989, p. 67). Regardless of how writing is taught in the instructional program, however, Reading Recovery teachers must understand how writing is approached so that the instructional programs they design can help children function within the boundaries of the classroom setting.

The way writing is approached in first grade has as much impact on what children learn as parents, books, and materials did in establishing the foundations of literacy in the home. In one study of three different first-grade classrooms from three different theoretical orientations to reading, DeFord (1986) found that the materials and practices that each teacher used together had a strong impact on the strategies children used in writing. The literature, or basal reading program, that was used in the classroom for teaching reading had the strongest impact on what children wrote. Children borrowed from or improvised upon what was available to them as literacy models in writing.

But not all schools view language teaching as different from what might have occurred in home settings. In a description of the writing contexts in literacy-rich classrooms, Sulzby, Teale, and Kamberelis (1989) described the teachers as individuals who encouraged children to (1) write for ownership, (2) use writing in their play, (3) use writing in response to literature they hear or read, (4) share their writing and respond to other children's writing, and (5) use writing to communicate with other people.

In classrooms such as these, the interactive nature of conversations around writing established the rights, roles, and responsibilities wherein literacy could be learned through participation in a literate culture. These become the contexts in which "instructional conversations" (Tharp & Gallimore, 1988) occur, in which everyone learns.

Dyson (1989) describes written language as a tool that helps the characters who populate a child's world accomplish social ends. In her framework for how children become writers in school, she argues that "children's written language learning is both social and developmental; its purposes, features and processing demands are learned as they encounter writing in meaningful activities" (p. 5). How the teacher uses the resources of a child's experiences, language, and imagination is an integral part of the development of an instructional program in Reading Recovery.

What Children Know About Writing at School Entry

The average child entering school, surprisingly, is able to write his or her name in part or in full, but this is about the limit of the child's constructive skill in written language (Clay, 1975). While this statement was made about New Zealand children in general, its veracity was made clear in a study conducted by Pinnell, McCarrier, and Button (1990) of kindergarten and first-grade children in Columbus, Ohio. In an analysis of the Diagnostic Survey (Clay, 1985) administered to the children in this study, 141 kindergartners from six urban schools provided a sample on which stanines were established. The average kindergartner knew four to seven of the upper- and lowercase alphabet letters at the beginning of the year. Out of 24 possible items on the Concepts About Print task, the average kindergartner accurately responded to 4. Kindergartners were able to orient a book in a "right-side-up" fashion, understand basic concepts of left-to-right and top-to-bottom directionality in book reading, but were usually unable to match spoken and written words. In terms of writing, the average child could not write any vocabulary items or represent any phonemes in the sentence: "The bus is coming. It will stop here to let me get on." The average child could not point and read to the text "*No! No! No!*" in a highly predictable children's literature book. They were more likely to read *No* or invent a language pattern such as "He's not in there!" in response to the teacher's prompt to point and read.

When these same children were assessed at the end of their kindergarten year, the majority had entered into the "literacy community" (Smith, 1988). The average child knew approximately 50 upper- and lowercase letters, had acquired many book-handling skills, scoring 13 to 14 out of a possible 24 points on the Concepts About Print task, and had the ability to write 10 to 14 vocabulary items in a 10-minute time period. They could also hear and record 15 to 21 out of 37 phonemes in the sentence "The boy is riding his bike. He can go very fast on it." In text reading, the average child was able to read a predictable story in an interactive experience with the tester where the pattern was established for the child. These results suggest that the average kindergarten child is well able to enter into the more formal reading and writing instruction offered in any first-grade classroom, no matter the instructional emphasis.

The First-Grade Writing Curriculum

The curriculum for writing in first grade varies across the nation. There are curricula for mastery learning, writing-process classrooms, traditional basal approaches, literature-based or whole-language classrooms, and systematic phonics. As you may note, many of these approaches have grown out of a way to teach reading, but they may also include recommendations for teaching writing. We will deal first with those approaches based in reading, and then with the writing-process approach, because of its most recent impact on classrooms.

Most traditional basal approaches, mastery learning, and systematic phonics include writing as a means of "practicing" vocabulary or skills established in the reading program. Figure 6.4 illustrates the types of practice exercises typically found in first-grade classrooms. In Figure 6.4a, an open writing assignment for "creative writing" turns into a simple vocabulary-writing exercise, with the writer paying little attention to creating a meaningful message. In Figure 6.4b, a letter constructed by the teacher, with "blanks" for sentences the child may fill in individually, is copied from the board. The child draws a picture, and the letter is sent off to a pen pal. Unfortunately, the child includes the teacher's original blanks as well. Figure 6.4c shows a common copying activity. The words come from the vocabulary in the basal program.

Copying, sometimes practiced as overwriting or underwriting, is a mainstay of early instructional activities in many classrooms. The copying activities may be written on the board, and children have to visually shift their focus from long to short distances; they may have difficulty keeping their place or keeping their attention on the task the teacher intends. Or the children may be given worksheet copying exercises, as in Figure 6.4c. Clay (1975) indicates that copying may not consolidate correct directional behaviors and that repetitious copying may lead to deterioration rather than improvement. She says that "copying may help the child to form his first few letters or words, but it is a rather slow and laborious way to extend one's repertoire" (p. 13).

Literature-based and whole-language approaches to reading have been strongly influenced by writing-process research (Calkins, 1986; Graves, 1983; Hansen, 1987). A major emphasis in these classrooms is on the literature that children can use across the school curriculum. Writing is integrated into the world of narrative and information as children use books from which to learn about reading and writing. The variety of writing that is an outgrowth of this approach is illustrated in Figure 6.5. Stories that evolve from stories read—as in the Figure 6.5 stories about the three bears and the elf and the shoemaker—as well as signs, invitations, letters, science logs, lists, surveys, and poetry are likely outcomes of literature-based and whole-language classrooms if there is a broad range of books present in the classroom (DeFord, 1986). Many of these classrooms will also include writing based on writing-process research.

As one example of a writing-process curriculum for first grade, Calkins (1986) suggests that opportunities for writing development be fashioned around the major aspects of the writing process: rehearsal, drafting, revision, and editing. According to Calkins (1986):

Rehearsal for a first grader centers around drawing and talk. In the same way the child plays at blocks, and says, "I'm making a tower," he can be drawing a person, and suddenly announce, "This is gonna be my brother. He's fighting." The

FIGURE 6.4. Classroom Writing Activities in First Grade

(A)

I will run and run,
we will ried and
We will and
We and run and run
We will we will
run and run

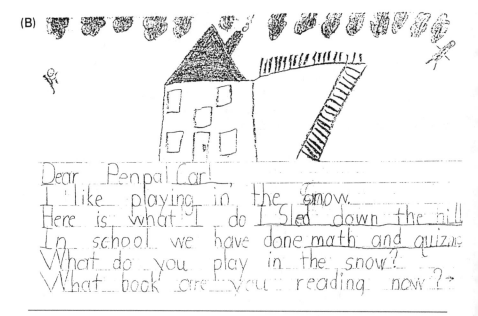

(B)

Dear Penpal Carl,
I like playing in the snow.
Here is what I do I Sled down the hill
In school we have done math and quizs
What do you play in the snow?
What book are you reading now?

FIGURE 6.4. (*continued*)

(C)

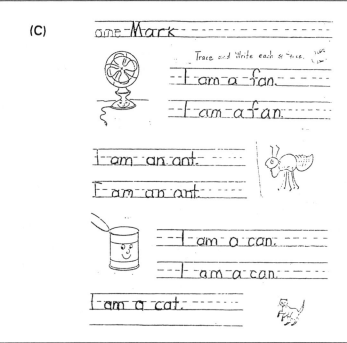

child writes for the sake of the activity in the "right now" rather than for any consideration of whether his message is good. (p. 50)

In the following scenario, Calkins (1986) captures the enormity of the task of writing for the young child. Chris, having drawn a picture of a person, decides to write *fighting* as a label for his picture:

> He sounds it out: "Fight-ing." He isolates a sound, /f/, then asks, "How do you spell /f/?" When no one answers, he scans the alphabet, guesses at a letter, and puts it onto paper. Meanwhile, he's forgotten what he wanted to write. (p. 50)

Much of the meaning Chris wants to impart is in the drawing that accompanies his written text. Pictures help the child select ideas to write about and elaborate meaning, and so they constitute the major part of a first grader's rehearsal strategy.

Drafting is a difficult process for children early in the year, but they gain fluency and skill as they write across the year. In order for them to represent

FIGURE 6.5.   The Impact of Literature on First-grade Students' Writing

(A) the thee litle bares.
One bday the thee litle bares Went
Owt to playx they had fun.
then they went bakin Side.
They Ahad fun in side they
playx games. They aet lunch at
the haws. Then they went to
toms hawsx they sisidahi
to tomx HI tom!
Then they had fun. The end!

(B)   The shoe makr
and theelvs.
Thine onec.
livd a. shoe makn
he. ha

the messages they want to write, they have to maintain their message in memory while they graphically represent that message. Because of the nature of writing and the difficulty previously discussed in children's ability to detect and manipulate phonemes, especially in a sequential manner, their messages are initially incomplete. Their choices of letters are not always correct, although they are logical (Calkins, 1986).

Clay (1985) discusses how children must learn to say words slowly, to hear and articulate sounds, and to represent the sounds they hear. Most children learn to articulate the major consonants, then some vowels, and finally to use a growing repertoire of visual information to extend the previous strategy of representing the sounds they hear. Calkins (1986) states that "As children become more fluent, the gap between their speech and their writing decreases, and they are more apt to write without verbal accompaniment" (p. 58).

Drafting involves the writer in experimentation and reflection and also provides an excellent opportunity to learn things about written language that will apply to reading settings. Revision for the early writer is often part of drafting. If given the chance to share their written pieces with a responsive listener, children often realize they have more to tell. Calkins (1986) found that "one way to support young children's growth in writing, then, is by encouraging them to read what they have written to the children working alongside them, and most of all, to themselves" (pp. 60–61). These conversations can also lead them to make their texts more explicit as the teacher or their peers indicate that information was left out of their message.

Finally, Calkins encourages teachers to help first graders think about editing with questions such as "Is this my very best? Am I done, or do I have more to say?" This may lead the children to reread their message one more time, to reflect on what they have written.

Flower and Hayes (1981) set forth a model that divides writing into three interacting processes in a proficient writing process for older writers: planning, translating, and reviewing. The first-grade writing curriculum as described above guides children into more proficient, mature use of this writing process. During the planning process, the writer must generate an idea, consider a way of organizing the message, and establish some goals. Translating is the process of putting ideas into visible language. The writer's task is to translate meaning, organized in a complex network of relationships, into a linear piece of written English. There may be conscious demands of mechanics, spelling, or grammar that interfere with the process of planning. Reviewing occurs when writers read what they have written in order to evaluate or edit the text. Reviewing can also occur when the writer encounters a problem within the text or within the recursive cycles of planning. Editing, evaluating, and generating can occur at any time in the act of writing, but they are influenced by the writer's knowledge of the topic, audience, and writing plans as well as what the task demands. The child oversees and monitors the whole process, becoming what Flower and Hayes (1981) refer to as a "strategist," who determines moves within the process. These aspects of the writing process are similar to the ones recommended by Calkins—rehearsing, drafting, revising, and editing. Young children, however, have particularly unique problems with learning to use this process that are different from those of older writers.

Problems Young Children Encounter with the Writing Process

In research on writing with the young child, Scardamalia and Bereiter (1982) have shown that difficulties in using the writing process can occur with young children because so little of the process is "automated" and they have a general lack of fluency with "executive routines," which would promote switching between aspects of the process and the sustained generation of ideas.

Speaking, problem solving, and writing all have a common reliance on idea generation (Caccamise, 1987). While the very youngest children have a foundation in speaking, problem solving, and idea generation, their experiences with writing in relation to problem solving and idea generation are less well developed. Therefore the task demands they encounter may place powerful constraints on the writing process. Research conducted on idea generation (Caccamise, 1987) indicates that when writers are generating ideas about familiar topics, they produce more ideas than when the topic is unfamiliar, with better organized texts.

An interesting study of 6- and 8-year-olds, mostly from low-income families, writing in an after-school program found that these children did not write on days when the writing researchers were not present (McLane, 1990). While the group workers attempted to encourage writing when the researchers were not present, they knew little about how to provide the help these children needed throughout the time they were writing. McLane (1990) stated:

> It seems probable that most beginning writers will continue to need such support for some time. How much support they will need, and how long they will need it, probably will depend on individual children's experience with writing, on their writing competence, on their confidence in their writing ability, and on whether or not there are peers who can take on some of these adult functions for them. (p. 317)

Children who do not come to school with sufficient literacy experiences or adult attention to important aspects of literacy knowledge need adult mediation in order to understand the uses and purposes of written language as well as to master its mechanics and techniques (Gundlach, McLane, Stott, & McNamee, 1985).

As part of the instructional program in first grade, then, children become more proficient at planning, drafting, revising, and editing their written messages. But in order to do so, they must be involved in both reading and writing experiences, since the two processes have been shown to develop in mutually supportive ways.

THE RELATIONSHIP BETWEEN THE READING AND WRITING PROCESSES

The literature-based, whole-language, and writing-process approaches to integrating writing into classrooms have a common thread. They maintain purposeful writing as a necessary part of the ongoing curriculum, and they support the integration of reading and writing as the means through which children become literate. Basic to the theoretical assumptions underlying their instructional recommendations is the belief that readers and writers learn about both processes as they use books and writing as tools in their learning. Butler and Turbill (1984) outline the nature of this relationship (pp. 11–14):

What Readers Do Before Reading

The proficient reader brings and uses knowledge
- about the topic
- about the language used
- about the sound symbol system

The proficient reader brings certain expectations to the reading cued by
- previous reading experiences
- presentation of the text
- the purpose for the reading
- the audience for the reading

What Writers Do Before Writing

The proficient writer brings and uses knowledge
- about the topic
- about the language to be used
- about the sound system

The proficient writer brings certain expectations based on:
- previous writing experiences
- previous reading experiences
- the purpose of the writing
- the audience for the writing

What Readers Do During Reading

The proficient reader is engaged in
- draft reading
    —skimming and scanning
    —searching for sense
    —predicting outcomes
    —re-defining and composing meaning
- re-reading
    —re-reading parts as purpose is defined, clarified, or changed
    —taking into account, where appropriate, an audience
    —discussing text, making notes
    —reading aloud to "hear" the message
- using writer's cues
    —using punctuation to assist meaning
    —using spelling conventions to assist meaning

What Writers Do During Writing

The proficient writer is engaged in
- draft writing
    —writing notes and ideas
    —searching for a way in, a "lead"
    —selecting outcomes
    —re-reading
    —revising and composing meaning
- re-writing
    —re-writing text as purpose changes or becomes defined, clearer
    —considering readers and the intended message
    —discussing and revising text
    —re-reading to "hear" the message
- preparing for readers
    —reading to place correct punctuation
    —proof-reading for conventional spelling
    —deciding on appropriate presentation

What Readers Do After Reading

The proficient reader
- responds in many ways, e.g., talking, doing, writing
- reflects upon it
- feels success
- wants to read again

What Writers Do After Writing

The proficient writer
- gets response from readers
- gives to readers

- feels success
- wants to write again

The instructional writing samples and descriptions of the type of writing experiences that are typical of first-grade writing curricula that we have presented in this chapter make certain assumptions about young writers. For example, one basic assumption is that learning to write is a process of making and using finer and finer distinctions about print so as to represent written messages with greater sophistication. There is also an assumption that writing is risk-free, that young children will engage readily in the process from the outset. There is an expectation in the first-grade classroom context that children will be able to progress in a forward direction within and across writing tasks, well able to monitor their own work, ask for help as necessary, and solve problems independently or with the help of their peers. While teacher input is important, the teacher is most often characterized as a facilitator or, at times, as a curriculum manager.

The above literature would suggest that for children who are just engaging in learning about writing, certain ingredients are critical in an instructional setting:

1. The setting should combine adult-guided interactions around written messages that are familiar to the writer.
2. Children will benefit from support in developing their understandings of idea generation, translation, and reviewing of their written messages.
3. Developing their problem-solving abilities, fluency, and knowledge of how text is organized will facilitate children's learning about the writing process.

The writing component in Reading Recovery lessons was devised to provide the highly supportive mediation that children who have not actively begun to engage in reading and writing by the time they are in first grade may need. They are at risk in most instructional programs. The information available on children's language learning and research on what good writers have learned in the first few years of formal schooling were integrated into the procedures described below.

WRITING IN READING RECOVERY LESSONS

Writing is a critically important component of Reading Recovery lessons. "Many of the operations needed in early reading are practiced in another form in early writing" (Clay, 1985, p. 63). She goes on to say that:

Children's written texts are a good source of information about a child's visual discrimination of print for as the child learns to print words, hand and eye support supplement each other to organize the first visual discriminations. When writing a message, the child must be able to analyze the word he hears or says and to find some way to record the sounds he hears as letters. (p. 35)

Writing should not be a copying task; rather it should be a process of going from ideas to spoken words to printed messages—in essence, the child should develop facility with the writing process, to produce his or her own written stories.

Within the lesson framework, the writing component is surrounded by reading events; first with the reading of previously read text, and finally with the reading of a new text. The purpose of embedding writing within the flow of reading is to relate writing to reading, to place writing in close proximity to reading so that the greatest opportunity is available to the child to create important conceptual links between reading and writing. Writing should be thought of as a resource for reading, and vice versa (Clay, 1991). Writing allows children to attend to the details of print in ways that they do not do in reading (Clay, 1991; Smith, 1988).

In the Reading Recovery lesson, the teacher and child work together to generate a topic for writing. The topic may come from something the child has done, a story he or she has heard or read, something that interests him or her, an experience he or she has had with the teacher, and so forth (Clay, 1985). As the following transcript illustrates, the teacher helps the child generate ideas and plan how best to organize the message. Early in Matthew's program, the demands of selecting a topic and using language to structure the message needed the teacher's mediation:

TEACHER: What can you talk about today? What would make a fun story?
MATTHEW: Um . . .
TEACHER: You've got it—what is it?
MATTHEW: I . . .
TEACHER: Okay . . .
MATTHEW: Can look . . . the . . .
TEACHER: You could look for something.
MATTHEW: I can look for . . .
TEACHER: For . . .
MATTHEW: My . . .
TEACHER: My who? Remember yesterday we were pretending that we had a big dog like Horace.
MATTHEW: Yeah.

TEACHER: Maybe you can look for somebody like that for today. What could you say? I can look for my . . .
MATTHEW: Dog.
TEACHER: Dog, where? Where are you going to look for him? I can look for my dog under . . .
MATTHEW: Under the . . .
TEACHER: Where is he going to be hiding?
MATTHEW: The chair.
TEACHER: Under the chair. Say it again to make sure I got it right.
MATTHEW: I can look for my dog under the chair.

As the transcript suggests, once the child has generated the story to be written, the teacher then notes the message in the daily lesson record, and the teacher and child begin to construct the message together. The teacher makes notes in his or her lesson plan about the child's contributions, approximations that are important to note as signs of the child's development, and what techniques might have been used, such as taking words to fluency, generating new items from known vocabulary, and what words were used in hearing sounds in words.

After the message has been completed in the writing book, the teacher usually writes the sentence on a sentence strip, then cuts the sentence apart for the child to reassemble. The child becomes a reader, then, of his or her written message.

The writing portion of the lesson is highly scaffolded. At this time, teachers are cautioned to observe children closely, watch their eyes and behavior so as to support the children in doing what they can for themselves, but always to be ready to do for the children that which they cannot do for themselves. The adult judges the complexity of the task in light of the child's participation, moving in and out to assist, participating with the child at points of difficulty, or stepping back as the child negotiates control.

Bruner (1975) has called this kind of interaction "scaffolding," where the adult "enters only to assist, making it possible for the child to participate in the learning event" (p. 12). Cazden (1988) suggests that this interaction is "a very special kind of scaffold that self-destructs gradually as the need lessens and the child's competence grows" (p. 104). The purpose of this scaffolding, however, goes beyond interactional support. The adult must structure the situation so that the child grows into increasingly more complex actions. The child must understand the intricate nature of the writing activities and processes shared with the adult and become independent in using these processes at a later date.

The sentence that Matthew constructed with the help of his teacher and the practice page illustrate how the teacher and child work together (Figure 6.6).

FIGURE 6.6.   Matthew's Writing Book

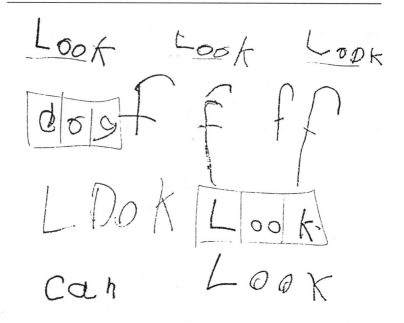

Practice Page

The message, written at the bottom, is spelled conventionally since the writing will be used on subsequent days as a reading experience. The child's approximations are dealt with through conversation as the teacher and child work at the top of the page. The teacher takes note of sounds heard appropriately (underlining sounds the child heard), sequences of sounds heard (numbers indicating sounds he or she heard first, second, third, etc.), and approximations made (what the child attempted to do when asked to hear and record what he or she heard).

The teacher and child will take high-frequency words to "fluency" by practicing them on the top portion of the writing book. They will attempt new words using boxes for hearing sounds in words, a technique adapted from an aural task by Elkonin (1973). The teacher analyzes the word to be attempted for the level of analysis the child is capable of (sound boxes or letter boxes), and then guides the child to do the analysis so that as much of the sound or letter framework as possible is provided by the child. The teacher may also use a known word that might be helpful, or ask the child to think of a word he or she might know that could help. In this way, new words are generated from known elements. The child is urged to reread the message, to monitor his or her own work, and to continue working independently at a variety of levels. The teacher asks questions and generally supports the child so that the writing process moves forward and the child is guided toward greater use of his or her own resources and problem solving toward independence in writing.

Figure 6.7 illustrates Matthew's writing across the year. The samples show that he is always at the edge of what he can do, and this helps to challenge him in ways that lead him to do more and more complex actions. His contributions are underlined in the samples. Across the year, the teacher can see some observable changes in sentence writing. Many of these shifts are evident in Matthew's writing from September through January. Matthew can control more high frequency words, and he shifts from laborious writing of known words to more fluent writing. At first he can hear sounds but not write them, and then he can hear and record some of the dominant consonants. He then hears and records the first and last consonants, and finally he begins to represent more of the consonant framework, along with some vowels. The next important learning event is when he uses what he knows about letters and words to generate new problem solving. At first, he responds to his teacher's initiation to get to new words. But then he sees relationships of a word he wants to write with something he has already written. Finally he initiates use of what he knows about letters and words to get to new learning.

As his understanding of the spelling system develops, he begins to use certain conventions, such as the final *e* on the end of words. He then adds

FIGURE 6.7. Matthew's Writing from September to January

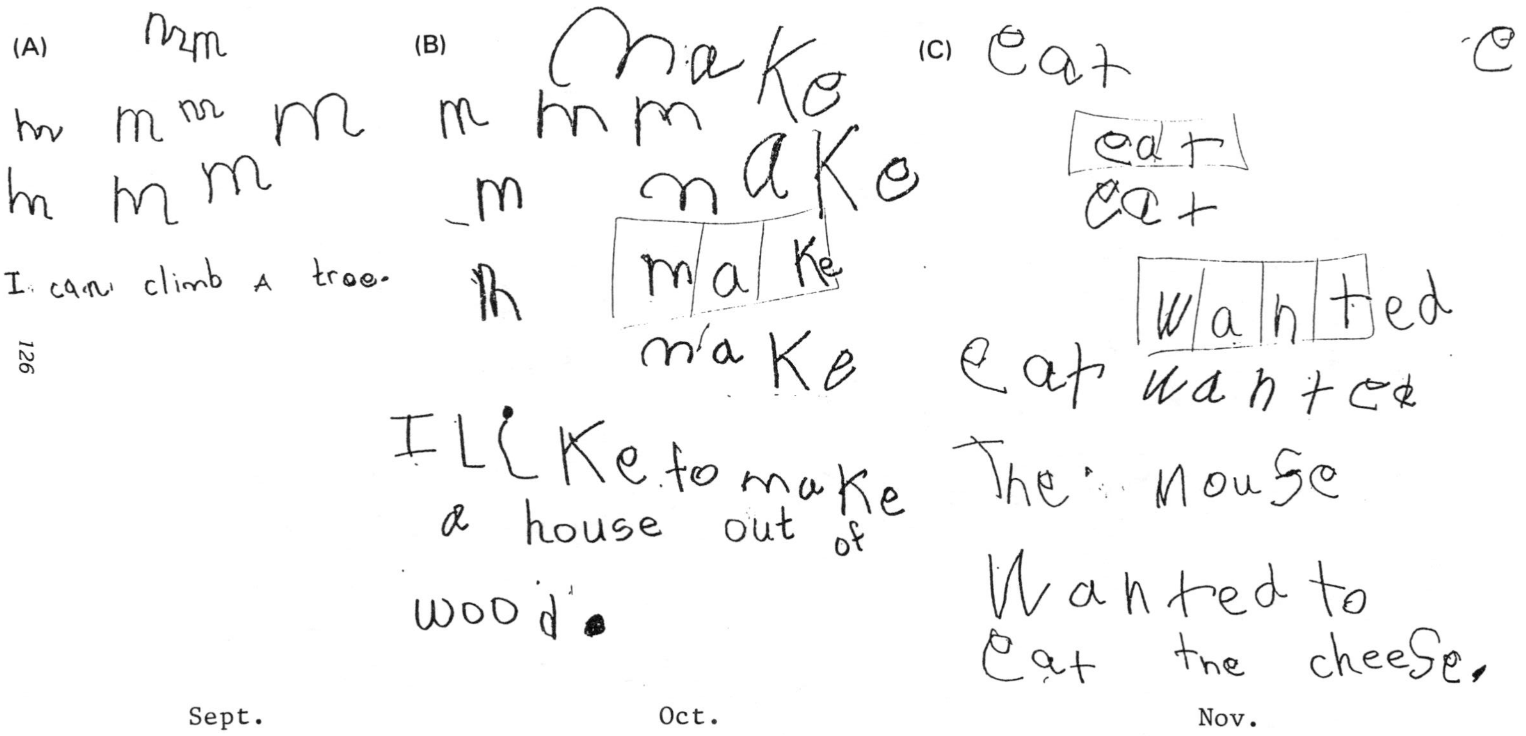

(A)

m m m
m m m m m
m m m m

I can climb a tree.

(B)

make

m m m make

make

make

ILKe to make
a house out of
wood.

(C) eat

eat
eat

wahted

eat wahted

The mouse
wanted to
eat the cheese.

Sept.   Oct.   Nov.

126

(D) Plat
Can
ran
tah
ran
Plat man ‖Play‖
it

(E)

The man
Went Out to
Play with the
balloon.

Dec.

‖hoPed‖
it

the Rabbit hoped
to the Tree to eat.

(F) | h

| i h | | J|ump|ed |
i'h

i'h

Obadiah Jumped
In the fire.
He jumped Out of
the fire.

Jan. 10th

Jan. 26th

127

inflections more easily and uses analogies or spelling patterns quite deliberately to problem solve new words. This leads Matthew to write increasingly
longer and more complex sentences, using better spacing and size of print.
There may also be an increase in legibility. In the next chapter, we will describe
the complexity of teacher and student interactions across a child's program
in Reading Recovery that facilitated these changes.

1. Reading Familiar Books—The child is able to orchestrate complex strategies. The teacher supports the overall meaning of the story.

2. Reading Familiar Materials—The teacher supports appropriate use of strategies and sources of information. In this instance, she supports the child in using what she knows (*it*) in problem solving new words (*sits*).

3. Running Record—The child reads yesterday's new book independently while the teacher notes "in-process" reading behaviors. The teacher records important information to be used in making instructional decisions, selecting teaching points to be emphasized after the running record.

4. Teaching Points after the Running Record—Using instructional records, the teacher quickly selects one or two important points that will support the child's developing strategies.

5. Writing—The child composes a message about a book read or a personal experience. Through joint problem solving, the child and teacher work together to write the child's message. The child writes as independently as possible.

6. Writing—As the child constructs the message "The children were scared seeing the terrible tiger," the teacher notes the child's inventions, and guides her to use what she knows to solve her own problems. In this writing session, the child wrote *The*, *were*, *seeing*, and *the* independently. They jointly constructed *children*, *scared*, and *tiger*. The teacher wrote *terrible* to save time.

7. The Cut-up Sentence—After writing the story the sentence is written on a sentence strip and cut up. The child uses knowledge of the sentence to search and monitor for visual, syntactic, and meaning cues while reassembling the message. The child re-reads the sentence to make a final check on her work.

8. Reading the New Book—The teacher introduces a new book, providing a framework for the meaning and language structures the child will meet. This book should offer a little bit more challenge than previous books read in the lesson, but be well within the child's reach. The child reads the new book as the teacher observes or offers support at difficulty.

Chapter 7

Teaching for
Problem Solving in Writing

The social nature of young children's construction of literacy was documented in the previous chapter. The research suggests that particular types of adult–child interactions with print support developmental events in literacy learning. While investigating parent–child storybook interactions, Sulzby and Teale (1984) identified a dynamic, interactive event they have called *obuchenie,* a Russian term that simultaneously means teaching and learning. Within this event, teaching and learning are seen as inseparable components of the dialectic. Both the parent and the child contribute to the interplay of ideas and the creation of the event. The child contributes what he or she can, and the adult contributes in such a way as to sustain the event. The research emphasizes both the children's personal construction of literacy and the activeness of adults in contributing to children's developing understandings of print (Cochran-Smith, 1984; Heath, 1983; Schieffelin & Cochran-Smith, 1984; Wells, 1986).

Clay and Cazden (1990) state that "as children engage in reading and writing, they are working with theories of the world and theories about written language, testing them and changing them" (p. 207). The adult judges the complexity of the task in light of the child's participation, moving in and out to assist, participating with the child at points of difficulty or stepping back as the child negotiates control.

Close observations of students' reading and writing behaviors provide teachers with insight into the strategies students use as they create meaningful text. Viewing these behaviors in terms of strategies provides a means for analyzing the children's knowledge of the complexities of written language. However, Clay and Cazden (1990) suggest that "the nature of the scaffold provided in the instructional setting must change, continuing the support offered, always at the cutting edge of the child's competencies, in his or her continually changing zone of proximal development" (p. 219).

Vygotsky (1978) coined the term *zone of proximal development* to refer to the "distance between the actual developmental level as determined by independent problem solving and the level of potential development as determined through problem solving under adult guidance or in collaboration with more capable peers" (p. 86). This concept provides a way of looking at instruction—adult guidance that takes into account the nature of what a child knows, the problem-solving processes used, and an understanding of what needs to be learned in order to strive for the potentials available to the child. Scaffolding is inherent to this definition, as is the notion of developing strategies, or in-the-head operations for using sources of information to act on text. In this chapter we describe how Reading Recovery teachers create contexts that support students so that they can develop effective problem-solving strategies in writing. We explore the complex nature of teacher–student interactions and explain what children with limited writing experiences learn to do under the guidance of a professional who understands intimately what it means to assist the child in achieving independence in writing.

TEACHING FOR PROBLEM SOLVING

The teacher plays an important part in supporting the child as he or she constructs a literacy system that works. This is done through joint activity, with the teacher always gauging how this system of strategies is operating, thinking about the questions the child is seeking answers to, and making decisions about "what next?" in terms of both instructional actions and the child's learning. For the child with little facility in manipulating language in the way that writing requires, there is much to learn. Clay (1991) indicates that children must be active in constructing knowledge about a host of things:

1) The aspects of print to which they must attend;
2) The aspects of oral language that can be related to print;
3) The kinds of strategies that maintain fluency;
4) The kinds of strategies that increase understanding;
5) The kinds of strategies that detect and correct errors;
6) The feedback control mechanisms that keep their reading and writing productions on track;
7) The feed-forward mechanisms (like anticipation or prediction) that keep their information-processing behaviors efficient;
8) And most important of all how to go beyond the limits of the system and how to learn from relating new information to what is already known. (p. 326)

The teacher can offer many forms of assistance in this constructive process. Tharp and Gallimore (1988) describe six means of assistance in their theory of teaching: modeling, contingency management, feeding back, instructing, questioning, and cognitive structuring.

Modeling

Through modeling, the teacher illustrates an action such as how to read a text and point to each word, a process such as checking on oneself to detect error, or something as simple as writing a word fluently. The child then is asked to do the same thing. In this way, new behaviors are initiated. This is not necessarily a low-level operation. In their discussion of modeling, Tharp and Gallimore (1988) suggest that observation of complex actions allows the learner to transform the action into new uses: "Through observation, a person can form an idea of the components of a complex behavior and can begin to visualize how the pieces could be assembled and sequenced in various other settings" (p. 48).

Thus, as the learner builds a network of strategies, direct action may not have to be taken in order to learn about a complex set of modeled operations. As Bandura (1977) has noted, however, "observers whose conceptual and verbal skills are underdeveloped are likely to benefit more from behavioral demonstrations than from verbal modeling" (p. 40). The teacher must decide what the nature of the activity is and determine the child's ability within that task in order to structure the setting so that modeling can be powerfully used to assist the learner. In the following example from one of Matthew's writing lessons, the teacher and child have written all but the last word of the sentence, "I can look for my dog under the chair." The teacher asks him to "say the word slowly . . . ch-air. Say it with me," providing letters he does not hear in the word *chair*. Both of these teacher actions are forms of modeling.

MATTHEW: "I can look for my dog under the chair."

TEACHER: Say the word slowly . . . *ch - air*. Say it with me. What do you hear, Matthew?

MATTHEW: I hear a *c*.

TEACHER: That's right [she knows he is using some visual information rather than sound–letter correspondence]. There is a *c* at the beginning of the word and then there's this letter that comes after it. (She writes an *h*.)

MATTHEW: An *a*.

TEACHER: An *a* and that's the next letter. Put it in. That's good, Matthew. And here is the next letter (she writes an *i*.) and you say it so we can hear the end. Stretch it with me.

TEACHER AND MATTHEW: *Chair.*

TEACHER: Let's do it again.

TEACHER AND MATTHEW: *Chair.*

MATTHEW: An *r*?

TEACHER: That's right. You hear another *r* at the end of the word just like we heard an *r* at the end of *under*. Read your story, Matthew.

Contingency Management

Contingency management—that is, praise or punishment—is an important part of assisted performance, although praise is used more often than punishment in educational settings. Tharp and Gallimore (1988) state that "social reinforcements of praise and encouragement are like props or buttresses that strengthen each point of advance through the Zone of Proximal Development, preventing loss of ground" (p. 53). Praise is used to encourage an action that is emerging or was purposefully done, but it cannot be used to originate new behaviors. Only modeling, instructing, and cognitive structuring or questioning will initiate new learning. The major purpose of praise, then, is to propel the learning process forward. "In the absence of praise and encouragement, learning may be fitful and unsystematic; only with adequate praise can progress be forward moving" (Tharp & Gallimore, 1988, p. 54).

Feeding Back

It is natural to ask for an evaluation of performance in a learning situation. Evaluation is termed *feeding back* in Tharp and Gallimore's (1988) model of teaching. This type of information helps learners to initiate self-correction and refine their actions. For information to be considered feedback, it must include a standard and the learner's performance must be compared to the standard. In instructional conversations in Reading Recovery, the teacher often compares what a reader does to the standard of a good reader. Another segment of Matthew's writing lesson can illustrate how this might look. He has dictated the sentence "I can look for my dog under the chair." Matthew then begins to write his sentence.

TEACHER: That is a good sentence. What's your first word?
MATTHEW: "I." (He quickly writes the word *I*.)
TEACHER: You write the next word. Think before you start. Where are you going to start your next word? (Matthew writes the word *can* very close to the word *I*.)
Take a look at it. (She points to his paper.) Does it have enough space? Take a look at the book and let's see. Let's take a look at the book, what it says here. You see there's a word and there's a word. See that space in between the words? Do we have enough space?
MATTHEW: (Looking carefully at his paper.) No!

In this instance, the teacher wanted the student to monitor for himself whether he was putting adequate spacing between words. So she used a verbal cue after he wrote his next word too close to the first one: "Think before you start. Where are you going to start your next word." She then asked Matthew to think about his own spacing *as compared to* the standard of one of his own books. Her comments provided the necessary amount of feedback to enable him to correct the spacing in his text. Teachers can use modeling to set standards and then provide feedback through simple instructions to initiate self-correction.

Instructing, Questioning, and Cognitive Structuring

Instruction and questioning are means through which teachers introduce or initiate new behaviors. Instructing, telling about something or directing actions in particular ways, calls for specific action on the part of the learner. Questioning, on the other hand, calls specifically for an active linguistic or cognitive response, thereby assisting the learner's thinking. The third form of teacher behavior that can initiate new actions is cognitive structuring. It does not call for a specific response or an action. Rather, this form of teacher action or language provides a structure for organizing new information and compares it to like instances. Therefore cognitive structuring helps the learner make comparisons, group new information, and evaluate and sequence actions or perceptions into their existing knowledge framework.

The integrated use of instructing, questioning, and cognitive structuring are intended to transform new information into independent action. Instructing and direct teaching have sometimes been overused in some management schemes. This overuse has given a negative connotation to these terms. However, since a learner is assisted by a teacher, instructing is a very important part of the learning process.

> The instructing voice of the teacher becomes the self-instructing voice of the learner in the transition from apprentice to self-regulated performer. The noninstructing teacher may be denying the learner the most valuable residue of the teaching interaction: that heard, regulating voice, a gradually internalized voice, that then becomes the pupil's self-regulating "still, small" instructor. (Tharp & Gallimore, 1988, p. 57)

In the previous example of Matthew writing "I can look for my dog under the chair," the teacher's use of instructing, questioning, and cognitive structuring were interwoven. The teacher instructed the child in the following way: "You write the next word. Think before you start. Where are you going to start your next word?" She fully intended that this type of verbal language would help guide him in this instance and would eventually become the internal cues he would follow on his own. Later, he might write too close to the previously written word and say "Oops," indicating that the internal cues are beginning to be used.

The teacher also questioned Matthew, but the questioning contained implicit instructions and she expected a linguistic response. The teacher in our example wanted to hear, "No, I didn't leave enough space." When he did not respond, she shifted back to instructing in order to help him understand the nature of her original question. Once she did this, and the child understood what she was asking, he was able to respond, "No" and also take appropriate action. Because questions call up the use of language, they assist thinking. As they call for the student to use language, the response allows the teacher to observe the student's processing.

Tharp and Gallimore (1988) indicate that there are questions that assist and questions that assess. In assessing, the teacher inquires in order to discover the level of the pupil's ability to perform without assistance: "What do you need to do next?" To assist, the teacher questions to produce a mental operation that the pupil cannot or will not produce alone: "Did you check the picture?" The assistance of the question prompts the learner to use the necessary mental operation. The above transcript illustrated this questioning process in action.

Cognitive structuring refers to the provision of a structure for thinking and acting. This contributes to the child's theory of the world, understanding, and strategy development. Tharp and Gallimore (1988) state that "it is an organizing structure that evaluates, groups, and sequences perception, memory, and action" (p. 63). Two types of structures that occur during this process are structures of explanation and structures for cognitive activity. The first, structures of explanation, are represented by the boxes during the writing portion of the Reading Recovery lesson. The use of Elkonin (1973) boxes structures the activity and provides an explanation of what the child is asked to do. The teacher draws boxes for the sound frame of a given word, such as *food*. In this instance, three boxes are drawn, and the teacher demonstrates by pushing pennies for each phoneme—/f/, /oo/, and /d/. The child is then asked to perform the same procedure. The motions are fluid and help the child locate and visualize where the sounds are occurring within the frame of the word—beginning, middle, and end. If the child can hear and represent the *f* and the *d* he or she is asked to write them in the first and last box regardless of the order in which they were heard.

As the child begins to map visual information acquired through reading and writing experiences onto the growing sound–graphic matches he or she has made, the teacher shifts to a box for every letter. If the teacher and child were working with the word *food* later in the child's program, there would be four boxes drawn, one for each letter. Because there are three sounds but four letters in this word, the child runs his or her finger under the boxes while saying the word, putting in the sounds heard and the letters he or she now expects to see. The child begins to develop cognitive structures for words with similar onsets and similar rimes (e.g., *g-ot* and *h-ot*), generating new categories of words from those that are known and verbalizing observations such as, "I don't hear this, but I bet there is an *e* at the end." The boxes for hearing sounds in words, then, serve as a means of helping the child organize actions and theories about how to represent the visual symbols for the messages he or she wishes to communicate. Eventually, the boxes will be used less and less as the child can independently orchestrate the complex, serial order activity of problem solving around new words. The following example illustrates structures of explanation and structures for cognitive activity through the teacher's explanations and actions around the use of Elkonin boxes.

While writing the sentence "I can look for my dog under the chair," Matthew has independently written *I can look for my dog* and hesitates when he comes to the word *under*.

TEACHER: *Under*. Matthew, wait just a minute. What do you hear?

MATTHEW: A *d*.

TEACHER: Say the word with me and push up the pennies.

TEACHER and MATTHEW: "Und-er."

MATTHEW: I hear a *d* right here. (He points to the third box.)

TEACHER: You do hear a *d*. In front of the *d* there are these two letters. (She writes *un*.) Now we're ready for a letter *d*.

MATTHEW: (Writes the *d* backwards.)

TEACHER: Can you make the *d* look just like this one? (She places a magnetic letter on the practice page, and Matthew writes the letter *d* correctly.)

TEACHER: Good for you. Let's say the word and see if we can hear how it sounds at the end. Say it with me slowly.

TEACHER and MATTHEW: (Matthew pushes the pennies into each box saying the word slowly.) "Un-d-er."

MATTHEW: I hear an *r*.

TEACHER: In front of the *r* is this letter (writing *e*). Now you make an *r* right at the end. There is an *r* at the end of the word *under*. Read your story, Matthew.

This conversation shows how the teacher assisted Matthew in hearing and analyzing the sounds in the word *under*. Tharp and Gallimore (1988) describe this type of experience as follows:

The teacher assists the pupil to organize the raw stuff of experience—both that which is at hand and that deriving from like instances. . . . For the child, the resulting cognitive structures organize content and/or functions and *refer to like instances*. The learner does this for himself as well, by offering explanations and hypotheses, which the teacher will seek to confirm or extend through mutual participation. (pp. 65, 67)

It is clear from the above interactions that the teacher is guiding Matthew in all aspects of the writing process. She helped him generate a sentence and use the language and sense of the story to guide his problem solving as he worked at representing his thoughts. She guided him in placing his message as he worked out spacing principles and represented sound–letter relationships. He used his visual memory for how words looked, developed fluency in writing, and reread to monitor where he was in the process. As Figure 7.1 illustrates, in the sentence "The dog got stuck in the bridge," which was written later in his program, Matthew was able to hear and represent 19 of the 25 letters, independently writing five out of the nine words, almost 76% of the total message. The teacher did nothing for Matthew that he could not do for himself, encouraging him to solve problems using his background knowledge and his sense of meaning. Using a dynamic combination of teaching moves, this teacher was able to support yet challenge this child as a writer. In the following section, we explore the research that documents the impact of assisted performance on the children who were initially at risk in the instructional program.

RESEARCH ON STRATEGIC TEACHING IN WRITING

In strategic teaching, a high degree of flexible decisionmaking is required as the teacher observes and interacts with a child. As the previous chapters on teaching for problem solving in reading suggested, the teacher's responses, prompts, reinforcing statements, and actions are critical. Teachers of children who made significant progress attended in a balanced way to all components of the reading process, shifted their teaching priorities over time, facilitated children's problem solving, and promoted more student action as children became able to take more responsibility.

In order to explore actions and decisionmaking that facilitate children's achieving rapid progress in learning about writing in Reading Recovery lessons, a team of three expert teacher leaders conducted an analysis of teacher–student interactions during the writing portion of the lesson. The research team analyzed the same videotapes used in the reading analyses reported in Chapters 4 and 5. Writing portions of lessons taught by two teachers with higher student outcomes and two teachers with lower student outcomes were analyzed to determine the nature of the teacher–student interactions and

FIGURE 7.1. **Matthew's Writing Book and Practice Page in January**

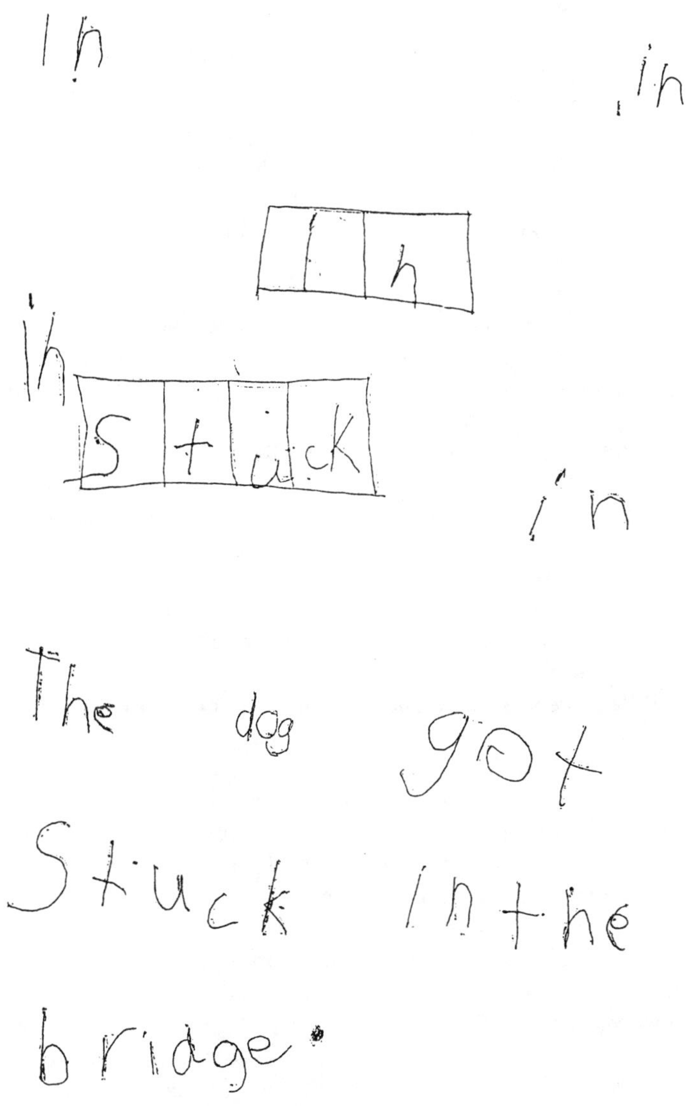

teacher decisions that may have made a difference in children's overall progress in learning about writing.

Teacher and Student Interactions

In a study conducted by DeFord, White, and Williams (1991), video-taped lessons of Reading Recovery teachers ($N = 4$) who achieved high and low student outcomes were analyzed at the beginning and end of the 70-day study. High and low student outcomes were determined by a comparison of pre- and post-test gains in text reading and dictation. Three experienced teacher leaders viewed the writing portions of videotaped lessons and developed a coding system that would classify prompts, responses, and actions during writing. These researchers were interested in investigating: (1) what prompts were used, what actions were initiated, and how students responded to teacher prompts and actions within the writing component for children achieving higher and lower outcomes, and (2) whether there were differences in teacher interactions with students achieving higher and lower outcomes when the sentences were generated and written. A taxonomy (see DeFord, White, & Williams, 1991) was then used to code student and teacher actions and prompts from the research tapes to uncover strategic teaching practices.

The analyses of teacher and student responses for shared responsibility (i.e., how children initiate and respond, and how teachers prompt and act) revealed little difference between the two groups (Table 7.1). Regardless of student outcomes, the number of prompts and actions by Reading Recovery teachers were similar within the writing component of the lessons. The one important difference was that higher-outcome students initiated actions more often. The lower-outcome children initiated actions to a lesser degree, with only 12.41% initiations. These data suggest that teachers and children are sharing the writing and problem-solving responsibilities in similar ways; however, the degree to which children initiate actions independent of teacher prompts is different. Teachers of higher-outcome children foster independent actions within the writing component of the lesson.

As we examined the interactional patterns as sentences were generated and composed, we found different patterns of prompting and actions for teachers achieving high student outcomes as compared to teachers achieving low student outcomes. What the teacher focused on in these instructional conversations, and what this led children to do, distinguished the groups.

A comparison of the most frequently occurring teacher prompts for teachers of high- and low-outcome students revealed that teachers of high-outcome students prompted for a greater variety of student responses or actions. For example, in generating sentences, teachers producing high outcomes prompted

TABLE 7.1.   Mean Percentage of Time Teachers and Students Shared Responsibility During the Writing Portions of Lessons

Category	High Student Outcome	Low Student Outcome
Initiates	21.38	12.41
Responds	29.09	33.43
Prompts	28.75	32.67
Acts	20.78	25.43

children to write about the book they had just read as well as to write from personal experience. The teachers producing low outcomes most often prompted their children to write from personal experience. The teachers of higher-outcome children also prompted the children to work on the practice page as a means of solving problems with new words or with writing words or letters fluently; they prompted children to say the word slowly, to reread, to check on their work, to identify a sound or sounds they had heard, and to write in their text. These prompts accounted for 62% of their total prompts. Teachers producing lower student outcomes, however, most often prompted students by asking them to identify a sound–letter relationship or to reread a word in the sentence. These two prompts accounted for 50% of their total number of prompts. They did not ask the child to say the word slowly, and only seldom prompted the child to write on the practice page.

These two aspects of the writing lesson—learning how to say a word slowly so as to represent the sounds within it and to use the Elkonin boxes on the practice page—are important cognitive structuring activities. They are the very tools that will help the young writer become independent. The fact that the teachers producing low outcomes in students were not utilizing these tools in a powerful way may be one reason why their children tended to initiate less as writers. They were not supporting the child in independently analyzing and writing words.

The examination of teacher actions within these videotaped lessons also produced an interesting contrast. The teachers producing lower student outcomes performed a broader range of actions *for* children than did the teachers producing higher student outcomes. These teachers reread words for children, said the words slowly, and generated the next word in the sentence for the child in 40% of their actions. They also tended to write letters and words on the practice page for children, a behavior that was not encountered with the teachers producing higher student outcomes. The teachers achieving higher student outcomes confirmed appropriate student responses most often, and this category accounted for 26% of their actions within writing lessons. While these teachers sometimes said words slowly and generated the next word in the sentence for the children, they monitored what was written by the child to a greater degree than did the teachers producing lower student outcomes. Most importantly, they asked the children to monitor for themselves. None of the teachers producing low student outcomes stressed student monitoring.

These differences in teacher prompting and actions had an impact on what children did in lessons. For higher-outcome children, saying words slowly, writing in their texts independently, finger pointing, identifying sound–symbol relationships, and generating the next word in their message were the most frequently occurring self-initiated actions in writing. The lower-outcome students' most frequently occurring actions were finger pointing and rereading their sentence to generate the next word.

The high- and low-outcome students responded in similar patterns to teacher prompts. Both groups of students responded most often to teachers by stating or identifying a sound–symbol relationship. The high-outcome students wrote more on the practice page and said words slowly to a greater degree in response to teacher prompts. The lower-outcome students also "spelled" words out more frequently than they said words slowly. Spelling words is a very different task, one not intended to be used in Reading Recovery lessons. It places a greater emphasis on memory than on problem-solving strategies. From the analysis of videotapes, it was clear that the higher-outcome children were more independent in writing lessons than the lower-outcome children. It was also apparent that the teachers' actions within these lessons were intended to move the children to action rather than to accomplish actions for them.

As was reported in Chapter 4, there were different time allocations given to the writing portion of the lessons by teachers achieving higher student outcomes. Early in lessons, for example, they spent a higher proportion of their lesson time on writing (44%) than did the teachers producing lower student outcomes (29%). This led us to consider the long-term outcome of these teacher behaviors. Consequently, we decided to examine the teachers' records and student writing books across the children's Reading Recovery program. A careful analysis of teacher records across two children's total program in Reading Recovery revealed the long-term results of these trends.

The Impact of Strategic Teaching Over Time

In order to determine the long-term effects of strategic teaching on students' writing progress, an in-depth case study of teacher–student interaction during the writing portion of the lesson was conducted at the beginning, middle, and end of the program. Extensive data from one high-outcome and one low-outcome student were examined. For purposes of comparison, two students with similar entry scores on the six subtests in the Diagnostic Survey (Clay, 1985) were selected. An examination of the high- and low-outcome students' entry scores reveals similar entry scores for each of the six subtests; the exit scores for each student, however, show a sharp contrast, especially for the word test, writing vocabulary, dictation, and text reading (Table 7.2). A close examination of the daily lesson records and writing books of each child throughout his program suggested how and why these differences occurred.

The writing portions of the teachers' lesson records—produced within time boundaries of beginning (the first one-third, etc.), middle, and end of the Reading Recovery program—were used, along with student writing

TABLE 7.2.   Entry and Exit Scores of High- and One Low-Outcome Student

Student Scores	Letter ID	Word Test	CAP	Writing Voc	Dictation	Text Reading
Entry						
High Outcome Student	46	2	12	5	7	A
Low Outcome Student	38	0	11	1	2	A
Exit						
High Outcome Student	53	20	22	40	35	18
Low Outcome Student	50	1	15	7	9	2

FIGURE 7.3. Student Writing Book Analysis of Shared Responsibility in Writing

Student	X̄ Sentence Length	Responsibility	Time in Program		
			Beginning	Middle	End
High Outcome	8.0	Child	57%	69%	71%
		Joint	34%	31%	29%
		Teacher	9%	0	0
Low Outcome	7.6	Child	27%	24%	36%
		Joint	52%	54%	54%
		Teacher	21%	22%	10%

samples, by three researchers. Analysis focused on the length of the written sentences, the words the children wrote independently, the words that were jointly constructed, the words the teachers might have written, and how the practice page was used. Using these events, the researchers determined whether the child or teacher had major responsibility for writing and how they shared this responsibility. The results provided some insight into why there may have been different outcomes for the two students (Table 7.3).

The mean length of the sentences the high- and low-outcome students produced across their program was very similar (low-outcome student, 7.6; high-outcome student, 8.0). Across the beginning, middle, and end of their program, the students' sentences increased in length in similar ways (low-outcome student, 5.4, 8.6, 8.05; high-outcome student, 6.0, 7.9, 8.72), with the high-outcome child writing slightly longer sentences toward the end of his program (low-outcome student, total 405; high-outcome student, total 503). Within their programs, however, the similarity ends with these surface features.

From the very beginning, the teacher with higher student outcome required the student, Matthew, to write as much of the message as he could. She also increased the corpus of vocabulary the student could write by having him practice words for fluent writing and helping him learn how to say and represent the sounds he heard in words through the use of Elkonin boxes. During the beginning of his program, Matthew produced independently 57% of the total number of words written. In the middle and end portions of his program, he produced 69% and 71% of the text by himself. The written vocabulary items were also built across reading experiences, since Matthew was writing consistently about books he was reading. The teacher wrote very few of these for him, writing only 9% of the text in the beginning of his program and not writing any whole words throughout the rest of his program. She elected to write such words as *salad, bear, chocolate,* and *climb.* Many of the high-frequency words he was learning to write were worked out on the practice page and written several times in fluent writing practice on the practice page. However, the greatest majority of them emerged out of joint problem solving and out of reading experiences. There were 196 entries on the practice pages of Matthew's writing book, with 75 instances of the teacher using boxes and 58 instances of the teacher using a known word, such as *make,* to help Matthew see how he could make an unknown word, such as *cake,* on his own. All other entries were for the purpose of establishing fluent writing of high-frequency items.

A very interesting characteristic that was unique to Matthew's program was the occurrence of miscues in writing. His most frequent problem with writing was in letter reversals, as when he went to write *is* and wrote *si.* At first the teacher drew his attention to these instances, but very soon Matthew was self-correcting independently. There were 23 instances of miscues produced in writing such as letter reversals, and 14 of them were self-corrected. The teacher taught him how to monitor for himself, supported him in this checking behavior, and then prompted him to check to make sure he was right. This type of assistance helped him develop the ability to monitor his own progress in writing. By the end of his program, Matthew was beginning to notice chunks of information, for example, words that ended consistently in *s, ed,* or *ing.* He was then able to use consistent spelling patterns to solve problems for himself, using information from what he expected words to look like. He wrote *tree, king, today, fly, forgot, outside, into,* and *play* by combining skills in hearing sounds in words and his growing visual analysis abilities. Goswami and Bryant (1990) describe this sophisticated writing ability in the following way:

> We suggest that the experiences which children have while reading influence the way that they spell, and that their knowledge of spelling affects their reading. . . . At first when children begin to read and to spell words, they make hardly any connection between these two activities. They carry them out in rather different ways, and they often seem unable to use their knowledge about reading to help them spell a word, or their knowledge about a word's spelling to help them to read it.

Later on, after roughly two years' experience of learning to read, they begin to connect reading and spelling. One consequence of their making this connection is that they no longer specialize. They no longer confine global strategies to reading, and they are readier than before to use their awareness of sounds when they read as well as when they spell words. Thus at around this time there are qualitative changes in the ways that they read and spell. (pp. 148–149)

The fact that Matthew was developing this ability at the end of his first-grade year is significant. This, in our view, is the only way a child who is at risk can enter into the mainstream educational culture. The ability to connect reading and writing and to learn about each process within any act of reading or writing is an important part of what Clay describes as a "self-extending system."

Steven, on the other hand, has been unable to develop into an independent writer, and there were important characteristics in the shared writing experiences he had in his program that may have caused his lack of progress. While Steven was dictating sentences that were equally as long as Matthew's, he was involved in the writing of these messages in a very different way. Steven's teacher wrote far more of his message than did Matthew's teacher. At the beginning of his program, she wrote 21% of the sentences; then she wrote 22% of the sentences in the middle portion of his program. At the end of his lessons, she was contributing 10% of the words in his written text. This is in contrast to Matthew's teacher, who wrote no individual words for him after the beginning of his program. The highest percentage of the text produced in Steven's lessons was jointly constructed (52%; 54%; 54%). What was interesting, however, was that almost all of this construction activity took place within Steven's written message. There were only 37 instances in which the teacher asked Steven to work on the practice page, and in only 12 of these instances were Elkonin boxes used. There were 22 instances of fluent writing practice and 3 instances when the teacher wrote on the writing page for Steven to copy. It is our hypothesis that by not using the boxes and counters to help Steven learn how to hear and represent the words he wanted to write, she kept him dependent and severely hampered his strategy development in both reading and writing. In the first 20 lessons, Steven wrote only seven vocabulary items by himself: *I, a, my, to, Mom, turkey, eat.* The word *I* was written a total of 20 times across those 20 lessons. While he was generating sentences such as, "I went on vacation," "I walked to my reading group," "When I come home from school I watch television," he was contributing on an average of 27%, 24%, and 36% of the text by himself in the beginning, middle, and ending portions of his program. It would appear that the teacher, by not having him write at least some of his messages around the books he was reading, might not have been facilitating the same links between reading and writing that Matthew's teacher sought to build.

RECIPROCAL GAINS BETWEEN READING AND WRITING

This close look at the teachers' lesson records and student writing books supports the analysis of the videotapes, but it also illustrates the dramatic influence that a teacher's decisionmaking during the writing portion of a lesson can have on student progress. What books the teacher uses, what sentences the student generates, and how the teacher and child work together are terribly important for the developing writer. The fact that the most effective teachers spent a greater amount of time with writing early in the children's program and blended reading and writing experience suggests the reciprocal gains that can be achieved through strategic decisions by making direct links between the two processes. Through assisted writing experiences, Matthew learned to look at print and to use this knowledge to help him in both reading and writing. In this way, the act of writing provided a cognitive structure that supported his learning—about reading, about writing, and about spelling. The actions that students engage in while writing slow down the process and facilitate their developing a sense of how print operates.

These data suggest that there may be an important difference in the writing conducted in Reading Recovery that is critical for the child who has not engaged in learning how to read. When the child writes alone and the teacher observes his or her invented spellings after the act of writing, that teacher can develop a good sense of what the child can do alone. However, by interacting with the child during writing, the teacher can serve as a catalyst to advance the concepts the child is developing. By strategic use of modeling, praise, feeding back, instructing, questioning, and cognitive structuring, every opportunity to learn can be powerfully utilized to bring about advances in the child's learning.

Teaching for problem solving in writing involves the child and the teacher in collaborative roles that are very similar to the scaffolded exchanges between parents and children in early literacy-learning experiences. These exchanges have been described by Rogoff (1986) as involving demonstration, direct feedback, and shared participation. The scaffolds provided in Reading Recovery lessons have the same characteristics, allowing the child to do more and more each day, but with the teacher constantly shifting the task demands so that the child is developing a self-extending system (Clay, 1991).

Teacher comments within the writing segment of the lesson provide for a host of problem-solving responses on the part of the child: "Do you know how to start writing *help*?" or "Say it slowly and see if you can hear what's at the end of that word." The teacher praises attempts, even if they are not totally correct: "You're right, *catch* could begin with a *k*, but this time it's a *c*." The teacher asks the child to use what he or she knows about print to predict new forms: "You know how to write *got*, so what would you have to do to make it *hot*?" The teacher may also introduce new information: "Let me show you how the word *eight* is written. It doesn't sound at all like it looks." In these prompts, teachers help the children to know what they know, use what they know to find solutions to their own dilemmas, and risk trying with greater confidence.

As Vygotsky (1962) has stated, "the only good kind of instruction is that which marches ahead of development and leads it; it must be aimed not so much at the ripe as at the ripening function" (p. 104). Reading Recovery is designed to take the lowest-achieving children in first grade and provide daily challenges that are well within the children's grasp. This can only be accomplished by supporting children in learning about that which they are just beginning to grasp. For those at greatest risk in our educational system, it may be an important chance to reach for their highest potential.

Chapter 8

How Teachers Learn to Understand Responsive Teaching

For the last two decades, the debates about effective teaching have centered on the teacher's ability to know, manage, and explain subject matter, formulate and ask appropriate questions, and respond to student answers (Adams, 1990). The underlying assumption was that effective teaching occurred when students sat silently, listened to and understood the teacher's directives, read the assigned material (usually basal texts), responded correctly to the teacher's questions, completed "dittos" that reinforced the material presented in the basal texts, and passed the required tests. The *teacher* controlled the context; the student was required to adjust to the environment created by the teacher.

Naturalistic studies of classroom environments (e.g., Au, 1990; Barr, 1987; Green, 1983; Jackson, 1968) have provided evidence that knowing and managing the content, asking questions, responding to students' answers, and testing students' knowledge is only a small part of effective teaching. Good teachers create social contexts that support teacher–student interaction. Students, in collaboration with teachers and their peers, are actively engaged in meaningful activities. Studies of Reading Recovery teachers (DeFord, Tancock, & White, 1990; Lyons, 1991a; Lyons & White, 1990) showed that the most effective teachers offered more opportunities for students to construct meaning through conversation with the teacher.

In the preceding chapters, we took an in-depth look at the kind of teacher–student interactions that enabled students to construct meaning through conversation. We saw how effective Reading Recovery teachers learned to reflect on their own teaching and work with children in order to assist a student's performance. According to Gallimore and Tharp (1990), if teachers are going to learn how to assist a student's performance effectively, they must themselves engage in the learning process. Without a program designed to change teaching behaviors, there is little chance that teachers will abandon their viewpoint that students are supposed to learn on their own.

In this chapter, we explore the different phases of learning teachers go through in their year of professional development in Reading Recovery. By examining teachers' reflections and analysis of their own teaching, we gain insights into the contexts that support continued growth in their understanding and ability to become more effective. It is clear that learning is socially constructed, not only for children, but for adults.

CHANGING TEACHERS' DISPOSITIONS ABOUT LEARNING AND TEACHING

A considerable body of evidence indicates that participating in the Reading Recovery program changes teachers' disposition and view of learning and teaching (DeFord, 1993; Lyons, 1992; Pinnell & Woolsey, 1985). The research suggests that teachers refine, expand, and change their views of learning and teaching because they refine, expand, and subsequently change their views of literacy, specifically how children learn to read and write. Reading Recovery is thus more than a program for children. It is a program for teachers that changes their way of viewing the process of becoming literate. The model of literacy underlying the Reading Recovery program and the model of training upon which the program is delivered go hand in hand. When teachers' dispositions and interactions with students are consistent with the model of literacy underlying Reading Recovery, they become effective.

Just as children learn through conversation with their teachers, so too do teachers learn through conversation with their colleagues and mentors. Teachers' and students' ability to think and learn is mutually constructed in supportive conversation within the Reading Recovery lesson. Vygotsky (1978) argues that the higher cognitive processes, such as problem solving and self-regulating strategies that enable individuals to develop productive independent behaviors, are first learned in social interactions. In these interactions the more knowledgeable individuals model the problem-solving processes and talk about what they are doing while engaging in the act. This talking while doing makes visible the normally invisible cognitive processes required to develop a self-regulating and self-extending system. In other words, teacher–student talk and teacher–teacher leader conversations eventually become inner dialogue, or subconscious thinking, that directs the learners' cognitive behavior. Although Vygotsky's work related primarily to children, the same processes can be applied to adult learning. This chapter describes teachers' progress as they learn to be effective Reading Recovery teachers.

STUDYING THE PROCESS OF BECOMING A RESPONSIVE TEACHER

We conducted a study to investigate how teachers shift in their understanding and ability to assist failing readers effectively. Previous research

(Lyons, 1993) suggested that a teacher's ability to assist a student *effectively* changed when the teacher shifted from wanting to know what to do and when to do it in order to get correct performance, to recognizing behaviors that indicate partially right and partially wrong responses. Once the teacher understands how to make a facilitating response to the child's half-right and half-wrong response at the most powerful point in time, he or she becomes effective. We wanted to document beginning teachers' thinking and reasoning during their transition from less effective to more effective responding.

Six Reading Recovery teachers in training (five women and one man) participated in this study. Participants tape-recorded, analyzed, and evaluated lessons throughout the year. In weekly discussions held after the behind-the-glass demonstration lessons, the teachers exchanged views about the effect of their actions and reactions while facilitating the students' learning. In weekly individual sessions with their teacher leader, colleagues, and the researcher, they shared the reasons for their decisions and how their teaching may have hindered and/or helped the student to develop a self-extending system. Within the research group, they discussed alternatives to the decisions that were made and why some alternatives may have been more effective. As the teachers progressed through the training program, they became more sensitive to and aware of reading and writing behaviors that signaled students' development of inner control. By sharing and discussing their personal reflections and analysis of their own teaching with colleagues and mentors, the teachers began to acquire an inner control over their teaching. They began to shift from less effective to more effective responding to the students' developing competencies. These shifts in understanding represented a continuum of learning that changed and was refined over time.

The ongoing analysis of the teachers' reasoning and decisionmaking processes throughout the year seemed to progress through six distinct but interrelated phases, or shifts, in learning. In the following section we describe and discuss each phase of learning and the teachers' understanding of their learning processes over time.

SHIFTS IN TEACHERS' UNDERSTANDING DURING THE YEARLONG TRAINING

Learning How to Become Astute Observers of Student Behaviors

Early in their training program, the Reading Recovery teachers learn how to observe students' behaviors. They are introduced to this difficult task during the assessment training and a two-week period called "roaming around the known," when teachers do not teach but watch for and record what the child already knows. Using many easy texts, which are either read to or with the child, teachers learn how to observe closely and record what the child knows. They then provide opportunities for each child to become fluent with what he or she knows so that they can use this information in different ways. For example, after Kathy observed that Matt could read *Cat on the Mat* by Brian Wildsmith (1982) independently, she asked him to generate a message based on the text. Kathy and Matt wrote together "Matt sat on the mat." This shared writing experience provided an opportunity for Matt to write what he could read; the teacher wrote the rest of the message. By writing and rereading the message, Matt began to understand the relationship between reading and writing and to understand that both should make sense.

Learning how to observe, record, analyze, and then respond to the child's behavior is a difficult and complex task, yet accomplishing this goal is essential if teachers are to provide the assistance students need to develop self-extending literacy behaviors. There are three basic reasons why teachers in training find it difficult to learn how to respond to a child's behavior. First, it is hard for them to abandon their preconceived ideas about what beginning readers need to know in order to learn how to read. Change is so difficult because teachers previously followed basal manuals that present a hierarchy of reading skills in a prescribed sequence. Second, it is hard for teachers to divorce themselves from transmitting information and move toward following the child's lead, perhaps because they feel responsible for selecting, managing, and presenting a predefined curriculum for students to learn. Third, teachers need to learn how to engage in conversations with the students and become responsive to them, a difficult process because the teachers have little or no training in observing children's learning behaviors and recognizing the most powerful teaching opportunities. Instead they have been taught to present the material outlined in the graded course of study to the average students in the class, to "water down" the curriculum for the below-average students by presenting the material in bits and pieces, and to provide the above-average students opportunities to enrich their learning experiences.

Kathy, a Reading Recovery teacher in training, remarked, "Throughout the 'roaming around the known' period, I kept asking myself how Matt was ever going to learn to read when he didn't recognize one word and he could only write the first letter in his name." Kathy believed that word recognition and remembering high-frequency words were essential processes in beginning to read. Her view was supported by the presence of the controlled vocabulary in basal texts she had been using for the last 16 years. This teacher, who was in her second week of training, found it difficult to follow the child's lead, as illustrated by an excerpt from the first session in "roaming around the known":

KATHY: Today's story is called *Cat on the Mat*. Look at the last word
in the title; that word is the same as your name, isn't it?

MATT: I don't know.

KATHY: Sure it is, your name is Matt, isn't it? And this word is *mat*,
except this word only has one *t* instead of two *t*'s like in your
name. I will read you the story and you read along. "The cat sat
on the mat." What does this say?

MATT: "The cat is on the rug."

KATHY: No. "The cat sat on the mat." Okay, let's look at the next
page. Here the words say: "The dog sat on the mat. The goat sat
on the mat. The cow sat on the mat. The elephant sat on the mat.
SSSppstt." Can you sound out those letters?

MATT: ssssss. ttttt

KATHY: Good. I'll finish the book now: "The cat sat on the mat."

This brief excerpt illustrates how Kathy's view about reading instruction controlled her selection of the book to read to Matt. She believed that if she selected a book that had a known word in the title (in this case, the child's name), he would be able to read the text more easily and thus progress in the program at a faster rate. The teacher had a predetermined rationale for selecting the book and a predetermined agenda for how she was going to read the text to the child. She did not teach Matt anything in a direct way, but the context she provided did not provide opportunities for Matt to show her what he knew. The following conversation, recorded six days later, documents a noticeable shift in the teacher's approach to the same book.

KATHY: Do you remember when I read this story to you about the cat
that sat on the mat?

MATT: Yeah, you read it the first day we met.

KATHY: That's right. (She opens the book to the first page and draws
Matt's attention to the first picture.) Here is the picture of the cat
sitting on this big red mat. Point to the words as I read them.
(Matt successfully points to the words as the teacher reads.) "The
cat sat on the mat."

MATT: (Spontaneously.) "The cat sat on the mat."

KATHY: I like how you made the words match what you were saying;
good job, Matt. Let's look at this page. Who joins the cat on the
mat?

MATT: The dog.

KATHY: Yes. Point to the words as I read them.

MATT: I can read them. (Reading the words while pointing.) "The dog
sat on the mat."

KATHY: You made your voice and words match again; I'm really proud of you. What happens next?

MATT: (Looking at the picture and pointing.) "The goat sat on the mat."

KATHY: You're right, you read the sentence all by yourself and you looked at the picture to help you read the sentence. I liked how you pointed to the words while you read them! Can you go on?

MATT: Yeah. (Looking at the picture first and then reading.) "The cow sat on the mat."

KATHY: Matt, I am so proud of the way you are checking the picture and matching what you read with the words you see on the page.

MATT: (Looking at the picture.) Boy, the rug, I mean the mat, is getting crowded. (Reading.) "The elephant sat on the mat."

KATHY: You were right when you said the rug was getting crowded because there isn't much room on the rug now. But you quickly changed the word "rug" to "mat." What made you change your mind?

MATT: Because when I read the other pages I said "mat" and this word (points to the word *mat*) looks the same.

KATHY: You are so right. Go on, I bet you can read the rest of the story by yourself.

MATT: "Sssppstt! The cat sat on the mat." The story ends like it started.

KATHY: What do you mean?

MATT: This part (goes back to the first sentence in the book) is the same as the end of the story.

KATHY: You are absolutely right. You have certainly taught me many things that you can read and notice.

This discussion reveals how Kathy shifted her stance, this time following Matt's lead and engaging in a conversation that enabled him to use what he knew in different ways. For example, he monitored his reading and self-corrected in order to change "rug" to "mat." He then commented that the word *mat* looked like the words he had read previously, suggesting his ability to visually scan information "on the run" while reading. Kathy's comment at the end of the interaction suggested that Matt was noticing some things about the text that she did not know he knew. As a result of reading this text a second time, new and useful behaviors began to emerge that neither the teacher nor Matt had known existed. She attributed the dramatic change in her behavior to last week's Reading Recovery class, which included a "roaming around the known" demonstration lesson.

When I saw Mary controlling the child's reading of the book and trying to make him guess at words that she wanted him to know, I thought of myself and knew that I had done the same thing when I was working with Matt. I listened as our teacher leader asked questions to help us discover what strengths the child had. I was surprised by the comments from the other RR teachers observing the lesson. They were noticing behaviors that I had not thought of. When the other teachers admitted that they found it "difficult to stop themselves from teaching," I felt much better. Our teacher leader then helped us understand that we needed to follow instead of lead the child and helped us understand how to accomplish this goal. I couldn't wait to try some of the techniques the next day. I'm only sorry that I didn't start sooner.

Learning How to Follow the Student

In order to help children make maximum progress, Reading Recovery teachers must become sensitive observers of student learning and learn how to *continue* to follow the child throughout his or her program; that is, they must learn how to observe children's behaviors and determine strengths and possible sources of confusions. It is unlikely, especially at the beginning of a program, that a Reading Recovery student would be able to be explicit about confusions. The following example illustrates how Janice enabled a Japanese child to understand and use the English word *hug*. The conversation took place during the introduction of a new book. After a few introductory comments, the teacher discovered that Shiko did not understand what was meant by the word *hug*, which appeared many times in the text. Their conversation illustrates the problem.

> JANICE: Let's look at our new book. This is a story about a little girl who wants a hug. I bet your mom and dad give you many hugs, don't they? (The teacher reads the title of the book.) *Give Me a Hug* (Cowley, 1988a).

The teacher was inviting the child to respond to the new book by drawing from some of his own experiences. The child, however, did not respond and sat motionless.

> JANICE: Let's see what happens. Here is the little girl and she is asking . . . (pausing) Who is she asking for a hug?
>
> SHIKO: (Looking at the picture of an elephant on the page.) She's asking the elephant.

> JANICE: What is she asking the elephant for?
> SHIKO: A ride.

In the following conversation, she attempted to link the plot of the story with the child's own experience.

> JANICE: She doesn't really want a ride, she wants a hug. Did you ever want a hug from your mom or dad?
> SHIKO: I don't know. What is a hug?
> JANICE: Look at the little girl's arms. She's holding them out like this isn't she? (The teacher stretches her arms out.) Can you stretch your arms out like I am doing? (The child complies.) That's right. You are ready to give me a hug, and I am ready to give you a hug. Can I give you a hug?
> SHIKO: Okay. (The teacher and student hug.)
> JANICE: What is a hug?
> SHIKO: It is putting arms out and squeezing.
> JANICE: Yes, when you give a hug you put your arms around someone and that person puts their arms around you. It's a good feeling, isn't it?
> SHIKO: Yes, I liked it.

Realizing that Shiko might not have had identical personal experiences to relate or, more likely, have a label for the experience, the teacher provided it. Now that the child had some understanding of the meaning of *hug*, the teacher began to explore the theme of the book.

> JANICE: Thank you for giving me a hug. Let's see who the little girl is asking for a hug. (Turning the page.) Look here she is asking the elephant but he is . . . (pauses).
> SHIKO: Too big.
> JANICE: You're right. Is there something wrong with the next animal she asks for a hug?
> SHIKO: Yeah, the bug is too little to hug and it has no arms.
> JANICE: You're absolutely right. (The teacher and child peruse the rest of the pictures, pausing several times to allow the child to predict what is occurring before turning the page.)
> JANICE: Who does the little girl finally find to give her a hug?
> SHIKO: Her mother.
> JANICE: Yes, the little girl and mother are giving each other a hug just like you and I did, aren't they?

SHIKO: Yeah.

JANICE: Let's read this story. The title of the book is *Give Me a Hug*.

Through their conversation, this teacher became aware of the prior knowledge Shiko needed to construct meaning. Additionally, their conversation about the story assisted the child in building a context for understanding the plot of the story. By providing the structure through demonstration and questioning, Janice enabled Shiko to assemble the information needed to read the text. Until the student internalized the concept of hug with the language, he needed assistance. Without a linked personal conversation to support the text, this internalization would not have occurred.

The preceding transcripts document how teachers create and sustain instructional conversations throughout the lesson. Through instructional conversation, confusions were uncovered and resolved. The quality of the teacher–student conversations had a direct influence on how much the child learned. Clay and Cazden (1990) and Chapter 3 in this volume argue that effective Reading Recovery teachers engage in meaningful conversations with children and are responsive to what students do. They are consistently aware of and monitor the student's transition from assisted to unassisted performance, realizing that this transition is not abrupt and takes time. Reading Recovery teachers make similar transitions while learning pedagogical skills that support effective decisionmaking. The third phase documents another transition Reading Recovery teachers experience as they learn to become more effective.

Learning How to Assist Students' Performance Through Demonstration and Explicit Teaching

When children first enter the Reading Recovery program, many have very limited understanding of the reading situation and the task or the goal to be achieved when they read. The teacher's role is to provide assistance through demonstration until the student's response is initiated. If, after repeated modeling, the student does not initiate the needed behavior, more explicit encouragement and teaching are needed. For example, if, after demonstrating for the child how to match what he or she says to the words in the text (one-to-one matching), the child does not match the words read with the words printed, the teacher might explicitly teach the procedures.

The teacher might say: "Read it with your finger" or "Did that match?" or "Were there enough words?" Through demonstration, explicit teaching, talking about the process to be learned, and the use of memorable, powerful examples to initiate the procedures, the student will come to understand the way in which the words on the page relate to one another and thus begin to understand what it means to read. This understanding develops through conversation and collaboration during the reading of the book. In the following transcript, Sue learns a valuable lesson about her role in helping Nancy to control her visual attention to print.

> SUE: Yesterday we read the story *The Ghost* (Cowley, 1983b). What was the story about?
> NANCY: The little girl saw stuff through her mask?
> SUE: That's right. Let me hear you read the story. "*The Ghost.*"
> NANCY: "the door" [Text: *I see the door.*] "a moon" [Text: *I see the window.*]
> SUE: Why don't you start over and read it with your finger.
> NANCY: "Here is a door and" [Text: *I see the door.*]
> SUE: "window" [Text: *I see the window.*]

Nancy did not understand Sue's direction to "read it with your finger." Sue could not assist Nancy's performance because the suggestion was beyond the child's level of understanding, something her performance revealed. Self-analysis and discussion with the research group illuminated the problem. By asking Nancy to "read it with your finger," the teacher provided an instructional context that was outside the student's zone of proximal development. Sue realized that she should have provided a clear demonstration by taking Nancy's finger and matching the words in her speech to the words in the text. If Sue had modeled the task and required Nancy to point precisely to the words after saying "read it with your finger," Nancy would have come to understand how oral language and visual information relate to one another. Once Nancy understood what she was supposed to do, she could be assisted by other means, such as a question or prompt. The following excerpt, which occurred two weeks later, demonstrates Sue's developing understanding of responsive teaching.

> SUE: Here is one of your favorite books. Can you read it all by yourself? Remember to point to each word as you read *Yuk Soup* (Cowley, 1986).
> NANCY: "In go some snails." (Pointing to each word.) [Text: *In go some snails.*] (Hesitating.) "In go all of the feathers." [Text: *In go some feathers.*]
> SUE: What's wrong?
> NANCY: I don't know.
> SUE: Were there too many words?
> NANCY: Yeah.

SUE: Read the sentence again and use your finger to match the
words with what you say.

NANCY: (Correctly matching print to language.) "In go some feathers."

SUE: I liked how you stopped and noticed something was wrong. You
knew that you said more words than there were on the page.
Then you reread the line, this time matching what you said with
the words on the page. That was excellent work.

Sue decided to ask "Were there too many words?" because Nancy hesitated
after realizing that what she had said did not match the number of words on
the page. She believed that Nancy could resolve this problem without much
guidance, so she said "Read the sentence again and use your finger to match
the words with what you say." Her response enabled Nancy to resolve her
conflict. Once she reread the line correctly, Sue restated what Nancy had done
and thus reinforced the behavior that led to the self-correction. This interaction demonstrates that Sue was beginning to understand Nancy's level of
performance and thus was able to scaffold her behavior promptly. Sue was
becoming a responsive teacher. The fourth phase expands on and develops
more fully this concept of responsive teaching.

Learning How to Question Effectively
or Prompt Students Based on Available Information

Once they begin Reading Recovery lessons, teachers are introduced to a
series of procedures that have been shown to support students' developing
ability to learn how to read. Using many little books and sentences the students have written, teachers learn how to help students make decisions on
the basis of the available information. For example, suppose that after looking at the picture of a lion and a giraffe, the child reads the text as follows:
"The *like* tells the giraffe." The teacher, noticing that the child had examined
the picture prior to attempting to read the text but had not made use of that
available information, decides that the most effective way to help the child *at
this moment* is to direct the child's attention to the meaning of the story. Saying
"Look at the picture; is that what is happening in the story?" should accomplish this goal. The process of enabling the child to use the illustrations to
confirm the meaning of the story and then cross-check this meaningful prediction with visual information (how the word looks in print) is actively fostered by the teacher who has learned how to use specific questions or prompts
that focus the student's attention. Helping teachers develop the skill and ability
to observe closely what the child is doing, decide what kind of information
the student needs to attend to, and *then* select the prompt or question that
will help the child accomplish this goal takes much practice and experience.

During the first few months of training, teachers' range of knowledge about how to question effectively and how to elicit desired responses is narrow; that is, their understanding of how to prompt or ask questions to direct children to three sources of information (semantic, syntactic, and/or visual) is limited to a few questions. "Does ___ make sense?" is intended to focus the child's attention on the meaning conveyed in the pictures. "Does ___ sound right?" is designed to help the child search for cues from the language structure of the sentence. "Does ___ look right?" is intended to draw the child's attention to the visual and auditory information available in the words and letters on the page. Teachers in training try out these questions and prompts; with weekly feedback from more experienced colleagues and mentors, they learn to develop and refine their skills and thus become more responsive to the students' behaviors. They learn how to raise the level of prompt to a more general level in order to promote independent problem solving by the student with less support from the teacher. For example, if the teacher knows that the child searches for all types of cues and cross-checks the meaningful language structure with visual information, he or she might say, "Try that again." Teachers use this prompt because they know that the child can resolve the conflict and have confidence that he or she can solve the problem without a more specific prompt.

The following conversation took place after the student, John, had read the text *Dan, the Flying Man* (Cowley, 1983a). Patty, his teacher, decided that John needed to learn how to use visual information to confirm the meaning and structural information that he used most frequently. Patty selected a clear example to teach the student how to check himself by searching for additional visual information. This excerpt documents how the teacher's intentions backfired.

JOHN: "All the people chased and chased." [Text: *All the people ran and ran.*]

PATTY: You read "All the people chased and chased." Let's take a look at this word. (The teacher rereads the line of text, stopping at the word *ran* in an attempt to get the student to predict that the word is *ran* by sounding out the first letter.) "All the people r . . . r . . . r . . . "

JOHN: "All the people r . . . r . . . r . . . "

PATTY: What did all the people do? "All the people r . . . r . . . r . . . r . . . "

JOHN: "All the people . . . All the people . . . " (The student rereads the line several times stopping at the word *ran.*)

PATTY: What are all the people doing? (The teacher points to the picture of the people running after Dan.)

JOHN: They are chasing Dan. "All the people chased Dan."

PATTY: The word is *ran.* (The teacher points to the word *ran* and then reads the sentence.) "All the people ran and ran."

Patty, lacking experience in knowing how to use John's strength to teach him to confirm the visual information, tried to sound the first letter of the word *ran.* When he did not respond appropriately, she tried to direct his attention to the picture, which showed the people running after Dan and asked him to guess what the word might be. John's answer made sense—the people chased Dan. Patty finally resorted to telling him the word and rereading the sentence. Her understanding of this predicament and the questioning techniques that would have been more effective are revealed in the following reflective commentary.

> I knew that John had already checked the picture and that he had the concept of the people running after or chasing Dan. That is why I focused on the word level and tried to sound the first letter of *ran.* What I should have done was use his meaningful prediction "chase" by saying "I like the way you checked the picture and made it make sense," thus verifying his use of meaning and language structure. Then I should have said, "Now read it again and make sure this word (pointing to the word *ran*) looks right." This prompt would have provided an opportunity to cross-check his prediction "chase" with the word in the text. This prompt would also have provided him an opportunity to keep the initiative rather than being overwhelmed and confused by my interjections, plus I would have had more opportunity to observe his behavior in response to my prompts. My questions needed to be very specific and follow what the child attended to. I saw him looking at the picture, so I should have supported this behavior. But I missed this opportunity. A teacher's prompt must also acknowledge what the student has attempted. My hasty response ignored his attempts to make sense. I knew he needed to attend to visual information, and so I prompted a letter sound at the expense of his meaningful substitution. Meanwhile he was trying to reread, a valuable behavior that I completely missed until I listened to the tape.

Gradually, through daily one-to-one tutoring and weekly peer discussion during live behind-the-glass demonstration lessons, the teachers begin to understand their teaching in a broader sense. They learn when, why, how, and under what conditions questions can and should be asked and how to tailor questions to fit the demands of the text and specific student needs. By reflecting on the use and misuse of questions in particular contexts, Reading Recovery teachers gradually come to understand how one question can straighten out or interfere with a child's attempts to understand. Helping teachers learn how to become sensitive to students' learning and to make skillful, moment-by-moment decisions based on observed behaviors develops with experience. Observations of teachers during this phase of development are presented next.

Learning How to Observe Behaviors to Make Informed Decisions

Midway in their training program, Reading Recovery teachers start to learn the importance of understanding the sources of and reasons behind a child's response. They learn how to prompt or ask questions to confirm their hypotheses for the child's behavior and then use this information to inform teaching. In other words, they begin to understand that the more formal knowledge outlined in *The Early Detection of Reading Difficulties* (Clay, 1985) is based on assumptions and experience concerning what the teacher believes to be the source of the child's previous response. Barbara, the teacher in the following example, took a major step in understanding the value of using Susan's *observed behaviors* to inform her instruction.

BARBARA: Today's story is *Boots for Toots*. Can you read it all by yourself ?

SUSAN: "These boots are not right." [Text: *These boots are too big.*]

BARBARA: That makes sense, doesn't it? Look at the words to see if they look right?

SUSAN: "These boots are too loose."

BARBARA: (Points to the word *big*.) Does this word look like *loose*?

SUSAN: "These boots are too . . . These boots are too . . . " Oh, now I know. "These boots are too big."

BARBARA: How did you know this word (pointing to *big*) had to be *big*?

SUSAN: I looked at the first letter. (Continues reading the text.) "These boots are too little." [Text: *These boots are too small.*] (Rereading and self-correcting.) "These boots are too small."

BARBARA: How did you know the word was *small* instead of *little*?

SUSAN: I looked at the first letter.

Barbara was beginning to wonder if her teaching had become a routinized pattern. Was she really following the child? Her analysis revealed some powerful shifts in her understanding of how to use *behaviors,* not expected responses, to inform her teaching.

During our behind-the-glass discussions, we were cautioned about getting into a routine question–answer format where the teacher asks routine questions and expects routine answers, which the student gives. After listening to the tape of my teaching, I could see how Susan and I had fallen into this mechanistic pattern. Her reading of this story was very typical. She read for meaning and at times ignored visual information if her substitutions fit the meaning and structure of the sentence. My questioning and reinforcing patterns were predictable. First, I would support her attempts to make sense; second, I would focus her attention at the word or letter level. Third, I would comment on her attempts to respond at the word or letter level (no matter what she did). Fourth, I would ask her how she knew the word (expecting her to respond that she looked at the first letter). Finally, I would comment on her routinized response, "I looked at the first letter," by saying "I liked how you looked at the first letter to predict what the word might be."

After listening to our conversation, I can see so much emphasis on the *word* level and *visual* accuracy. While the ultimate goal is to enable the child to be able to use all cueing systems strategically, I wasn't really helping the child know how to cross-check one source of information with another. I was valuing accuracy over the process of predicting and checking. By being so consistent with my prompts for the cue that had been ignored, I had actually trained the child to read until I found an error, then respond with the expected "I used the first letter" after I told her where to attend. I had attempted to simplify a very complex process, to a quick, letter level response behavior, thinking that this process was helpful. Susan was clearly "filling in the gaps" in my teaching.

After analyzing this conversation, I also began to wonder if she understood the question, "Does ___ look right?" Every time I asked that question, Susan reread the sentence. She exhibited this behavior five different times in this short lesson segment. By rereading, she was probably attempting to regain meaningful language structure, but I ignored this behavior and instead focused her attention at the word level. I then followed my directive by commenting on her attempts to analyze the word or letters. I did this on three different occasions. I then asked her how she knew the word and expected her response, "I looked at the first letter." I ignored the fact that she probably got the word *big* because she reread the sentence two times and the pictures clearly showed that the boots were too big for Toots. Her comment, "Oh, I know," was probably the result of her ability to use the meaningful language structure, not the letter name or sound. I should have supported her rereading and commented on how she used the language structure to predict the word *big*. I then should have reinforced and supported her attempts to confirm the prediction by cross-checking it with the first letter. But instead, I asked my usual question, "How did you know the word was *small* instead of *little*?" And she gave me the routine answer, "I looked at the first letter."

From now on, I will pay very close attention to behaviors and allow the behaviors to dictate my plan for teaching. I will be sensitive to all of the student's behaviors, not just behaviors I want and expect to see. I will also try to understand a student's sources of information, asking for this information when I need to confirm my own hypothesis of how he or she may be thinking. Once I have a clearer picture of the child's processing, I will be able to use this information to focus my teaching. This analysis has really helped me to look for and examine routine question–answer patterns of behavior. If the patterns of behavior are evident, teachers must examine their teaching and student's responses and ask themselves what they are doing or saying to encourage these behaviors.

At this point the teacher was beginning to understand not only the importance of following the student's behavior but the need to develop skills that would enable her to examine the student's way of making sense. Barbara was moving to the final phase of learning.

Learning How to Examine the Student's Way of Making Sense

This last learning phase is exemplified in Bill's reflection after Peter read *Rosie's Walk* (Hutchins, 1971).

PETER: "Rosie the hen went for a walk
around the pond
over the haystack
past the mill
th . . . around . . . th . . . "(long hesitation) "over, over, over, through the fence."
BILL: You worked hard on this page. Where was the tricky part? (The student points to the word *through*.) Look at the picture and tell me what she did.
PETER: She went over the fence.
BILL: It could be *over*, but check to see if what you read looks right.
PETER: No, it's not *over*.
BILL: How do you know?
PETER: There's no *v*.

BILL: Good checking. What would make sense?
PETER: I don't know.
BILL: Would *through* make sense?
PETER: Oh, yeah—"through the fence."

Bill's comment following this episode is revealing. He was surprised that Peter attempted to substitute *over* for *through* on three different occasions, even though he had read the word correctly earlier in the story. He also expressed surprise that the student could not get the word after he had attempted to search for the initial letters. Bill thought that a cross-checking meaning and visual cues would have given Peter the word. Upon reflection, however, Bill understood his source of confusion better.

> I think that Peter lost the meaning of the story because he spent so much time on the page. He forgot it was Rosie who was taking a walk. So when I asked the question, "Look at the picture and tell me what *she* did," Peter didn't know who I was talking about. I noticed that he was looking at the fox, not Rosie. Once I realized that Peter's response was due to the fact that he was looking at the fox, I began to have a better understanding of the source of his confusion. The picture in the text showed the fox going over the fence, not through the fence. Another source of confusion was that Peter knew the word *over* had a *v* in it and the word that he was trying to read did not have a *v*. If I had asked him to reread the entire story stopping at this particular point in the text, I believe that Peter would have regained meaning and would have been more likely to self-correct. A child needs to read fluently to maintain the meaning of the text, and once the reading slows down, the student is more likely to guess at the words and rely on visual information. I did not provide Peter an opportunity to read the text fluently to regain the meaning of the story. I feel confident that if he had regained the meaning of the story, a simple question such as "Try that again and see if what you said sounds right, makes sense, and looks right" would have enabled him to self-correct.

Bill's analysis of his conversation with Peter enabled this teacher to step out of his own perspective and understand the student's perspective. Bill was beginning to hypothesize about the source of the student's confusion. The teacher's reflections demonstrate how he might respond to unexpected answers in the future. He was considering whether his questions were based on the student's responses and attempts to make sense or on his own preconceived notions of how the student should respond based on *his* view of making sense.

DISCUSSION AND IMPLICATIONS
FOR PROFESSIONAL DEVELOPMENT

Marie Clay (1991) says that "sensitive and systematic observation of behavior is really the only way to monitor gradual shifts across imperfect responding" (p. 233). Although Clay was talking about the development of children's behaviors, the same notion can be applied when describing teachers' change in behavior. The study illustrates that as Reading Recovery teachers monitor their own behavior across imperfect responding while teaching, they develop skills in responsive teaching and become more effective teachers. Thus the fundamental process of development and learning is generic and applies to learning in general. The instructional activity of teaching and learning "is good only when it proceeds ahead of development. It then awakens and rouses to life those functions which are in a stage of maturing" (Vygotsky, 1956, p. 278).

The data presented in this chapter suggest five general principles of learning and teaching that, once understood and effectively practiced, can help teachers improve their instruction.

First, all learners have zones of actual development (what they can do without assistance) and zones of proximal development (what they can do with assistance). Through assisted performance by a more capable other, individuals expand and reorganize their understandings in order to create new meanings and learn how to learn.

Second, the language that surrounds events within a Reading Recovery lesson mediates performance and creates systems of change. At the beginning of their training, teachers struggle as they attempt to translate and use the theories of language and literacy learning underpinning the program to inform their practice. However, when paired with mentors or peers who ask specific questions about the learning behaviors of students while observing and reacting to a single observation, teachers in training acquire practical and theoretical knowledge. The teachers appear to have a difficult time engaging in this activity alone, but the necessary cognitive activities are "awakened" through social interactions with mentors and colleagues while viewing the behind-the-glass demonstration. Through conversations, behavior changes, and over time, teachers internalize and transform questions and comments from their colleagues to direct their own performance. This qualitative change in teachers' practical reasoning and performance affects students' acquisition of literacy.

Third, conversation must assume a prominent role in teachers' learning. Transactions take place and higher cognitive processes are initiated and instantiated through dialogue. It is important that teachers have opportunities to share their thinking with one another and with more experienced teachers and mentors through colleague visits and school visits, in addition to the regularly scheduled class. By talking with one another, teachers become aware of their own understandings and misunderstandings. Through mutually constructed conversation, more experienced colleagues explain and clarify concepts that are not clear to some individuals while promoting the acquisition of more complex understandings for other individuals. These ongoing discussions serve to scaffold teachers' understandings and mediate performance by providing bridges between what the teacher already knows and needs to know to support students' further literacy learning.

Fourth, when teachers, students, mentors, and colleagues form collaborative partnerships, everyone benefits. Collaboration enables teachers to develop theoretical and practical knowledge. In doing so, they develop competencies for dealing with and resolving a variety of instructional problems that have a direct impact on students' abilities and interest in resolving their own problems. Just as high-risk students acquire literate behaviors through social interactions with teachers, teachers acquire effective problem-solving skills and become responsive teachers through social interactions with colleagues and mentors.

Finally, the major shifts in teacher theorizing are occasioned by learning to teach Reading Recovery and are greatly influenced by the in-service course. The yearlong course provides teachers many opportunities to acquire a disposition about learning, teaching, and beginning reading instruction that is different from the one they had prior to the training. This model of learning enables teachers to internalize and transform psychological processes in learning how to learn into their own instructional repertoires. Through this process, lifelong learning occurs. One teacher captured her own development of theoretical and practical knowledge to inform her teaching through the Reading Recovery program:

> The major shift in my understanding occurred when I had the sense that the child was muddled and confused. His voice got louder and he seemed irritated and annoyed. He started to yawn and I remember how he sat back in his chair, pulling away from me and the text. While I was very dissatisfied with the student's passive behavior, I didn't know what to do about it. That evening, while listening to the tape and reflecting on my one-sided conversation, I began to think about what went wrong. I remembered when the student began to withdraw. It was after I attempted to teach for an accurate rendition of the word *ran* (rather than *chased*) without realizing that I could have accepted a partially correct response and then prompted the child to cross-check with visual information. I shared this reflection with my colleagues the next day and together we discussed why this

may have happened and alternative ways that I could have resolved the situation. My example provoked a discussion about similar interactions my colleagues had experienced with their students. By sharing our experiences and frustrations with our own inadequacies, we grew to understand that we had not behaved in a way that was consistent with our view of reading as strategic behavior. We had all abandoned, at one time or another, the theoretical framework of the learning process provided in Vygotsky's (1978) work and the reading process inherent in Clay's (1991) work. We could recite the principles and theories of learning and reading that support the Reading Recovery program without difficulty, but we couldn't act on them. I believe our group was at a point in our development that we could scaffold each others' understanding. I doubt that I could have come to this understanding on my own. I needed teaching experience, experience with the reflective process, which I gained in analyzing the audiotapes of many lessons over time, participating in the weekly behind-the-glass discussions, and having ongoing conversations about the effects of my decisionmaking with informed colleagues and more experienced mentors. It was this myriad of experiences that supported my learning and enabled me to become a more responsive and thus effective Reading Recovery teacher.

In this chapter we described the processes teachers experience and engage in as they learn to become responsive teachers. We also documented beginning teachers' thinking and decisionmaking as they became more effective. Reading Recovery, however, is not just a label for a successful program; it is much more. Reading Recovery is a disposition, a way of viewing the world. The program instantiates a conceptual frame for understanding effective learning and teaching. In the next chapter we take a closer look at that conceptual frame through the eyes of experienced and successful teachers.

Chapter 9

Understanding Teacher Change

The theory of learning and instruction inherent in the Reading Recovery program implies a demanding standard for teachers: The most powerful teaching occurs when the learner's performance is assisted. In Reading Recovery, teachers are required to reconstruct and/or transform their understandings of the learning, reading, and teaching processes. This process begins during the initial year of training and continues as long as the teacher is involved in the program. It consists in the refinement of old and development of new high-order cognitive processes that guide intelligent, purposeful action and interaction. For example, Reading Recovery teachers learn how to organize the events in a lesson according to specific goals they expect the child to achieve. They learn how to plan, problem solve, think, and act according to the child's responses during the lesson. The teacher's cognitive processing (i.e., problem solving) while engaged in the act of teaching is similar to the strategic problem solving we have detailed in our discussion of students' cognitive processing while engaged in the act of reading and writing.

Transforming and reconstructing knowledge are not surprising or unfamiliar processes. Individuals usually rethink information to gain additional insights. And they develop more complex reasoning skills at a later point in time after they have had these new kinds of experiences. It is not likely, for example, that a first-year engineer would proceed to design a robot for an automobile assembly line in the same way as more seasoned engineers. Senior engineers, who have been involved in initial research and development for the industry, have had more opportunities to acquire the thinking skills necessary to design state-of-the-art robotic equipment. Nor is it likely that experienced tennis players would have the same swing or make the same mental errors they made during their first games. As tennis players gain more experience, they rethink how they are hitting the ball in order to understand why they are having trouble with a particular shot. Thus, through experience individuals acquire higher-order problem-solving skills that enable them to monitor their own behavior and resolve their own conflicts.

In Chapter 8 we described our study of six recurring transformations of beginning teachers' thinking processes and practice. As the teachers acquired more knowledge and experience working with children, mentors, and colleagues, they made more powerful teaching decisions. In this chapter, we take an in-depth look at why those transformations occur and the conditions that support their development. Using a Vygotskian perspective, we examine the social context and nature of teachers' cognitive development.

VYGOTSKY'S INFLUENCE ON STUDYING LEARNING AND TEACHING

During the last decade, Vygotsky's work has received much attention. His writings have greatly influenced scholars interested in describing learning and teaching (Moll, 1990; Wood, 1988) and the important role teachers play in students' learning (Rogoff, 1990; Tharp & Gallimore, 1988). One reason for this renewed interest in Vygotsky's ideas may be that he has provided an analytic way of thinking about a complex phenomenon such as how individuals learn that is otherwise hard to understand and describe. A second reason may be that his theories have helped educators think about the importance of the teacher's role in the process.

Clay and Cazden (1990), for example, have interpreted students' and teachers' processing in Reading Recovery lessons from a Vygotskian perspective.

> The metaphorical term *scaffold*, though never used by Vygotsky, has come to be used for interactional support, often in the form of adult–child dialogue that is structured by the adult to maximize the growth of the child's intrapsychological functioning. In their shared activity, the teacher is interacting with unseen processes—the in-the-head strategies used by the child to produce the overt responses of writing and oral reading. For one child, the Reading Recovery program as a whole is such a scaffold. On a more micro level, we have seen many examples of the child functioning independently, in both reading and writing, where earlier collaboration between teacher and child was necessary. (p. 219)

DeFord (1993) and Lyons (1993) have used Vygotsky's theories to describe the transformation of teachers' implicit ideas about reading instruction and student learning during the Reading Recovery staff development course. These descriptions have not, however, fully explained the mechanisms that support Reading Recovery teachers' learning as they make this transformation. A more detailed examination of two Vygotskian theoretical principles of learning and teaching will be used to explain and discuss changes in Reading Recovery teachers' development of the complex, self-regulatory cognitive processes necessary to maximize student learning.

The Theory of Cognitive Development

The first principle we will explore is Vygotsky's (1978) theory of cognitive development. Vygotsky believed that cognitive development is a transformation of basic biologically determined generic processes into higher psychological functions. The theory suggests that the infant is endowed by nature with the capacity to perceive, to attend, and to remember. These basic processes, however, are substantially transformed to higher-order cognitive processes as the child begins to control and regulate his or her behaviors. This capacity to regulate one's own behavior is a social process mediated by language.

Children learn language because they have a basic need to make themselves understood, to express their wants and needs. They acquire language through interaction with more competent speakers (older children and adults) who communicate with them and enable them to use language as an intellectual tool for thinking. These more competent speakers do not intentionally teach children a language. Instead, they attempt to understand what a child means, what he or she is thinking, and then respond to the child's utterances in order to sustain the conversation. Children, therefore, construct their knowledge (learn) through language, initially assisted by others, until they can assist themselves. Thus language plays a critical role in developing a child's capacity for thinking and making him- or herself understood. As the child is supported by others through conversation, he or she develops higher-order, self-regulatory cognitive processes. A 2-year-old child, for example, would have little trouble verbally directing a parent to buy the jelly-filled donuts instead of the plain donuts. An 8-month-old child, however, would find it difficult to communicate his or her wants through words.

Such a view of children's development of higher-order thinking is supported by language research (Lindfors, 1987) and classroom discourse (Cazden, 1988). Evidence from these studies suggests that children understand more than they can produce, but through interaction they build systems of understanding and strategies for generating further learning. Clay (1991) has called language a "self-extending system" that fuels its own learning.

Vygotsky's theory of cognitive development, which emphasizes the role of social interaction through language, has also been described as a theory of education because it emphasizes the social organization of instruction (Bruner, 1986). In Vygotskian theory, instruction is a "unique form of cooperation between the child and the adult that is the central element of the educational process"; by this interactional process "knowledge is transferred to the child in a definite system" (quoted in Moll, 1990, p. 2). Vygotsky's theory of instruction suggests that teachers and students share activities so that the learner can complete tasks with the help of the teacher that he or she could not complete alone. The learner is supported at the beginning through conversation with the teacher, but gradually the learner develops the higher-order cognitive skills that enable him or her to complete more alone. Teacher–student collaboration, supported by language around a specific learning activity, allows the learner to "construct some inner generating system, which will initiate and manage learning of this kind independently on future occasions" (Clay, 1991, p. 42).

Within the Reading Recovery yearlong staff development course (with follow-up support in subsequent years), teachers acquire reasoning skills that enable them to construct a self-generating system for making powerful teaching decisions. This process is initiated early on in the training program as more experienced mentors transfer information and knowledge to novice teachers through conversation while observing teacher–student interactions during live demonstration lessons. One teacher, for example, commented that she had never understood when she should shift from introducing a new book with help to a minimal book introduction until the teacher leader focused the class on book introductions.

> During the observation lesson, our teacher leader provided us opportunities to discuss behaviors to look for that suggested the student was on his way to independence and ready for minimum help from the teacher. We were able to observe, discuss, and explain why the minimal book introduction was powerful in the first lesson and not successful in the second lesson.

Language research also documents how children, in collaboration with teachers and parents, construct shared meanings through language as they engage in specific events (Wells, 1986). A trip to the zoo to see panda bears from China, for example, should stimulate much discussion and a specific language to describe and explain what the children and teachers are seeing. Without the trip to the zoo and conversation around the event, this expanded vocabulary may not be generated.

Reading Recovery teachers also acquire a language to construct a shared meaning that often only those involved in the program can understand. Teachers learn new meanings for terms (e.g., *strategies, cross-checking, monitoring*). The specificity of their language plays a critical role in enabling them to build and think about a concept (e.g., teaching for the strategy to search for additional information). Conversations with informed others develops teachers' ability to recognize, assess, and resolve problems as events occur. In Chapter 8, for example, Patty may not have been able to think about, articulate, or provide a possible explanation about why John was having a problem reading *Dan, the Flying Man* without a shared language to discuss the phenomenon. Through experience, knowledge, and conversations with informed others, she was able to develop the more complex reasoning processes needed to resolve John's conflicts as well as her own. Earlier in her training program, Patty would not have been able to do this.

The Zone of Proximal Development and Learning

The second principle we found helpful in explaining Reading Recovery teachers' change process is the concept of the zone of proximal development (ZPD). The ZPD is the distance between what an individual has learned, that is, what he or she can do without help from others, and their level of potential learning, that is, what he or she can do with support from others. Vygotsky proposed that an individual's ability to learn how to regulate his or her own behavior is for the most part a language process that develops from social interaction within the ZPD. He argued that the essential feature of learning is that it creates the ZPD and thereby awakens a variety of internal cognitive processes when the individual is interacting with people in his or her environment or in cooperation with peers. According to Vygotsky, these higher mental functions first appear on the social level, between people (intercognitive), and later on the individual level, inside the learner (intracognitive). Once the processes are internalized, they become part of the learner's independent developmental achievement.

The concept of the ZPD is usually used to describe a child's cognitive development. Clay and Cazden (1990) describe changes in the child's forms of mediation during a Reading Recovery lesson:

> According to Vygotsky, major turning points in development are connected with the appearance, or transformation, of new forms of mediation. Reading Recovery is designed to help the child accomplish just that: the integration of the semiotic codes of oral language and English orthography, plus world knowledge, into the complex operations of reading and writing. It includes the presence of stimuli created by the child (in the self-composed sentences) as well as those given to the child in teacher-selected texts. And it includes a shift from pointing as an external psychological tool (Wertsch, 1985, pp. 77–81), which the child is asked to use to focus his attention on each word in sequence, to later internalization, when the teacher judges the child to be ready to try with "just his eyes." (p. 219)

We would argue that the concept of the ZPD can also be used to discuss conditions that apply to Reading Recovery teachers' learning of new teaching skills. This application is generally not obvious because adults have already acquired many types of higher functions and can think conceptually. They can abstract information from print and generalize what they have read to other domains. They can also construct their own understandings and develop a self-generating system to learn from those newly acquired understandings.

But learning in the Reading Recovery program requires reorganization and often reconstruction of teachers' theoretical understandings about the learning process. Acquiring these new abilities involves learning a new language to describe, assess, explain, and interpret phenomena. Skillfulness in these activities depends on a flexible, reflective approach to instruction. It also involves the teacher in an ever-changing dynamic process with students, colleagues, and mentors.

As teachers acquire skill in making more effective teaching decisions, their thinking and ability to regulate their actions follows a developmental course that parallels the development of Reading Recovery student self-regulation. We will use Vygotsky's theories of self-regulation, as described by Tharp and Gallimore (1988), to discuss the development of self-regulatory teaching skills among Reading Recovery teachers.

The Zone of Proximal Development and Teaching

According to Tharp and Gallimore (1988), the developmental progression of teachers' ability to regulate their teaching performance can be viewed as a continuum of five stages within and beyond the ZPD: (1) assistance provided by more capable others; (2) transition from assistance by others to self-assistance; (3) assistance provided by the self; (4) internalization and automatization; and (5) deautomatization and recursion. The first four stages of teachers' development recur over and over again in the lifetime of an individual as new capacities are developed. Furthermore, at any point in time, the performance of an individual will reflect a mix of regulation by others, self-regulation, and automatized processes. We will explain Reading Recovery teachers' development in terms of these five phases.

Assistance Provided by More Capable Others. The notion that Reading Recovery teachers' behavior is initially regulated by teacher leaders in social interaction is discussed and described through case reports in Chapter 8. The teacher leader's primary goal is to provide assistance by focusing teachers' attention on specific principles (e.g., following the child's lead) that need to be understood early in the training. The behind-the-glass demonstration provides many opportunities for novice teachers to observe and mentally record a child's behavior and his or her attempts to problem solve through interaction with a more experienced teacher. The interactions between the teacher and student in this first phase of development allow students to participate in literacy activities that would be impossible for them on their own. The novice teachers learn how to make powerful teaching decisions that support and advance the child's learning through conversation with the teacher leader and peers. Language provides teachers a powerful tool for both thinking and communicating around verbal and nonverbal behaviors that the teacher leader focuses on throughout the lesson.

Transition from Assistance by Others to Self-Assistance. As the weeks progress, the teacher leader's responsibility and direction steadily decline and there is a corresponding increase in the teachers' proportion of responsibility. The teachers ask questions about observed behaviors and initiate discussions about the effect of the teacher's questions and/or prompts on students' learning. One teacher commented that without observing and discussing the routine teacher questions and student responses during a live demonstration lesson, she would not have examined her interactions with students. After listening to audiotapes of lessons, this teacher discovered that her routine pattern of behavior did not challenge, but rather constrained, the children in the process of posing and solving problems. She did not engage children in stretching their understanding and problem-solving skills to apply to more challenging texts. The teachers in transition from assistance by others to self-assistance begin to function as their own consultants, providing assistance to themselves. The teacher leader shifts the responsibility for thinking and strategic problem solving about their teaching skills to the teachers. The teachers undergo the transition from regulation by others to self-regulation, which generally produces high levels of stress and anxiety. Tharp and Gallimore (1988) describe this transition as follows:

> In the beginning, the apprentice may only vaguely appreciate the goal toward which the collaborating pair is moving. Indeed, the predominant experience of the apprentice is likely to involve confusion, anxiety, and self-doubt. Attention is focused almost exclusively on small portions of the capacity to be acquired. Only gradually does the apprentice come to understand the way that the parts of the activity relate to one another and to understand the meaning of the performance. Ordinarily, in training a teacher, this understanding develops through conversation about the task to be performed or modeling of the skill in question. When some conception of the overall performance has been acquired through language or other semiotic process, the apprentice can be assisted by other means—questioning, feedback, and further cognitive structuring. (p. 250)

Teachers' transcripts in Chapter 8 provided several examples of frustration. Barbara was upset that she had let herself get into a routine question–answer pattern, and Patty was concerned that she had ignored John's attempts to make sense and instead focused his attention at the letter level. One teacher's comments about her feelings of frustration seemed to represent the group's disposition.

> It took me several months teaching four children on a daily basis to feel comfortable about my analyses of the students' strengths and their level of processing. But deciding which strategy to focus on and what question will enable the child to acquire that specific strategy is very hard to learn. I wasn't able to think fast enough to get the right question or prompt to correspond to a specific strategy. I would realize that the child needed to learn how to cross-check a meaningful prediction with visual information and ask "Does _____ make sense" instead of "Does _____ look right." I just couldn't seem to put it all together yet. I couldn't control the way I responded to what the child was doing. It was so frustrating! I was wasting the child's time and my time. He wasn't progressing because I wasn't progressing.

Although these feelings of frustration, stress, and anxiety are disheartening, they are to be expected. "Self-regulatory cognition was predicted by Vygotsky to occur under conditions of learning, stress, and disruption" (Tharp & Gallimore, 1988, p. 252).

Assistance Provided by the Self.   Transformations in teachers' thinking and decisionmaking continue to be refined and expanded as they gain more knowledge and experience. They begin to realize that their role is to be the observer who gathers information about each student's processing system. They start to discern behavior signals or evidence of the student's processing and create tentative hypotheses from these observations (e.g., Bill's hypotheses about why Peter might have been confused while reading *Rosie's Walk* in Chapter 8). The teachers begin to understand that because the instructional conversation during a lesson is responsive and because children and their language and behaviors are so various, it is not possible to routinize teaching acts; for example, Barbara's realization of the dangerous situation she had established with routine questions.

Developing the cognitive processes necessary to assist yourself is a complex skill that takes time. Teachers need first and foremost to develop a theoretical understanding of the reading and learning processes. They need to learn how to use these theories to make careful observations of student behaviors and develop a flexible, tentative attitude that allows for continually creating and discarding hypotheses about the student's literacy processing.

Although the responsibility for observing and determining the child's level of processing, as well as for determining the most powerful questions and prompts to support the developing competencies, is shifting from the teacher leader to the teacher at this point, performance is not fully developed or automatized. That is because the regulating function (what question to ask and when to ask it) is an overt verbalization, often in the form of self-directed speech.

One teacher commented that she often asked herself the same questions that the teacher leader asked the class.

"What does the child control?"
"Who is controlling the process, the teacher or the child?"
"What sources of information is the child attempting to use?"
"What are the child's strengths?"

She would jot down things to look for prior to listening to audiotaped lessons. For example, she noted what she did when the child found it hard to continue reading. She listened for her reinforcing comments and questions she asked after the child hesitated, made an error, or self-corrected.

When teachers start to assist themselves, rather than asking the teacher leader or others for guidance, there are significant gains in their teaching performance. What was once regulated by a more experienced teacher or teacher leader is now regulated by the teacher him- or herself. This form of self-regulation generally appears as self-talk, self-instruction, self-questioning. Examples of self-directed speech obtained from teacher interviews illustrates how Reading Recovery teachers assist themselves. "I should have done _____ but instead I did _____." "I missed an opportunity when he came to this part of the story to teach him something he needed to know." "I really didn't need to ask her a monitoring question; she was already monitoring." "I was asking him something he already knew; I should have asked a higher-level question." "When I did _____ the student did _____." Bill's retrospective account of possible reasons for Peter's confusion and what he should have done to enable Peter to resolve the confusion is a good example of a teacher talking himself through a problem.

Internalization and Automatization.   Teachers progress through two major transitions before their behavior is internalized and automatic. First, they are assisted in learning the program by more capable others, notably the teacher leader who directs their learning. One teacher referred to the teacher leader as her subconscious.

For the first four months of my training program, my teacher leader became my subconscious, my inner voice. I felt like I had a split personality. There was a two-way conversation going on inside my head when I worked with the children and when I was thinking about their progress while analyzing records. My teacher leader would be asking me questions—"What strengths does the child have?" "Is he monitoring his own reading or are you monitoring for him?" "What could you ask him to help him learn how to cross-check two sources of information?" Not only would I hear the questions, I would respond to them out loud. I think that talking to myself after imagining that my teacher leader was talking to me helped me learn how to follow the child and select the most powerful question to help the child learn how to use his strengths.

A second transition occurs when the teacher leader's voice becomes the teacher's voice. The teacher makes the transition from the regulating voice of the other (the teacher leader) to self-directed inner speech. After these two transitions take place, the skill (e.g., asking the most powerful question to support a child's flexible use of reading strategies) is internalized and automated. The self-directed inner voice is silent, and self-examining consciousness is reduced. Tharp and Gallimore (1988) describe this process in the following way:

> In theoretical terms, once self-directed assistance disappears, we may presume that the individual has emerged from the ZPD for the task at hand. Task execution is smooth and integrated, and its regulation has been internalized and automatized. Assistance, from others or the self, is no longer needed and would now be disruptive. Even self-consciousness itself can interfere with the smooth integration of all task components. Self-control and social control are no longer required. The performance capacity is not developed: Vygotsky used a vivid metaphor—"fossilized"—to describe its fixity and removal from the social and mental forces of change. This fixity, however, is not permanent. (p. 257)

Reading Recovery teachers who are operating at an automatic level of problem solving have internalized a repertoire of actions with which to react and make powerful decisions. They can easily move up and down a hierarchy of prompts or questions to support the child's processing because they have internalized this repertoire of information and knowledge. Donna, for example, an experienced Reading Recovery teacher, was carefully recording Scott's first reading of *Along Comes Jake* (Cowley, 1987a). Scott suddenly stopped reading. He was stuck on the word *then* in the sentence "Then along comes Jake." Donna reached for three magnetic letters (*t*, *h*, and *e*) and began to say, "You know the word *the*." Her idea was to help Scott use a known word, *the*, to get to the word *then*. In the middle of her sentence, Donna stopped. She noticed Scott rereading the sentence prior to the one he was stuck on (a technique she had previously taught him to use). Suddenly he read "Then along comes

Jake." Donna immediately put the magnetic letters away and commented, "I like how you reread the sentence, checked the picture, and got your mouth ready for the first word in the sentence. That was excellent work!"

In this example the teacher abandoned her first idea (focusing on the lowest level of information—letters) and shifted because she noticed Scott shifting. His rereading demonstrated that he was attempting to operate at the higher level (story meaning) of processing. He had not previously integrated the meaning (looking at the picture), language structure (rereading the sentence), and visual and auditory information (getting his mouth ready for the first letter). Scott did not need to drop down to the lower levels of word and/ or letters, and neither did his teacher. He was beginning to move flexibly among a hierarchy of levels of information in order to pick up cues from different sources and to use strategies to move from one level to another. Donna's careful observation, analysis, and interaction were done immediately, while Scott was engaged in the process.

Donna has developed a dynamic network of teaching techniques that are easily retrieved from her repertoire of knowledge. Because this repertoire of information has been internalized, or "fossilized," Donna's attention is free to pick up new information. She can call up and use this information and change direction at any point in time if the unexpected occurs. For example, when Scott demonstrated that he was processing at the meaning level, Donna quickly changed her original plan to help him read the word *then* by focusing at the letter level.

A teachers' ability to function automatically in a flexible way is a complex skill that requires a wide knowledge base. Teachers at this level of performance observe the students' performance, interpret the behavior, hypothesize about the student's internal processing, select several alternative teaching procedures to try to support the student's level of processing, and then act. If one procedure is not productive, the teacher can attempt an alternative plan. Plans B, C, and D are the norm, not the exception, because student's processing is so tentative and complex. The teacher's decisionmaking process happens very quickly while the student is engaged in reading and writing activities. The process is efficient when the teacher understands what the student needs to learn how to do in order to develop a self-extending system and can act accordingly.

The four phases of the learning process we have just described recur many times throughout an individual's life as he or she develops new capacities. In the following transcript, Beth describes her transition among the four phases of development as she progressed through the initial year of training and subsequent years.

When I started my training, I relied on my teacher leader for everything. I read and reread the theory outlined in *Reading: The Patterning of Complex Behavior* (Clay, 1972) and *The Early Detection of Reading Difficulties* (Clay, 1985) carefully. I studied the teaching techniques in the books and tried to apply them to the children while I was working with them. I made a list of questions or prompts to get the child to monitor, search additional information, and so forth, and then kept referring to the list while I was teaching the child. It was really hard to observe and match the child's behavior and select the best question to ask and then watch the behavior again to see if the question paid off. If the question wasn't effective, I had to search my list of questions for a better one. I kept thinking, how is this child processing, what is going on inside his head? Why is he or she doing this? How can I untangle this confusion? How can I help him learn how to help himself? When I had trouble coming up with a solution, I would reread the books, bring the question to class or discuss my question with the teacher leader or another peer. I could tell my teacher leader knew what to ask and could switch gears as a new or different behavior emerged, but I couldn't. I went on colleague visits and observed colleagues teaching their children and talked about what they did in response to the students' behaviors. My best learning opportunities took place during the behind-the-glass discussions. Our teacher leader challenged and stretched our thinking. I benefited from the groups discussion while we observed the lessons.

It is apparent from Beth's discussion of her own learning cycle that there is a shifting relationship between assistance by others and self-assistance. Yet she had not reached the point in her cognitive development where her performance had become automatized. In the following excerpt there is evidence, however, that this phase of Beth's learning has been reached and she has emerged from the zpd.

After several years of teaching children on a daily basis, observing and discussing teacher–student interactions behind the one-way glass, and making colleague visits you begin to realize that you can teach a child without thinking about what specific language to use to prompt for a desired behavior. You start thinking in terms of principles to be learned. For example, you might note that one child understands the principle of prediction and cross-checking with visual information in writing but he cannot transfer that principle to reading. You start to predict what may be going on in the child's head. You hypothesize about the child's level of processing and what strategies he may be using. Then you test out the hypotheses by setting a context using a specific text and think to yourself: If he does _____, that tells me he has control of _____; if he does _____, it means he doesn't have control of this strategy. You look for partially right and partially wrong responses or behaviors and then ask questions or use prompts to support a partially right response. Then you test out the newly acquired behavior (if you were successful in developing it) the next day by setting up another context. And the cycle repeats itself.

Beth's discussion of her own reasoning while teaching children suggests that she is making decisions and acting automatically. She has internalized a repertoire of actions and reactions that have been integrated throughout the lesson. The fact that she can operate at an automatic level frees her to deal with unexpected responses and behavior as they occur. These unexpected student responses often create the deautomatization of teaching performance that leads to recursion through the ZPD.

Deautomatization and Recursion. According to Gallimore and Tharp (1990), deautomatization and recursion occur so regularly during the learning cycle that they constitute a fifth stage of the normal developmental process.

It often happens that self-regulation is not sufficient to restore performance capacity, and a further recursion—the restitution or other-regulation—is required. Whatever the level of recursion, the goal is to reproceed through assisted performance to self-regulation and to exit the zone of proximal development anew into automatization. (p. 187)

Reading Recovery teachers often comment that they learn the most from children who are difficult to teach. When students' processing is hard to infer, predict, interpret, and understand, teachers engage in more complex reasoning. They become more sensitive to partially right responding to determine what students can do without help—what it is they know. They use students' emerging reading and writing behaviors to hypothesize about the nature of the students' processing. Then they apply theoretical knowledge and understanding of learning and the reading process to select the most powerful teaching techniques to assist students in constructing a self-extending system. Beth, for example, discussed how Michael helped her develop an understanding of the role of serial order in student processing.

Most of my Reading Recovery children had little difficulty learning directionality. Once I demonstrated how to read the words with their finger, they easily learned the procedure. Michael, however, was different. He had difficulty developing consistency in matching what he read with what he said. If his language structure overrode the words in the text, he didn't know what to do. Michael's behaviors were puzzling and I started to reread *Becoming Literate: The Construction of Inner Control* (Clay, 1991) to look for some explanation for his inconsistent behavior. By interpreting and inferring Michael's behaviors in light of the theories presented in *Becoming Literate,* I began to understand how directional learning fits into an explanation of reading and writing acquisition. I then discussed these new understandings with colleagues, and they shared their experiences and reasons for using specific teaching techniques and discarding others. Without Michael, I would not have known what questions to ask my colleagues and in the process learned with them.

Michael's behaviors presented a new set of circumstances that enabled Beth to learn how to assist herself. She needed to reenter the ZPD—assistance by others and self-assistance. The more opportunities she has to teach children who have difficulty learning about directionality, the more likely it is that she will develop automatized cognitive structures to deal with this situation.

CONCLUSION

Vygotsky's (1986) theory suggests that learning never stops and is always recursive. The more we know, the more we do not know, and the more we need to seek assistance to grasp new knowledge and insights. It is through assistance by more knowledgeable others that we are challenged to stretch our boundaries to learn more.

The Reading Recovery staff development course develops teachers' capacities for assisting performance. This lifelong process in renewed through continued work with students and ongoing professional development. A Vygotskian analysis of the Reading Recovery program for teachers is closely linked to Vygotskian theories of learning and instruction. As Vygotsky's work suggests, the substance and structure of the teaching activity within Reading Recovery take place in an enormously complex interactional setting that powerfully shapes the teacher's learning and, in turn, the student's as well.

Chapter 10

Making the Most
of What We Know

What we have learned from Reading Recovery has helped us think about ways to address the pressing problems of literacy education in the United States. It is strange that a program that has as its focus working with young, high-risk children might have implications for the general education of U.S. children. Reading Recovery serves first-grade students by immersing them in reading and writing. We do not advocate transferring Reading Recovery to classroom instruction; our research indicates that even if that were desirable, it is not efficient or productive. And most children do not need the intensive procedures of Reading Recovery. But what Reading Recovery offers us is more important than any particular method or procedure.

Reading Recovery provides a model that helps us understand some fundamental processes for enhancing the education of students, particularly those who find themselves at risk of failure in school. Reading Recovery is an intervention in the system of education provided for individual children. By implementing Reading Recovery, we change the system to provide the level of support needed by individual children at critical periods in their schooling. By finding out how Reading Recovery works and hypothesizing about why it works, we have developed some insights that are applicable to general education. As an intervention program, Reading Recovery itself will have an impact if it is implemented in a high-quality way with sufficient coverage. Figures from New Zealand Department of Education indicate that in 1988, 21.24% of the 6-year-old age cohort were served by Reading Recovery and .8% of these children were referred for special needs programs (Clay, 1989). Case reports (Lyons, 1991b) and data collected in one Ohio school district revealed that when 20% of the first grade population received Reading Recovery, .006% were classified as learning disabled (Lyons & Beaver, in press). Reading Recovery also has implications for classroom instruction and we can look to the design of Reading Recovery for assistance in restructuring other educational efforts. We believe that what we have gained from Reading Recovery goes beyond instruction of individual children. We have gained some important insights into the kinds of systems and adjustments that will enhance literacy education for all children. In our study, we found that superficial aspects of Reading Recovery were not as important as underlying factors, such as the teachers' knowledge base out of which decisions emanate. In this chapter we summarize our findings regarding the Reading Recovery context, how teachers and children learn, and how the system works. Then, we propose some ideas for restructuring literacy education based on our study and our experiences over the last eight years.

WHAT WE LEARNED

In our study we contrasted four interventions and their outcomes. We tested traditional Reading Recovery with fully trained teachers working in 10 school districts. We also tested three other interventions. The first, Reading Success, was a Reading Recovery–like tutorial provided by certified teachers who received an alternative form of training in which they learned the lesson framework and the application of procedures but did not participate in the yearlong process. A second treatment, Reading and Writing Group, involved a trained Reading Recovery teacher working in groups instead of individually with children. A third treatment, Direct Instruction Skills Plan, was provided by a certified teacher who provided daily, individual tutoring using a skills-practice model. Each treatment, across 10 districts, was compared with student outcomes of a randomly assigned control group. Results of our study indicated that traditional Reading Recovery with a fully trained teacher had the best student outcomes; based on the final scores, Reading Recovery was the best of the instructional contexts we studied. But such findings are not useful unless we go on to look below the surface, to discover how outcomes are related to underlying characteristics of the instruction. In other words, we need to know why certain characteristics of instructional programs are effective in order to help redesign education.

WHAT WE LEARNED ABOUT THE
READING RECOVERY CONTEXT

The instructional comparisons we established in the MacArthur Early Literacy Research Project allowed us to assess the impact of such aspects of Reading Recovery as one-on-one teaching, time spent on reading and writing, and the lesson framework. We discovered that some characteristics of the Reading Recovery context are necessary; but superficial factors are not sufficient to explain the results of Reading Recovery for high-risk children. Although factors such as content, time, and individual instruction are necessary to achieve the results of Reading Recovery, they are not sufficient to explain the results of the program. And adopted as superficial features, they would not guarantee success. In fact, many educators have used versions of the "lesson plan," for example, but ignored the fine tuning of teaching that is required during participation in the in-service course. When superficial aspects of an effective program are utilized as "formulas" for success, failure is usually the outcome. In our study, we learned more about this fine-tuning. In the next section, we discuss these necessary but not sufficient factors: content, time, and individual instruction.

Content

From our analysis of the videotaped lessons, we found that large segments of time within the half-hour lessons in Reading Recovery and Reading Success were spent with the child engaged in reading and writing tasks. This finding supports Clay's (1985) characterization of Reading Recovery as having a "bias towards text." This bias toward text—the reading of text and the construction of text—provided a rich context for these children as literacy learners.

In reading settings, for example, we found it was important to have high-quality materials to support children's problem solving on text. The children learned to use strategies, such as searching for additional meaning cues in pictures and monitoring the match between meaning and visual information, because the text itself supported the need for these strategies. They had good pictures that clearly represented the concepts and written language. Then, as the child developed more complex understandings of these strategies, the gradient of difficulty of the materials was increased. This combination of quality text and increasing challenge within a child's individual reading program enabled the child to become a problem solver in reading rather than simply acquiring a bank of items for remembering. In many remedial programs, the texts offered children are limited. They spend time on word practice and only occasionally read extended text (Allington & McGill-Franzen, 1989; Slavin & Madden, 1989). In our own study of one one-on-one tutorial and one small-group instructional contrast, children read very few books and they received poor results. Other research has related a similar dearth of reading time allotted for those very children who need to learn to read (Allington & McGill-Franzen, 1989). Reading Recovery children read many books and compose a written message every day. The Reading Recovery framework is a powerful instructional model that immerses children in massive amounts of reading and writing, even when they may appear at first to know very little about literacy.

Early in a child's learning, the reciprocal gains between reading and writing are important. Writing is critical to the development of reading strategy in early literacy experiences. Our most effective teachers, for example, tended to spend more time on writing early in the child's program and less time on writing at the end. It may be that, since writing slows down the process, it simultaneously allows the child to form concepts about how print operates. It is not that writing diminishes in importance as a child learns to read, but it may assume a different role in the life of the young literacy learner. Once the child has learned how to look at print and use visual information "on the run" while reading for meaning, the reciprocal benefits may be more complex, supporting comprehension and text construction.

The act of writing, in itself, facilitates the development of cognitive structures that support reading. The motor aspect of writing enables the children to attend closely to print and facilitates memory of how letters and words are made (Luria, 1970). For high-risk children, an adult scaffold that can take what they know as a strength and put that together with the most ready links in conversation will extend the children's capabilities. This instructional conversation is important while the children write for themselves. The teachers in this study consistently prompted the children to use strategies. The teachers insisted that the children monitor themselves by saying, "You check for yourself . . ." When support was necessary, however, they were ready to provide it.

The highly scaffolded instructional setting in Reading Recovery is different from process writing, where the child writes alone and the teacher uses the product to evaluate the child's developing understanding of writing. It is also different from the language experience process, where the teacher writes for the child and asks the child to read it. The child who has not engaged in the process of learning to read by the time he or she enters school has not noticed the detailed organization of print. The highly scaffolded interactions between teacher and child in Reading Recovery, then, help to frame an understanding of how print is organized and facilitates the child's learning of "how to learn" in new print settings. Again, assisted performance and increasing challenge are hallmarks of accelerated progress. Take the instance of a child's production of invented spellings. Invented spellings are approximations—they are the half-right possibility. These approximations show what the child has cognitively understood about phenomic representation. The use of boxes in the writing component of Reading Recovery sets a frame for the child to move in with the "half-rights." The teacher's job is to frame the approximations for the child so that he or she knows where to go next and how to continue analyzing in ever more complex ways. Then, the teacher uses his or her knowledge of the importance of the child's inventions to help the child move ahead.

The content analysis indicated that massive amounts of reading and writing are essential, particularly for children who are at risk. However, although the Reading Success teachers had the same overall profile for reading and writing content, they did not achieve the same results. So when we are designing programs, it is necessary to include a variety of rich experiences in reading and writing text; but text alone will not do the job. Writing and reading good children's literature are basic characteristics of good classrooms. However, the amount of time spent on and the quality of instructional conversations may also be important considerations.

Time

We examined all interventions for time spent on reading, writing, and other activities. This time analysis confirmed the well-established findings concerning time-on-task. Teachers with better results spend more time on reading and writing (Rosenshine, 1979). But our interpretation of these results does not support this simple conclusion. All too often, policymakers have turned over the schooling of at-risk children to teachers who are required to spend most of the day focusing on drill-and-skill literacy tasks. This practice has led to a narrowing of education and sometimes resulted in an excess of drill and practice, which conflicts with children's natural responses to meaningful activities. Our results should not be interpreted as supporting such actions. Too much attention to time-on-task might lead us to conclude that we should lengthen time spent reading and writing, and consequently to lengthen the 30-minute lesson. This may have deleterious results. However, we feel that it is the intensity and the appropriateness of teacher decisions in combination with time spent on worthwhile reading and writing tasks that makes the difference. Time is not the issue; it is important to provide powerful and meaningful activities surrounded by the kind of talk that supports learning.

All the interventions spent time on literacy activities, but some included more drill and practice on isolated items, with poor results. Even when tasks in reading and writing are holistic in nature, we should be cautious about ascribing results to the mere provision of time for reading and writing. Our Reading Success teachers spent massive amounts of time on reading and writing, but they were found to be less incisive in selecting and articulating memorable teaching points. Rather than lengthening the program, then, or including more time on reading and writing in the 30-minute Reading Recovery lesson, we suspect that lengthening the time would actually weaken the instruction by lessening the demand to select critical teaching moves. If there is time for everything, many weak actions might be encouraged and practice might be extended beyond the point where it is needed or effective. Clay (1991) talks about the program going to the child. That is what makes a program efficient and powerful. If the teacher structures the instructional conversation within the lesson to respond specifically to the child's needs, the time spent on reading and writing instruction will be the most powerful and memorable.

Individual Instruction

As we began this study, we were responding to the idea that the salient feature of the Reading Recovery program was one-on-one instruction. Couldn't any teacher working one-on-one achieve the same results as Reading Recovery? As we implemented Reading Recovery, people began to ask, Couldn't a trained Reading Recovery teacher working in groups achieve similar results? The answers have important implications for the use of funds in the education of high-risk children.

Our study indicated that individual instruction is a necessary characteristic of Reading Recovery if the school district wants the lowest-achieving children to make accelerated progress in reading. However, one-on-one interventions such as the Direct Instruction Skills Plan tutorial had poor results. Even Reading Success teachers who worked one-on-one using a Reading Recovery framework were less successful than Reading Recovery teachers, and the difference was a critical one. Children in Reading Success made progress, but not accelerated progress. Few became independent readers with reading processes that were self-extending. Even trained Reading Recovery teachers working in groups were unable to achieve accelerated progress. It may be that working one-on-one is a necessary context for teachers to make incisive decisions that will make a difference in the construction of a self-extending system. One-on-one is absolutely necessary, but again, not sufficient.

WHAT WE LEARNED ABOUT HOW
TEACHERS AND CHILDREN LEARN

The foundation of Reading Recovery is a theory explaining how children learn to read and write. Teachers are challenged to observe children's behavior in light of their theoretical understandings so that they can increase and enrich them. Interpretation of behaviors as signals of children's learning is considered to be an important teacher skill. In collegial groups, teachers engage in activities, sometimes called "sifting and sorting," during which they reflect on teaching procedures and talk about their consistency with theory and their appropriateness for individual children at particular times. In our study, the theoretical foundation emerged as an important element in the educational process.

Literacy education has traditionally been thought of as guiding students through a series of steps so that they acquire items of knowledge in sequential fashion. For example, young children would be expected to learn the letters and related sounds and then to read. They might also have lists of sight words, which they would then meet in simple texts, contrived to contain exactly the words used. Even in these circumstances, Clay (1991) believes that most young readers could learn items in orchestrated ways. They could take the information provided and incorporate it into their more complex ideas about stories and language, eventually bringing all systems to bear on the act of reading.

More holistic notions of reading instruction involve children in reading and writing text from the beginning, using approximation at first but asking children to check their predictions against the print on the page. Thus children engage in reading as a constructive act from the very beginning. They learn items as they proceed; for example, young children develop some knowledge of the letters or particular words they know and can produce. These islands of certainty in a sea of print help the reader work strategically to monitor his or her own reading. The important operation to the reader is the in-the-head problem solving that accompanies the use of item knowledge. It is this strategic behavior that makes for the development of the self-extending system. As Clay (1991) says, "a few items and a powerful strategy might make it very easy to learn a great deal more" (p. 331).

In recent years, educators and policymakers have moved toward curricula that immerse children in reading and writing with the idea that by providing children massive opportunities to engage in reading and writing meaningful text, they will be assisted in the construction of the reading process. A critical element in this process, however, is the knowledgeable adult who works alongside the child, providing feedback, demonstrating, and talking about the process. The teacher's role is critical. Children are not expected to work alone as they put together their ideas about reading and writing. But how do teachers learn how to support young readers skillfully? Previously in teacher education, we have used a transmission model. We have provided informational sessions to tell teachers about theory and suggest activities. Becoming a teacher meant first learning about teaching in university classes and then putting it together for yourself in your own classroom. Some interactions surrounded student teaching, but little coaching on the job took place, and that which existed usually focused on specific activities. Materials guided teachers through step-by-step procedures, but where was the time to examine why? Books such as *The Lonely Teacher* (Knoblock & Goldstein, 1971) have highlighted the solitary process of developing teaching knowledge and skill.

One of the most important findings of our study was the difference made by the Reading Recovery training model. Reading Recovery teachers, both those working individually and those who provided the Reading and Writing Group intervention, were acting on a different theoretical orientation from the rest of the teachers in the study, and they behaved differently. Reading Recovery provides a unique kind of model for teacher learning: Through language, teachers explore concepts together, thinking about theory and checking it with their observations. We need to examine the training model to uncover information about the learning processes involved. In this section, we look at how teachers and children learn in constructive ways and we examine the role of language in their learning.

Constructing Knowledge

Learning is a constructive process whereby people connect what they know to information they encounter in new experiences. Through a variety of literacy experiences children encounter written language; they link it with their own knowledge of oral language and their world experiences. Reading is a process of in-the-head problem solving in which the reader uses many different sources of information in an orchestrated way. Items of knowledge, such as individual words and letter–sound relationships, are important information to be used in connection with more powerful systems, such as implicit knowledge of language syntax and meaning during this searching and checking process. Knowledge is built up through meaningful and memorable experiences with print. The young learner creates "a network of competencies which power subsequent independent literacy learning" (Clay, 1991, p. 1). In literacy events, according to Wood (1988), learning takes place on two levels. First, the child is learning the particular task at hand. But more is happening on the second level: Children are also learning how to learn. They are building systems that help them structure their own learning and carry it forward. Clay (1991) has described a "self-extending system," one that allows readers to continue to increase their skills while reading. That is why, she says, the good readers get better and better.

Teachers build knowledge constructively while they teach. We could describe teachers' wisdom as built on a case-by-case basis as they encounter different classroom experiences. Teachers sometimes accept ideas from authorities, follow the adopted curriculum materials, or accept the "folk wisdom" of experienced teachers; but if they act as constructive learners, they check all ideas against their observations of children in their own schools and classrooms. For example, they should ask, Do my children actually do what authorities say they do as they read texts?

Seldom does teacher education, even in-service education, take advantage of this ability to construct knowledge out of the teaching act. Teachers receive information, but seldom are they supported in this constructive activity; thus they may be forced to rely on recipes or they may not have the confidence to challenge existing prescriptive curricula. With the impressive amount of information now available on children's initiative in constructing their own learning, some teachers may even be intimidated by the process. They may stand back, not knowing how to intervene or teach without interfering. They may provide materials and activities but not truly support students' learning at an appropriate level. In *Rousing Minds to Life*, Tharp and Gallimore (1988) make a challenging statement:

> In American classrooms, now and since the 19th century, teachers generally act as if students are supposed to learn on their own. Teachers are not taught to teach and most often they do not teach . . . all participants in the educational enterprise have shared an inadequate vision of schooling. (p. 3)

Teachers' construction of their own knowledge base is considered a critical element of Reading Recovery. Throughout the book we describe how the reflective process helped teachers make leaps in their own learning and translate their knowledge into more effective teaching. By reflection, we mean their understanding of alternative possibilities. Through behind-the-glass sessions in Reading Recovery, for example, teachers became acutely aware of children's behavior and the way it signaled internal processes. They could provide theoretical explanations that then implied selection of responses and the way they placed attention. Analysis of records helped them think through the programs of individual children and match it with their theoretical understandings. While learning how to teach their individual children, these teachers were also learning to structure their thinking while teaching. They were building a repertoire of responses, but more than that, they were learning alternative explanations for behavior and building the knowledge base. They were learning at two levels: first, they were developing expertise at a specific level for individual children; second, they were structuring their own learning about teaching and learning.

The Role of Language in Assisting Learning

Significant in the process of learning is a more knowledgeable expert who interacts with the learner in a way that supports the extension of concepts and ideas. In our study, language emerged as a powerful learning support for both children and teachers. For children, instructional conversations both demonstrated processes and confirmed their own attempts. Reading Recovery teachers and Reading Success teachers used similar time and content formats; but Reading Recovery teachers were teaching more powerfully through their conversations with children. Our interpretation of the data leads us back to the provision of a yearlong collegial training experience. For teachers, talking while observing and then reflecting with the guidance of the teacher leader played a major role in helping them structure their own teaching interactions.

Since reading and writing are language processes, it is not difficult to conceptualize the role of language in learning to read. After all, children use their knowledge of language throughout the process. They have learned oral language as a self-extending system, one that operates on a system of rules that can constantly generate new language the child has never heard. They use language to learn in order to constantly increase their world knowledge as well as their ability to use language in different ways. Encountering written language requires matching up this already extensive knowledge of oral language with a new system. Activities such as rereading texts and writing their own stories provide opportunities for children to link oral and written language and to monitor their own processes.

When Clay (1991) said, "I see no reason to make him do it alone" (p. 17), she was emphasizing the important role of the knowledgeable other in helping children construct literacy. Bruner and Vygotsky both consider instructional interactions as the "raw material" of learning. Through instructional conversations, the teacher helps the child bring prior knowledge to bear in making sense of the new experiences in literacy. Meaning drives the process; together, teacher and child surround reading and writing with meaningful talk. Tharp and Gallimore (1988) use the metaphor of "weaving" to describe how learners integrate new material into their systems of meanings and understandings.

> This metaphor of "weaving" is deeply connected to the basic processes of literacy. Consider the etymology of the word "text." Deriving from the Latin verb *texere* (to weave), "text" has come to mean the woven narrative, a fabric (*textile*) constructed by the relating of many elements. In the instruction of comprehension, the teacher herself is weaving a "text" composed of written and memorable materials. What we study, as researchers and students of the process, is that text created by the teacher–child interchange. That instructional conversation (the text that is continually becoming)—the fabric of book, memory, talk, and imagination that is being woven—that instructional conversation is the medium, the occasion, the instrument for rousing the mind to life. (p. 109)

They go on to say that this weaving process is especially critical for children whose emergent literacy experiences prior to schooling do not form the base for helping them put it together for themselves. Instead of learning items of knowledge in an orchestrated way, some children may not be connecting literacy learning to the meanings they understand in their everyday lives. We see evidence of this gap in children who move through text using initial letter cues heavily but producing something that sounds like nonsense. We also frequently see first graders using their language and story sense to "invent" text but not checking with cues in the visual display of print even though they know some letter–sound relationships. Instructional conversations help them to hook the texts they encounter with something that makes sense. These conversations guide the process. In Chapter 4 Matthew's teacher was persistent in talking about the way he approached text. He had predicted that the people in the story would go home for "lunch," but he changed his reading to "dinner." Through conversation, the teacher explored this self-correction, helping Matthew understand that the initial prediction had made sense. They could have been going home for lunch. He had changed his response because he checked with the visual information on the page. Thus the teacher, through conversation, drew attention to two important cognitive operations, using language and meaning to predict while reading text and monitoring and checking with visual cues. Learning the word *dinner* was not the goal, although it might eventually be a side product of learning.

Attending to and supporting the child's engagement in strategic operations was the teacher's objective. The instructional conversation acknowledges what is "half right" about the response and guides the learner to possibilities for new actions. The format of activities provided in the Reading Recovery lesson provides opportunity for the learner to act. Teacher demonstrations help to get them started before they have control of all of the complex processes that will be involved. It is conversation that helps the teacher develop awareness and independent control of the processes. Thus the reader moves from acts, with supportive interactions, to awareness that builds the self-extending system.

The theory does not prescribe an instructional model. Given this view of learners as constructing and teachers as assisting, prescription would be impossible. The hard question for teachers is posed in this statement, written by Clay (1991) in response to Bruner's work:

> How does one manage to support the child's control of literacy activities from the beginning, to interact with an inner control one can only infer, and to progressively withdraw to allow room for the child to control the development of a self-extending network of strategies for literacy learning? (p. 344)

To accomplish this lofty goal, the teacher must know the possible routes to literacy like a roadmap. Additionally, the teacher must have ways of checking on the child's progress that help him or her discover how the child is progressing. All of the children in the class may take slightly different routes.

They may attend to different items that form the important examples that help them check on themselves in reading. They have different favorite stories that they are willing to read over and over. Matthew noticed the *d* in the word *dinner* and used that information to check his prediction. His experiences helped him check on himself. Another child might pay attention to something else about the text. It is the teacher's job to think about what the child is paying attention to and to help him or her extend it.

Rogoff (1990) uses the idea of apprenticeship as a model for children's cognitive development. Children actively organize their own learning; they put themselves in a position to make sense of new situations. Others in the social environment help in arranging tasks and activities. They are skilled partners who take over some of the harder parts of the task so that the new learner can do the easy parts and learn how the task is organized. Apprentices, Rogoff suggests, learn to act in increasingly knowledgeable ways by performing tasks with more expert people. The problem solving is shared between this active learner and the more skilled partner. Rogoff outlines features of guided participation, including (1) the importance of routine activities, (2) tacit as well as explicit communication, (3) supportive structuring of novices' efforts, and (4) transfer of responsibility for handling to novices. In Reading Recovery, the lesson framework, with its shared reading and writing, establishes a predictable and routine context. Different messages are composed and written, and different books are selected and read; but the dyad have established times and ways of interacting. This secure context supports communication; teachers participate with children in the literacy events and sometimes talk about them, although there are a minimum of explicit descriptions of processes. Instead, teachers attend to powerful examples of behaviors that signal the development of inner control. New learning is demonstrated and supported so that learners can take it on, but as soon as possible, full control is transferred to the child.

Interacting with children in such a sensitive way requires self-awareness and knowledge on the part of the teacher. Teachers must simultaneously observe, interpret, and make decisions about their own behavior. The teacher's knowledge base is critical in the process of guiding children's learning. When progress is slow, it is likely that the teaching is not sufficient to meet the child's learning needs. In our study, powerful teaching transcended the use of routines or the lesson framework. Even one-on-one instruction did not necessarily guarantee powerful instructional interactions. The teacher's ability to follow the lead of the child, but be ready to shift as the child extends capabilities, is a critical context element in learning. The most effective teachers change their behavior in response to children; their patterns did not remain static.

Teacher education may not be providing the environment that teachers need to learn how to teach. Rather than learning *to* teach, teachers need to learn *through* their teaching, engaging in a process that helps them improve in responding to individual children. They need a self-extending system that continually adds to the teaching repertoire.

A knowledge base develops thought through language—to think, to articulate, and to be reflective. The Reading Recovery teacher education model capitalizes on a talking-while-observing process, which we described in Chapter 3. Teachers are asked to think out loud as they have a common experience in observation. Each week, they observe lessons, building knowledge on a case-by-case basis. Viewing lessons helps them to reflect on their own teaching, but it also offers material for co-construction of knowledge. The teacher leader's questions and challenges support this language process. Teachers use language to describe what they see, to pose new ideas, to challenge and argue about concepts. They begin to understand the complexity of children's learning and to recognize and use children's half-right answers to form their own instructional moves. Teachers also begin to be comfortable with their own half-right answers about what the child is doing and may need. As a social group, the class constructs meaning together. They are willing to say "I don't know" and to hold theories tentatively.

Teacher education is close to teaching and involves teachers in social construction of the meanings that underlie their actions. In our study, training appeared to make a difference. Traditional Reading Recovery training provided far greater opportunity for the use of language processes than did training experiences available to teachers in the other treatments in our study. It seems that training, which places emphasis on assisted learning on the part of teachers, played a major role in helping teachers to work effectively with the high-risk children in our study.

WHAT WE LEARNED ABOUT SYSTEM CHANGE

Reading Recovery is a system intervention that is designed to work by creating change. It is possible to interpret the results of our study in a way that accounts for this systemic aspect of the program. As a treatment, Reading Recovery achieved the best student outcomes. We hypothesize that these results can be attributed to the more powerful teaching occurring in Reading Recovery lessons. This powerful teaching transcended necessary but insufficient characteristics such as individual instruction and curricular frameworks. In the previous section, we gave the credit to the training program. Yet our experience suggests that the training program alone will not support teachers at the level they need.

Our Reading Recovery teachers had not only experienced a year of training; they were currently part of a network of communication designed to support their teaching. Other teachers in our study had supervisory visits to assist them, but these provisions did not duplicate the widespread "belonging-ness" engendered by Reading Recovery. Reading Recovery teachers develop collegial friends with whom they discuss their work in both formal and infor-mal situations, and this process supports learning. The delivery system of Reading Recovery provides for interaction at every level.

In describing Reading Recovery, Clay (1987) has said that the program works to achieve change along four dimensions:

> behavioural change on the part of teachers;
> child behaviour change achieved by teaching;
> organisational changes in schools achieved by teachers and administrators;
> social/political changes in funding by controlling authorities. (p. 36)

The system works together to assure that all aspects of the program are car-ried forward. Reading Recovery is not a tutoring program. Good tutoring may be provided by a teacher who is intuitive and reflective. Such a teacher may make good use of the descriptions of Reading Recovery procedures, but this would not mean that Reading Recovery is being implemented in his or her school district. Reading Recovery is an intervention in the system that pro-vides for those dimensions of change.

A powerful initial training is delivered by a trained teacher leader. As teachers meet and talk about their teaching, they shift their behavior and then reflect on their actions. The expectation is continued contact not only with the initial training class but with others involved in the program. Continu-ously, teachers are assisted in reexamining their work. Ways of analyzing, challenging, and interacting are taken over by teachers, and they use them independently in their work with other teachers. The leader is less necessary as teachers take over the structuring of their own learning. Of course, this process is imperfect and impacts individuals differently. Some teachers may enter into the process more deeply. We do not know the extent to which the teachers in our study were involved in the continuous learning available in the Reading Recovery network. These teachers worked in 10 different set-tings across a large state. They were influenced by factors in their local con-texts. Some were located geographically far from the center of Reading Recov-ery activities in the state. Yet it is possible that the inclusion in a system had an effect on their teaching and was an intervening factor in their learning.

Chapter 11

Restructuring Literacy Education

This book, like every good study, ends with some recommendations for practice. One of our goals in undertaking this study was to provide useful information at several levels—for teachers of young, at-risk children, for teacher educators, for administrators, and for researchers—and we see some important implications in this research. When we consider our findings in the light of our experience in implementing one innovative effort—Reading Recovery— we realize that we cannot simply talk about making a few small changes in instructional practice. Even small changes have a ripple effect in the educational system; therefore all of our recommendations have implications for system change.

Reading Recovery provides a demonstration of something new in educational efforts. Not all components of Reading Recovery are new; the instructional procedures and activities are familiar to many educators. Other programs use one-on-one instruction; many innovations feature massive engagement in reading and writing. Some favor holistic approaches; others focus on details of print. A few innovations have long-term staff development programs. Although we know of no other effort utilizing the "talking-while-observing" technique with peer teaching, other systems have used the two-way mirror for observation. But Reading Recovery is unique in its combination of powerful components: (1) in the way the program provides harmony so that components can work in combination, (2) in the insistence on high-quality implementation with long-term plans, (3) in the ongoing education and support for teacher learning, and (4) in the network of communication that supports systemic change.

Bringing Reading Recovery into an educational system such as a school, school district, or state system is almost certain to necessitate change. Clay (1987) has outlined four dimensions of change that must be achieved if Reading Recovery is to work effectively: (1) behavioral change on the part of teachers, (2) child behavior change achieved by teaching, (3) organizational changes in school achieved by teachers and administrators, and (4) social and political changes in funding by controlling authorities. Our experience suggests that the situation is even more complex than Clay has indicated. Implementing Reading Recovery requires U.S. and Canadian educators to rethink many aspects of the system of education we provide for at-risk students and perhaps for all students.

Some changes, such as thinking about ways to provide more time for reading and writing, appear easy. Even such a seemingly easy step, however, means rethinking schedules and materials, both of which have budget implications. A more difficult challenge may be persuading personnel in the system to take a completely different view of children having difficulty. Instead of slow, minute steps, we now want to help them make leaps in learning. Both teachers and administrators may have to struggle with their internal theories about such children. Policy change may be required to provide for one-on-one instruction; finding space in crowded schools is not a simple matter. Educators will have to think about establishing different rules for entering and exiting programs. So, in view of the fact that Reading Recovery requires change, it also makes a good demonstration and offers a learning situation for the educators and researchers involved. If we can accomplish changes to accommodate this program, we can learn how to make other changes occur. We have been learning through our ongoing teaching of high-risk students, through our involvement in the national Reading Recovery program, and by conducting research. In this chapter we discuss our recommendations for the teaching of at-risk students, for teacher education, for system change, and for further research. We begin with a brief discussion of the difficulty of change.

WHY IS IT SO HARD TO CHANGE?

Educational organizations, like all human organizations, have forces that work to perpetuate the system and help it operate. These forces have value in that they help a system to work efficiently, to maintain itself, and to accomplish its goals. One of the difficulties in educational innovation is that in order to effect real change, one must disrupt some of those same operations that people have used to keep the system going. For example, testing practices may have been used so long and so efficiently in a system that no one questions whether the tests are really giving teachers valuable information to help in their work with children. The scores simply go in every year. Changing assessment to provide a closer look at children's thought processes may lead to looking at children in new ways and will probably disrupt or at least cause some conflict with the existing system.

Sometimes rules and operations become so entrenched that they become ends in themselves rather than means to accomplishing goals. This kind of thing can happen when a system gets locked into a particular reading program. Moving through levels, taking tests, and going over exercises become ends in themselves. People can lose sight of the end goal, which is teaching children to read and understand extended text. Presumably, children are learning to read as best they can given their ability, developmental level, and home situations, so no one questions the program. Those in difficulty are presented with a slowed-down or repeated version of the adopted program, but no one takes a good look at their behavior or tries to figure out what might work better. Even new adoptions offer different materials but do not essentially change teaching beliefs or approaches. When children do not learn, it is assumed that somehow the child is at fault. The system perpetuates itself rather than engaging in the problem solving needed to attain the original goal for all children. We contend that the system has become "failure-oriented," and we have evidence that many of our schools are failure-oriented systems for at-risk children.

We admit that Reading Recovery is difficult to implement. It requires commitment, energy, resources, and a willingness to put aside previous assumptions and change. But, looking at it another way, it is no more difficult than continuing the struggle, with its attendant sense of frustration, that permeates failure-oriented systems. To many systems, Reading Recovery offers a first step toward changing primary literacy education. It has generated some valuable thinking about the nature of professional development for teachers and has helped educators think through priorities rather than simply preserving the status quo. In these times of financial crisis, Reading Recovery and other innovations can help us learn to move in new directions that have better results for our at-risk students.

RECOMMENDATIONS FOR THE DESIGN OF PROGRAMS FOR HIGH-RISK STUDENTS

Our study provides some fairly clear implications for producing good results with high-risk students. Our suggestions for teaching and for program design are discussed below.

Individual Instruction

The literature suggests that intervention, provided early, can help young students make leaps in learning that will have payoffs throughout their school careers. Our study was based on that premise; we investigated in depth several kinds of early interventions, creating comparisons that would let us look at characteristics of each. If we are to invest early in students' careers, we thought, we wanted to find the most productive kind of early intervention in literacy education. So, we looked at both individual and group efforts. In general, our findings indicate that working one-on-one is the most effective kind of help to give the readers having the most difficulty. We therefore recommend that the lowest-achieving students be provided individual instruction early in their schooling, just as soon as teachers can tell that they are falling behind. That point may vary within systems, depending on age and the traditional curriculum. The fact is that some children need a higher level of support than can be provided even in a good classroom; a wait-and-see approach can have devastating effects for some children.

Individual support is important, but since our study clearly shows that it matters what *kind* of one-on-one help is given, we have to look further. The social support provided in the individual setting may be the critical ingredient; that is, children may not be dependent on their own maturation and development as much as they are dependent on the experiences and opportunities afforded by their interactions with adults. Both Bruner and Vygotsky see instructional interactions between teacher and a student as the "raw material" of learning and development (Wood, 1988). By providing Reading Recovery, we adjust the social situation so that young learners with fewer previous experiences in literacy have a very rich and supported situation in which to learn. The evidence is that they learn rapidly under such conditions.

Program Components

District personnel who are investing in individual education for the lowest-achieving children want to be sure that they design programs for maximum results. Results of our study indicate that the framework of Reading Recovery, with its intensive engagement in authentic reading and writing, is a powerful influence on students' learning. Even Reading Success teachers and the Reading and Writing Group teachers, all of whom used frameworks similar to Reading Recovery, had some positive results, although our research does not support either of those two approaches as adequate for the neediest children.

We have said that Reading Recovery is a program with a "bias toward text"; that is, children spend most of their time either reading or writing extended written language. A general principle for enhancing primary literacy education is to engage children in reading and writing; they need many opportunities within the school day. But it matters what they read and under what circumstances. Here, we would like to make recommendations about matching children with texts, introducing them to texts, and supporting their efforts. We make these recommendations for general education, not just those children who are at risk.

Our study indicates that it is important for children to do their problem-solving work while reading texts that roughly match their current level of ability. These texts should be interesting and fun; they should offer challenge but not be so difficult that the reader must struggle and the process breaks down. Accomplishing this match is the responsibility of the teacher. While children may roam freely through many interesting and beautiful texts at designated times during the school day, there should be a time when they are expected and helped to read books selected by the expert in the situation. We do not believe that young children at the beginning of sorting out reading and writing, especially those having difficulty with that task, should have the sole responsibility of choosing books for themselves. They deserve assistance in this process.

Nor do we support the practice of consistently offering children books that are too difficult for them to read. That happens in different kinds of curricular approaches. In basal reader systems, for example, children having the most difficulty are consistently overplaced in reading material (DeFord, 1986). They are helped to read this too-difficult material by slowing down the instruction, often spending a week on one story, accompanied by numerous skill-practice exercises. Faster progress could be achieved by initially involving them with texts they are able to read and insuring that they read massive amounts of material, then by supporting them in ways that help them get effective strategies going. We are not advocating keeping low-achieving children on low levels, but it is essential to have them read effectively every day—and that is impossible if they are always struggling with difficult hard texts.

Inappropriate placement of children also happens in literature-based or whole-language classrooms. Some children may consistently select materials they can only approximately read; without guided reading to help them sort out their concepts about the processes, there is a danger that they will become confused. We recommend that teachers become highly aware of the difficulties in the individual texts that they offer to children and that they continually assess children's progress and provide texts that are appropriate. Running records or miscue analysis (see Goodman & Burke, 1972) are helpful tools in this process. Especially troubling are approaches that involve mass reading of too-difficult texts. No matter how high the quality of children's literature in such situations, children who are attempting to memorize in order to join in with the group will be at a disadvantage. We refer here to the practice of having a whole group read along with the teacher on a very difficult text. Such practice has erroneously been called "whole language"; it is actually whole-class instruction. Our study gives us no information about the efficacy of whole-class instruction, so we cannot comment on the approach itself. It does suggest that reading material must be within the reader's grasp and that individuals must be engaged in some problem-solving work rather than simply chanting along. Teachers who work in such situations should take a good look at the texts they are asking children to read. Some might be more appropriate as books to read aloud to the children and to discuss, while creating some simpler texts to support the beginnings of reading.

This research suggests that good teachers work to make texts accessible to children and that they introduce stories in ways that help children link them to their personal experiences. Orienting children to stories requires conversation between teachers and children. Sometimes it does not actually look like teaching, more like two friends talking together about what is going to happen in a book. The orientations we studied were different from two kinds of common practice: (1) preteaching words and asking children questions prior to reading and (2) reading the story *to* the children prior to reading. Neither, we feel, is as powerful as orienting children to stories. The orientation to the story helps children reflect on stories and begin to make judgments about them. Teachers in our study who were particularly effective in helping children gain access to texts did not "test" children by asking a series of questions; instead they conversed with children. Our recommendation is that classroom conversation about texts can support children's thinking about what they read.

We also recommend guiding children during reading. While most children do not need one-on-one instruction such as is provided in Reading Recovery, they do need high-quality interactions surrounding their reading. In Chapter 4, we described how highly effective Reading Recovery teachers try to draw attention to powerful and memorable examples. During any kind of reading instruction, teachers could think about the kind of attention they pay to children's reading. Our study suggests that the kind of interactions that are provided and the attention teachers direct has a powerful influence on children's progress. The most at-risk children are the most vulnerable (see Board, 1982). Every teacher of reading might consider reexamining the kinds of statements and questions he or she makes during children's reading, asking questions such as:

> What am I calling attention to; that is, am I neglecting meaning, or syntax, or visual information?
> Am I flexible in my approach?
> Do I help children notice more than one kind of information?
> Do I attend to strategic problem-solving moves rather than accuracy?
> Am I working to make children independent of me?
> Am I praising children for their partially right responses?
> Am I helping children to structure their own learning?
> Am I helping children learn something new every day?

There is clear evidence from our research about the power of writing in supporting young children's growth in reading. Excellent literacy programs provide for time in writing, both guided writing and independent writing. We recommend that those designing programs for at-risk students take particular notice of the potential of writing and include it in their programs. Our most effective teachers worked intensively on writing in early lessons, using this activity to help children notice the details of print. Writing offers a powerful demonstration of how written language works, perhaps providing for the young child the clearest examples of the building-up and breaking-down processes that are involved in both reading and writing.

In other research (see Pinnell & McCarrier, in press) we have explored a process that we call interactive writing, a guided situation in which teachers work with children to produce pieces of writing related to the texts that they hear read aloud or those that they read themselves. Adapted from shared writing, which is commonly used in whole-language curricula, interactive writing is a dynamic language event that involves the following: (1) group composition of a message or story; (2) repetition and rereading of the composed message; (3) "shared-pen" activity while writing the message; (4) teaching of early strategies such as directionality and word-by-word matching; (5) attention to hearing sounds in words and to visual detail in the construction of words in the message; (6) transformation of difficult texts to easy reading for the children involved; (7) connections between reading texts, children's own experiences, and writing; and (8) awareness of text characteristics (e.g., beginnings, common language, etc.) through group composition. Interactive writing provides a demonstration of writing that helps children move from their early reading experiences to noticing discrepancies between approximated renderings of text and the print on the page. It helps them match what they say to the visual display of print. Interactive writing is an example of the kind of group activity that may be helpful to teachers in demonstrating the connections among talking, writing, and reading.

Teaching as Shared Problem Solving

In a sense, the teacher is an expert assistant who makes it possible for the young child to move beyond his or her independent level of performance. Assisted learning is essential, whether the teacher is working one-on-one or with a group. The process is called shared problem solving. During reading and writing, the adult, or "expert," takes over the hard parts of the task while leaving the easier parts for the novice to accomplish. Together, they achieve a goal that the child could not achieve alone; in the process the student learns to structure his or her own learning. Key factors are routine activities that offer security and consistency, demonstrations that implicitly provide information, direct instructions at appropriate times, and turning over the task to the learner. Some changes can be made through decisions by program planners; others depend on the professional development offered to teachers.

RECOMMENDATIONS FOR THE PROFESSIONAL DEVELOPMENT OF TEACHERS

It would be impossible to implement the most important of the recommendations in the previous section without being concerned about enhancing teachers' knowledge base and decisionmaking power. In Chapters 9 and 10 we described the reflective processes that helped teachers in our study and in Reading Recovery make leaps in their own learning and translate their knowledge into more effective teaching. By reflection, we mean their understanding of alternative possibilities. Reflection involves rethinking one's teaching, a process made easier when one is assisted by someone with more experience and expertise. Here, too, we explore the concept of assisted learning. In Reading Recovery, the teacher leader represents an expert, but one who is still involved in his or her own learning and practice. The teacher leader teaches children daily and struggles to expand his or her repertoire and knowledge base to meet diverse needs of students. At the same time, the leader works to assist practicing teachers while they work with children (and/or observe peers working with children during behind-the-glass sessions). The leader helps teachers to think about their teaching and move beyond the kind of reflection they would do alone. Watching one another teach and talking aloud as they do it increases their observational powers and helps to link their understandings into a self-extending system that supports quick decisionmaking. In the class, teachers are encouraged to approximate, to generate hypotheses about behavior and learning, to challenge one another, and to reflect on their own responses and those of others. They do not simply share common wisdom, although that has its value. They consult reference materials and work together to develop a theoretical base that is grounded in action. They hold their theory tentatively, always checking their assumptions against children's behavior. *Coach* might be an appropriate term to describe this teacher-leader role. We have identified the following vocabulary to characterize the teacher leader's activities: to encourage, provide context, help, demonstrate, ask questions, affirm answers, give critical feedback, challenge, model, tell, explain, redefine and redirect, and summarize.

In our view, attention to teacher development has the greatest potential for remaking the educational future of at-risk children. A critical finding of our study was that training with particular characteristics made a difference in the behavior of teachers and in student outcomes. We recommend that policymakers place high priority on creating designs for teacher education that go further than the quick-fix workshops or lectures of the past. Teacher development programs should be intensive and long term; they should occur concomitantly with ongoing practice. Teachers need exciting situations that engage them simultaneously in theory building, observation of real situations, and examination of their own teaching. While we discovered no substitute for our behind-the-glass live experiences, we recommend exploration of technologies that can help teachers bring problem solving to bear on real situations. Current technology, including laser disks and interactive video, offer some potential. Teacher educators might consider new ways to take advantage of technology, always being careful to avoid transmission models that destroy the inquiry process.

RECOMMENDATIONS FOR POLICY CHANGE

What do policymakers have to do to make all this happen? First, our research suggests that policymakers need to look at the whole system and adjust it to the children being served. Providing high-quality instructional time for children at risk can be thought of as a safety net that captures children, offering more support at a critical time, so that they can fully profit from good, ongoing teaching in their school or district. That, in itself, will have impact on a system. With good coverage, almost all children can enter the world of literacy and begin early to use literacy in their learning of content.

Then, policymakers need to take a look at general education in the system. Is classroom teaching truly supportive? Are materials appropriate? We need curriculum frameworks and materials that set the scene for good teaching and take the program to the child. That means providing enough materials so that every child has many selections that he or she can read. It means issuing policy statements that provide for time to read and for children to write in their own language. Such an approach is more efficient than dragging students through a prescriptive curriculum in which learning cannot be assured and many fall through the cracks. More can be accomplished in a shorter period of time because children's attention is in the right place at the right time. It requires excellent teaching, an attainable goal.

Policymakers should ask themselves whether they are investing resources in good teacher development rather than in shallow in-service programs. If we think about cost-effectiveness, we have to opt for the kind of teacher development that helps teachers keep on learning and help their colleagues learn. Many districts spend the same amount of money year after year on workshops to communicate isolated techniques or to learn to use new materials. Investment in long-term, high-quality in-service programs initially can create learning communities among teachers and foster independence and ongoing development. In many instances, teachers who have been involved in observation and inquiry with colleagues go on to conduct their own research studies to improve education in the school or district. Keeping teachers in a dependent, "taking it in" position is not cost-effective in the long run and will not improve instruction for children.

We also recommend taking another look at assessment and accountability practices. Reading Recovery is a highly accountable system. Teachers keep records and graphs of progress for every child; data are gathered and analyzed so that teachers at each site can work together to achieve better results. Measures used reflect students' learning progress and mean something to the people who have to improve the program. The kinds of behaviors teachers observe are the kinds of behaviors we wish to see in independent readers and writers. So, while teachers are "doing" assessment (e.g., taking running records), they are also increasing their knowledge base and making sure that they attend to productive behaviors on the part of children. They are simultaneously accomplishing several goals. Thus it is possible to assess progress through activities that, in themselves, have instructional value for students.

We have stated that the measures Reading Recovery teachers use are designed for primary teachers and that many groups are using them productively. Other assessments can be used in the same way; teachers in some districts have designed and implemented their own systems. It is appropriate for educational systems to be accountable and to examine their work; we recommend harmony among assessment, learning expectations, and instructional tasks.

Another recommendation for policymakers is that they place high priority on developing teacher leaders in various areas. These teacher leaders need special learning environments to help them discover how to help adults extend their own learning. Independence is the goal for teachers as well as for children. Expert staff development support from people who themselves remain teachers of children can provide for assisted learning on the part of school staff members.

Finally, we think that policymakers can do much to create an environment in which continued learning and change can be expected. Reading Recovery creates a self-renewing system that requires everyone involved to reexamine their own teaching of children and adults. Data feedback helps implementers to reevaluate the systems on a yearly basis; colleague feedback is valued. Participants report that training varies from year to year as teacher leaders and university faculty learn more through their own teaching and through research. The expectation to change is part of a culture of learning that everyone involved in Reading Recovery tries to keep alive. Given this situation, it is expected that the program will continue to evolve and change.

Individual lessons for each teacher look different from year to year as they learn more about responding to children and as feedback helps them change their understandings. This kind of policy climate can be fostered in any organization if leaders schedule regular meetings to reexamine processes and procedures that have traditionally been accepted. Information, both student outcome data and systematic observational data, helps participants to look beyond their own perspectives. Another quality to foster in the system is the expectation that everyone at every level of decisionmaking will learn from colleagues.

RECOMMENDATIONS FOR FURTHER RESEARCH

Recommendations for further investigations are another outcome of research, and our study provides much for researchers to think about. Further studies of early interventions are needed, but these should probe beyond superficial characteristics of programs or program elements to examinations of teaching and learning within instructional designs. The methodology we designed for our study capitalized on approaches that looked in great detail at a few subjects (see for example, Dyson, 1981; Graves, 1983; Rowe, 1989). We expanded our numbers and used the qualitative approaches in connection with quantitative data. These techniques were productive, and they might be further expanded to large samples from diverse geographic areas.

Studies of Instruction

We need studies that look at instructional interactions in detail. Qualitative analyses of teacher–child interactions could be carried out on larger samples of teachers, so that the range of responses to individual children could be more fully explored. Detailed studies that relate moment-to-moment teaching moves to each child's responses could be productive. We also recommend observations of how interactions shift over time and relate to the text being read. We looked at teachers and children at several points in time, but with information from previous research and more resources, smaller shifts could be detected. Such studies would provide useful information for teachers as they reflect on their own practice and could also help teacher educators design professional development programs.

Studies of Teachers' Learning

We also need studies that follow teachers over time, finding out what influences their learning and how they translate learning in their work with students. We recommend undertaking a large number of longitudinal case studies that examine teachers' work in classrooms and other settings. It does little good to explore effective teaching when we know so little about how to help teachers learn to do it. Experience suggests that simply "telling" teachers what to do backfires into rigid and prescriptive ways of operating. Research on teacher learning may illuminate important learning processes.

CONCLUSION

As we write this book, we realize that the problems connected with literacy education are increasing with time, both for individual children who are moving along in the system and for educational systems as they search for new ways to help children they are failing to serve. This phenomenon lead us to research Reading Recovery in the first place and to probe deeper in this study, sponsored by the MacArthur Foundation. Our study has answered some questions, captured in the recommendations in this chapter, and raised others, projected in recommendations for future research. What we cannot do, however, is wait to act; neither can we support quick solutions. We need long-range plans based on the best knowledge we now have. What will it take to remove the phrase *at risk* from our discourse, so that no one ever has to say it again? Our research has provided some valuable information. The kinds of models we have discussed represent a piece of the whole; used in connection with approaches that address other school issues, we have a real chance to make a difference in the lives of young children. Further research will reveal more information. Meanwhile, back at the school, we should put to work what we already know. Investing in our children and our teachers is investing in our future. Failure to do so is not their failure but ours.

References

Adams, M. J. (1990). *Beginning to read: Thinking and learning about print*. Cambridge, MA: MIT Press.

Allington, R. L., & McGill-Franzen, A. (1989). Different programs, indifferent instruction. In D. Lipsky & A. Garther (Eds.), *Beyond special education* (pp. 3–32). New York: Brookes.

Alvermann, D. E. (1990). Reading teacher education. In W. R. Houston, M. Haberman, & J. Sikula (Eds.), *Handbook of research on teacher education: A project of the Association of Teacher Educators* (pp. 687–704). New York: Macmillan.

Au, K. H. (1990). Changes in a teacher's views of interactive comprehension instruction. In L. C. Moll (Ed.), *Vygotsky and education: Instructional implications and applications of sociohistorical psychology* (pp. 271–286). New York: Cambridge University Press.

Bandura, A. (1977). *Social learning theory*. Englewood Cliffs, NJ: Prentice-Hall.

Barr, R. C. (1973/1974). Instructional pace differences and their effect on reading acquisition. *Reading Research Quarterly, 9*, 526–554.

Barr, R. (1984). Beginning reading instruction: From debate to reformation. In P. D. Pearson, R. Barr, M. L. Kamil, & P. Mosenthal (Eds.), *Handbook of reading research* (Vol. 1; pp. 545–581). New York: Longman.

Barr, R. (1987). Classroom interaction and curricular content. In D. Bloome (Ed.), *Literacy and schooling* (pp. 150–168). Norwood, NJ: Ablex.

Berliner, D. C. (1986). In pursuit of the expert pedagogue. *Educational Researcher, 15*, 5–13.

Board, P. E. (1982). *Toward a theory of instructional influence: Aspects of the instructional environment and their influence on children's acquisition of reading*. Unpublished doctoral dissertation, University of Toronto.

Brophy, J., & Good, T. L. (1986). Teacher behavior and student achievement. In M. C. Wittrock (Ed.), *Handbook of research on teaching* (3rd ed.; pp. 328–375). New York: Macmillan.

Bruner, J. S. (1975). The ontogenesis of speech acts. *Journal of Child Language, 2*, 1–19.

Bruner, J. S. (1986). *Actual minds, possible worlds*. Cambridge, MA: Harvard University Press.

Burton, F. (1989). Writing what they read: Reflections on literature and child writers.

In J. M. Jensen (Ed.), *Stories to grow on: Demonstrations of language learning in K–8 classrooms* (pp. 97–116). Portsmouth, NH: Heinemann.

Butler, A. (1988). *The trolley ride.* Crystal Lake, IL: Rigby.

Butler, A., & Turbill, J. (1984). *Towards a reading–writing classroom.* Rozelle, New South Wales, Australia: Primary English Teaching Association.

Caccamise, D. J. (1987). Idea generation in writing. In A. Matsuhashi (Ed.), *Writing in real time: Modelling production processes* (pp. 224–253). Norwood, NJ: Ablex.

Calkins, L. M. (1980). Children's rewriting strategies. *Research in the Teaching of English, 14,* 331–341.

Calkins, L. M. (1983). *Lessons from a child: On the teaching and learning of writing.* Exeter, NH: Heinemann.

Calkins, L. M. (1986). *The art of teaching writing.* Portsmouth, NH: Heinemann.

Carnegie Foundation. (1986). *A nation prepared: Teachers for the 21st century.* Hayattsville, MD: Carnegie Forum on Education and the Economy.

Cazden, C. B. (1988). *Classroom discourse: The language of teaching and learning.* Portsmouth, NH: Heinemann.

Chall, J., & Feldman, S. (1967). *A study in-depth of first grade reading: An analysis of the interactions of proposed methods, teacher implementation and child background* (Cooperative Research Project, No. 2728). Washington, DC: U.S. Office of Education.

Clay, M. M. (1972). *Reading: The patterning of complex behaviour.* Auckland, New Zealand: Heinemann.

Clay, M. M. (1975). *What did I write?: Beginning writing behaviour.* Auckland, New Zealand: Heinemann.

Clay, M. M. (1979a). *Reading: The patterning of complex behaviour* (2nd ed.). Portsmouth, NH: Heinemann.

Clay, M. M. (1979b). *Sand or Stones.* Auckland, New Zealand: Heinemann.

Clay, M. M. (1985). *The early detection of reading difficulties* (3rd ed.). Portsmouth, NH: Heinemann.

Clay, M. M. (1987). Implementing Reading Recovery: Systemic adaptations to an educational innovation. *New Zealand Journal of Educational Studies, 22,* 35–58.

Clay, M. M. (1989). Concepts about print in English and other languages. *The Reading Teacher, 42,* 268–276.

Clay, M. M. (1990). The Reading Recovery Programme, 1984–88: Coverage, outcomes and education board district figures. *New Zealand Journal of Educational Studies, 25,* 61–70.

Clay, M. M. (1991). *Becoming literate: The construction of inner control.* Portsmouth, NH: Heinemann.

Clay, M. M. (in press). *The new observation survey.* Portsmouth, NH: Heinemann.

Clay, M. M., & Cazden, C. B. (1990). A Vygotskian interpretation of Reading Recovery. In L. C. Moll (Ed.), *Vygotsky and education: Instructional implications and applications of sociohistorical psychology* (pp. 206–222). New York: Cambridge University Press.

Clay, M. M., & Tuck, B. (1991). *A study of Reading Recovery subgroups: Including outcomes for children who did not satisfy discontinuing criteria* (Technical Report). Auckland, New Zealand: Ministry of Education.

Cochran-Smith, M. (1984). *The making of a reader.* Norwood, NJ: Ablex.

Comprehension Test of Basic Skills (CTBS). (1981). Forms U and V. Monterey, California: CTBS McGraw-Hill.

Cowley, J. (1980). *Mrs. Wishy-washy.* Auckland, New Zealand: Shortland Publications.

Cowley, J. (1983a). *Dan, the flying man.* Auckland, New Zealand: Shortland Publications.

Cowley, J. (1983b). *The ghost.* Auckland, New Zealand: Shortland Publications.

Cowley, J. (1986). *Yuk soup.* San Diego, CA: Wright Group.

Cowley, J. (1987a). *Along comes Jake.* San Diego, CA: Wright Group.

Cowley, J. (1987b). *Letters for Mr. James.* Bothell, WA: Wright Group.

Cowley, J. (1987c). *The poor sore paw.* San Diego, CA: Wright Group.

Cutting, J. (1988a). *Give me a hug.* San Diego, CA: Wright Group.

Cutting, J. (1988b). *Space journey.* San Diego, CA: Wright Group.

DeFord, D. E. (1980). Young children and their writing. *Theory into Practice, 19,* 157–162.

DeFord, D. E. (1981). Literacy: Reading, writing, and other essentials. *Language Arts, 58,* 652–658.

DeFord, D. E. (1986). Classroom contexts for literacy learning. In T. E. Raphael (Ed.), *Contexts of school-based literacy* (pp. 163–180). New York: Random House.

DeFord, D. E. (1993). Learning within teaching: An examination of teachers learning in Reading Recovery. *Reading and Writing Quarterly, 9.* Washington, DC: Hemisphere Publishing.

DeFord, D. E., Pinnell, G., Lyons, C., & Place, A. W. (1990). *The Reading Recovery follow-up study* (Technical Report, Vol. III). Columbus: Ohio State University.

DeFord, D. E., Tancock, S., & White, N. (1990). *Teachers' models of the reading process and their evaluations of an individual reader: Relationship to success in teaching reading and judged quality of instruction* (Technical Report, Vol. 5). Columbus: Ohio State University.

DeFord, D. E., White, N., & Williams, C. (1991). Analysis of the impact of writing in Reading Recovery tutoring settings. Paper presented at the American Educational Research Association annual conference. Chicago.

Duckworth, E. (1987). *"The having of wonderful ideas" and other essays on teaching and learning.* New York: Teachers College Press.

Dyson, A. H. (1981). *A case study examination of the role of oral language in the writing process of kindergarteners.* Unpublished doctoral dissertation, University of Texas, Austin.

Dyson, A. H. (Ed.). (1989). *Multiple worlds of child writers: Friends learning to write.* New York: Teachers College Press.

Dyson, A. H. (1990). *The word and the world: Reconceptualizing written language development* (Technical Report No. 42). Berkeley: Center for the Study of Writing, University of California.

Elkonin, D. B. (1973). USSR. In J. Downing (Ed.), *Comparative reading: Cross-national studies of behavior and processes in reading and writing* (pp. 551–579). New York: Macmillan.

Ferreiro, E., & Teberosky, A. (1982). *Literacy before schooling.* Exeter, NH: Heinemann.

Flower, L. S., & Hayes, J. R. (1981). A cognitive process theory of writing. *College Composition and Communication, 32,* 365–387.

Gallimore, R., & Tharp, R. (1990). Teaching mind in society: Teaching, schooling, and literate discourse. In L. C. Moll (Ed.), *Vygotsky and education: Instructional implications and applications of sociohistorical psychology* (pp. 175–205). New York: Cambridge University Press.

Gates–MacGinitie Reading Test. (1978). Lombard, IL: Riverside.

Geeke, P. (1988). *Evaluation of the Bendigo Reading Recovery Programme, 1984.* Victoria, Australia: Centre for Studies in Literacy, University of Wollongong.

Ginsburg, M. (1972). *The chick and the duckling.* New York: Macmillan.

Good, T. L., & Beckerman, T. M. (1978). Time on task: A naturalistic study in sixth-grade classrooms. *The Elementary School Journal, 78,* 192–201.

Goodlad, J. I. (1990). The occupation of teaching in schools. In J. I. Goodlad, R. Soder, & K. A. Sirotnik (Eds.), *The moral dimensions of teaching* (pp. 3–34). San Francisco: Jossey-Bass.

Goodman, Y., & Burke, C. (1972). *Reading miscue inventory: A procedure for diagnosis and evaluation.* New York: Richard C. Owen.

Goswami, U., & Bryant, P. (1990). *Phonological skills and learning to read.* East Sussex, U.K.: Erlbaum.

Graves, D. H. (1983). *Writing: Teachers and children at work.* Portsmouth, NH: Heinemann.

Green, J. L. (1983). Exploring classroom discourse: Linguistic perspectives on teaching–learning processes. *Educational Psychologist, 18,* 180–199.

Green, J. L., & Wallat, R. (1987). In search of meaning: A sociolinguistic perspective on lesson construction and reading. In D. Bloome (Ed.), *Literacy and schooling* (pp. 4–31). Norwood, NJ: Ablex.

Gundlach, R. A., McLane, J. B., Stott, F. M., & McNamee, G. M. (1985). The social foundations of children's early writing development. In M. Farr (Ed.), *Advances in writing research: Vol 1. Children's early writing development* (pp. 1–58). Norwood, NJ: Ablex.

Halliday, M. A. K. (1975). *Learning how to mean: Explorations in the development of language.* London: Edward Arnold.

Hansen, J. (1987). *When writers read.* Portsmouth, NH: Heinemann.

Harste, J. C., Woodward, V. A., & Burke, C. L. (1984). *Language stories and literacy lessons.* Portsmouth, NH: Heinemann.

Heath, S. B. (1983). *Ways with words: Language, life and work in communities and classrooms.* New York: Cambridge University Press.

Holmes Group. (1986). *Tomorrow's teachers: A report of the Holmes group.* East Lansing, MI: Author.

Hutchins, P. (1971). *Rosie's walk.* New York: Macmillan.

Jackson, P. W. (1968). *Life in classrooms.* New York: Holt, Rinehart & Winston.

Keenan, E. O., & Schieffelin, B. B. (1976). Topic as a discourse notion: A study of topic in the conversations of children and adults. In C. Li (Ed.), *Subject and topic* (pp. 335–384). New York: Academic Press.

King, M. L., & Rentel, V. M. (1981). *How children learn to write: A longitudinal study*

(Final report to the National Institute of Education, NIE-G-79-0137 and NIE-G-79-0039). Columbus: Ohio State University.

King, M. L., & Rentel, V. M. (1982). *Transition to writing* (Final report to the National Institute of Education, NIE-G-79-0031 and NIE-G-79-0137). Columbus: Ohio State University.

King, M. L., & Rentel, V. M. (1983). *A longitudinal study of coherence in children's written narratives* (Final report to the National Institute of Education, NIE-G-81-0063). Columbus: Ohio State University.

Knoblock, P., & Goldstein, A. P. (1971). *The lonely teacher.* Boston: Allyn & Bacon.

Kuhn, D. J. (1970). Behavioral objectives in the life sciences: A useful instrument in curriculum development. *Science Education, 54,* 123–126.

Lindfors, J. W. (1987). *Children's language and learning* (2nd ed.). Englewood Cliffs, NJ: Prentice-Hall.

Luria, A. R. (1970). The functional organization of the brain. *Scientific American, 66,* 67–78.

Luria, A. R. (1983). The development of writing in the child. In M. Martlew (Ed.), *The psychology of written language: Developmental and educational perspectives* (pp. 237–277). New York: Wiley.

Lyons, C. A. (1991a). A comparative study of the teaching effectiveness of teachers participating in a year-long or 2-week inservice program. In J. Zutell & S. McCormick (Eds.), *Learner factors/teacher factors: Issues in literacy research and instruction* (Fortieth Yearbook of the National Reading Conference) (pp. 367–375). Chicago, IL: National Reading Conference, Inc.

Lyons, C. A. (1991b). Reading Recovery: A viable prevention to learning disability. *Reading Horizons, 31,* 384–408.

Lyons, C. A. (1992). *The influence of Reading Recovery teachers' belief systems on instructional decisions and successful practice.* Manuscript submitted for publication.

Lyons, C. A. (1993). The use of questions in the teaching of high risk readers: A profile of a developing Reading Recovery teacher. *Reading and Writing Quarterly, 9.* Washington, DC: Hemisphere Publishing.

Lyons, C. A., & Beaver, J. (in press). Reducing retention and learning disability placement through Reading Recovery: An educationally sound cost-effective choice. In R. Allington & S. Wamsley (Eds.), *No quick fix: Redesigning literacy programs in America's elementary schools.* New York: Teachers College Press.

Lyons, C. A., & White, N. (1990). *Belief systems and instructional decisions: Comparisons between more and less effective teachers* (MacArthur Foundation Research Technical Report No. 4). Columbus: Ohio State University.

Macdonald, M. (1983). *Boots for Toots.* Wellington, Australia: Department of Education.

McLane, J. B. (1990). Writing as a social process. In L. C. Moll (Ed.), *Vygotsky and education: Instructional implications and applications of sociohistorical psychology* (pp. 304–318). New York: Cambridge University Press.

Meek, M. (1982). *Learning to read.* London: Bodley Head.

Melser, J. (1981). *Little pig.* Auckland, Australia: Shortland Publications.

Meyer, L. (1988). Research on implementation: What seems to work. In S. J. Samuels & P. D. Pearson (Eds.), *Changing school reading programs: Principles and case studies* (pp. 41–57). Newark, DE: International Reading Association.

Moll, L. C. (1990). Introduction. In L. C. Moll (Ed.), *Vygotsky and education: Instructional implications and applications of sociohistorical psychology* (pp. 1–27). New York: Cambridge University Press.

Ochs, E. (1983). Planned and unplanned discourse. In E. Ochs & B. Scheiffelin (Eds.), *Acquiring conversational competence.* London: Routledge & Kegan Paul.

Peek, M. (1985). *Mary wore her red dress and Henry wore his green sneakers.* New York: Ticknor & Fields.

Peterson, B. (1991). Selecting books for beginning readers and children's literature suitable for young readers. In D. E. DeFord, C. A. Lyons, & G. S. Pinnell (Eds.), *Bridges to literacy: Learning from Reading Recovery* (pp. 119–147). Portsmouth, NH: Heinemann.

Pinnell, G. S. (1991). Teachers and children learning. In D. E. DeFord, C. A. Lyons, & G. S. Pinnell (Eds.), *Bridges to literacy: Learning from Reading Recovery* (pp. 171–187). Portsmouth, NH: Heinemann.

Pinnell, G. S., Bradley, D. H., & Button, K. (1990). *High risk students' definitions of reading during participation in initial reading instruction* (MacArthur Foundation Technical Report, Vol. 3). Columbus: Ohio State University.

Pinnell, G. S., DeFord, D. E., & Lyons, C. A. (1988). *Reading Recovery: Early intervention for at-risk first graders.* Arlington, VA: Educational Research Service.

Pinnell, G. S., DeFord, D. E., & Lyons, C. A. (1990). *MacArthur Foundation research project instruments* (Technical Report, No. 11). Columbus: Ohio State University.

Pinnell, G. S., Lyons, C. A., DeFord, D. E., Bryk, A. S., & Seltzer, M. (in press). Comparing instructional models for the literacy education of high risk first graders. *Reading Research Quarterly.*

Pinnell, G. S., & McCarrier, A. (in press). Interactive writing: A transition tool for assisting children in learning to read and write. In E. Hiebert & B. Taylor (Eds.), *Getting reading right from the start: Effective early literacy interventions.* Needham Heights, MA: Allyn & Bacon.

Pinnell, G. S., McCarrier, A., & Button, K. (1990). *Constructing literacy in urban kindergartens: Progress report on the kindergarten early literacy project* (MacArthur Foundation Technical Report, No. 10). Columbus: Ohio State University.

Pinnell, G. S., & Woolsey, D. P. (1985). *Report of a study of teacher researchers in a program to prevent reading failure* (Report to the Research Foundation of the National Council of Teachers of English). Urbana, IL: NCTE Press.

Rogers, C. R. (1969). *Freedom to learn: A view of what education might be.* Columbus, OH: Merrill.

Rogoff, B. (1986). Adult assistance of children's learning. In T. E. Raphael (Ed.), *Contexts of school-based literacy* (pp. 27–40). New York: Random House.

Rogoff, B. (1990). *Apprenticeship in thinking: Cognitive development in social context.* New York: Oxford University Press.

Rokeach, M. (1979). Some unresolved issues in theories of beliefs, attitudes, and values. *Nebraska Symposium on Motivation, 27,* 261–304.

Rosenshine, B. (1979). Content, time and direct instruction. In P. Peterson & H. Walberg (Eds.), *Research on teaching: Concepts, findings, and implications* (pp. 28–56). Berkeley, CA: McCutchen.

Rosenshine, B., & Stevens, R. (1984). Classroom instruction in reading. In P. D. Pearson, R. Barr, M. L. Kamil, & P. Mosenthal (Eds.), *Handbook of reading research* (pp. 745–798). New York: Longman.

Rowe, D. W. (1989). Author/audience interaction in the preschool: The role of social interaction in literacy learning. *Journal of Reading Behavior, 21,* 311–349.

Scardamalia, M., & Bereiter, C. (1982). Assimilative processes in composition planning. *Educational Psychologist, 17,* 165–171.

Schieffelin, B. B., & Cochran-Smith, M. (1984). Learning to read culturally: Literacy before schooling. In H. Goelman, A. A. Oberg, & F. Smith (Eds.), *Awakening to literacy* (pp. 3–23). Exeter, NH: Heinemann.

Schön, D. A. (Ed.). (1991). *The reflective turn: Case studies in and on educational practice.* New York: Teachers College Press.

Scott, Foresman. (1979). Special practice books. Glenview, IL: Scott, Foresman.

Shannon, D. (1990). *A descriptive study of verbal challenge and teacher response to verbal challenge in Reading Recovery teacher training.* Unpublished doctoral dissertation, Texas Woman's University, Denton.

Shulman, L. S. (1987). Knowledge and teaching: Foundations of the new reform. *Harvard Educational Review, 57,* 1–22.

Slavin, R. E., & Madden, N. A. (1989). Effective classroom programs for students at risk. In R. E. Slavin, N. L. Karweit, & N. A. Madden (Eds.), *Effective programs for students at risk* (pp. 23–51). Boston: Allyn & Bacon.

Smith, F. (1988). *Understanding reading: A psycholinguistic analysis of reading and learning to read* (4th ed.). Hillsdale, NJ: Erlbaum.

Snow, C. E. (1983). Language and literacy: Relationships during the preschool years. *Harvard Educational Review, 53,* 165–189.

Sully, J. (1986). *Studies of childhood.* New York: Appleton.

Sulzby, E., & Teale, W. H. (1984). *Young children's storybook reading: Hispanic and Anglo families and children* (Report to the Spencer Foundation). Evanston, IL: Northwestern University.

Sulzby, E., Teale, W. H., & Kamberelis, G. (1989). Emergent writing in the classroom: Home and school connections. In D. S. Strickland & L. M. Morrow (Eds.), *Emerging literacy: Young children learn to read and write* (pp. 63–79). Newark, DE: International Reading Association.

Talwar, J. (1989). Behind the glass. *The Running Record, 3,* 3–4. Columbus: Ohio State University.

Teale, W. H., & Sulzby, E. (1986). Emergent literacy as a perspective for examining how young children become writers and readers. In W. H. Teale & E. Sulzby (Eds.), *Emergent literacy: Writing and reading* (pp. vii–xxv). Norwood, NJ: Ablex.

Tharp, R. G., & Gallimore, R. (1988). *Rousing minds to life: Teaching, learning, and schooling in social context.* New York: Cambridge University Press.

Vygotsky, L. S. (1956). *Izbrannye psikhologicheskie issledovaniia* [Selected psychological research]. Moskow: Izdatelstvo Akademii Pedagogicheskikh Nack.

Vygotsky, L. S. (1962). *Thought and language.* Cambridge, MA: MIT Press.

Vygotsky, L. S. (1978). *Mind in society: The development of higher psychological processes*. Cambridge, MA: Harvard University Press.

Vygotsky, L. S. (1986). *Thought and language*. Cambridge, MA: MIT Press.

Wells, G. (1986). *The meaning makers: Children learning language and using language to learn*. Portsmouth, NH: Heinemann.

Wertsch, J. (1985). *Vygotsky and the social formation of mind*. Cambridge, MA: Harvard University Press.

Wildsmith, B. (1982). *Cat on the mat*. Oxford, U.K.: Oxford University Press.

Wildsmith, B. (1983). *All fall down*. Oxford, U.K.: Oxford University Press.

Wiley, J. (1992). Analysis of learning: A hard-to-teach child or a hard-to-teach teacher. *The Running Record, 4,* 1–3. Columbus: Ohio State University.

Wood, D. (1988). *How children think and learn: The social contexts of cognitive development*. Cambridge, MA: Basil Blackwell.

Wood, D., Bruner, J. S., & Ross, G. (1976). The role of tutoring in problem solving. *Journal of Child Psychology and Psychiatry and Allied Disciplines, 17,* 89–100.

Index

About the Authors

Carol A. Lyons is an Associate Professor of Education and Director of the Martha L. King Language and Literacy Center at Ohio State University. She teaches courses in developmental and corrective reading, learning, and curriculum. She has published articles and chapters in books dealing with issues related to reading and learning disabilities, teachers' and students' learning, and instruction. She is editor of *Literacy Matters* and director of the National Diffusion Network Reading Recovery Program.

Gay Su Pinnell is Professor of Theory and Practice in the College of Education at Ohio State University, where she teaches courses on language development, literacy, and children's literature. She is editor and author of *Discovering Language with Children*; co-author of *Teaching Reading Comprehension*; and author of *Restructuring Education: The Reading Recovery Approach,* a Phi Delta Kappa fastback. For her article "Learning How to Make a Difference," she received the International Reading Association's Albert Harris Award for contribution to the education of children with learning difficulties.

Diane E. DeFord is a Professor in the Department of Educational Theory and Practice at Ohio State University. She coordinates the faculty of Language, Literature, and Reading and teaches courses in reading and writing methodology, linguistics, and evaluation. She has published articles in *Language Arts, Journal of Reading, Reading Research Quarterly*, and *Theory and Practice*, as well as many chapters in professional books.

In 1989, Drs. Lyons, Pinnell, and DeFord received the Ohio Governor's Award in recognition of their outstanding achievement in education for the Reading Recovery Program. They are also co-editors and authors of *Bridges to Literacy: Learning from Reading Recovery*. The colleagues have taught children in Ohio public schools and prepared teacher leaders and trainers of teacher leaders for implementing Reading Recovery since 1985. Under the auspices of a grant from the John D. and Catherine T. MacArthur Foundation, Gay Su Pinnell served as principal investigator and Diane DeFord and Carol Lyons were co-investigators for the research reported in this book.